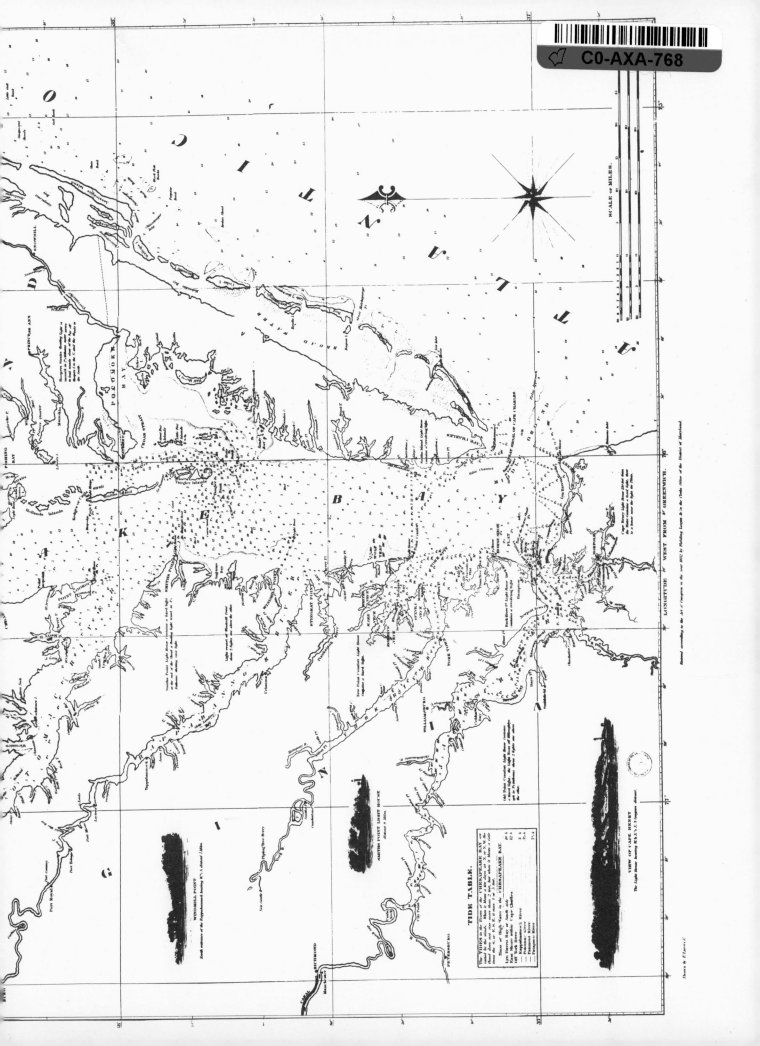

ST. MARY'S COUNTY, MARYLAND

IN THE AMERICAN REVOLUTION

CALENDAR OF EVENTS

Library of Congress Catalog Card Number 75 - 15395
Manufactured in the United States

BOOKS BY EDWIN W. BEITZELL

St. Mary's County, Maryland in the American Revolution
Calendar of Events

Life on the Potomac River

Point Lookout Prison Camp For Confederates

The Jesuit Missions of St. Mary's County, Maryland

Genealogies:

The Beitzell Family
The Weser Family
The Norris Family
The Gerard and Cheseldine Families
The Kinney Family
The Stanhouse Family
The Olive Family
The Boyd Family

ST. MARY'S COUNTY, MARYLAND IN THE AMERICAN REVOLUTION
CALENDAR OF EVENTS

Compiled from the Official Records of Maryland
for the St. Mary's County Bicentennial Commission

By Edwin W. Beitzell

This Calendar endeavors to put into sequence the
daily happenings in St. Mary's County throughout the
years of the American Revolution and to identify the
military and civilian personnel who were most directly
involved.

It is dedicated to those courageous patriots who
were determined to sacrifice their lives and their fortunes
rather than to surrender their liberty, and in particular
to the unknown dead of which there are many.

PREFACE

This book is one of several projects of the St. Mary's County Bicentennial Commission designed to memorialize those historic people and events of 200 years ago. We hope that this Calendar of the Revolutionary War in St. Mary's County will give you a picture of the great efforts on the part of our people here in St. Mary's to gain those liberties envisioned by the Founding Fathers. We hope too that the data provided will assist you in identifying your ancestors who fought in the Revolution or who assisted the military in civil capacities.

For 60 years the Major William Thomas Chapter of the Daughters of the American Revolution has endeavored to preserve and maintain our County history in the Revolution and to honor the memory of our men whom General Washington placed in the forefront of many of the crucial battles of the War. Perhaps this book will motivate some of you to join the DAR and others to form a local chapter of the Sons of the American Revolution. This would be a worthy and lasting accomplishment of this Bicentennial era which would help keep alive the memory of our patriots and would help preserve those ideas and ideals for which they fought.

This volume is the work of Commission member, Edwin Beitzell. It is merely the most recent of a series of tributes he has paid to his native county. It was a happy day, indeed, for St. Mary's County when Ed Beitzell returned from exile to dedicate his retirement years to the Mother County of Maryland. He is a gentleman and a scholar, liked by all who know him.

I would like also to thank The Enterprise and, in particular, Mrs. Vivian Lemon who typed the manuscript as a contribution to our Bicentennial activities.

Marvin C. Joy
Chairman
St. Mary's County Bicentennial
Commission

FOREWORD

The burning of the St. Mary's County Court House in 1831 was a tragic happening for the students of County history. Not only were the land records lost but also the records of the American Revolution, the War of 1812 and the Colonial records dating back to the founding of the County government in 1708. Fortunately, the will records escaped the fire.

Almost all of the County militia records in the American Revolution were lost, excepting the names of the officers, who were commissioned by the Council of Safety (later the Council of Maryland) in Annapolis. We are fortunate that the names of the officers were preserved in the State records, together with many of the muster rolls of the Independent Companies and the Continental Army, (the Maryland Line).

This Calendar has been compiled from these records, contained in the Archives of Maryland, Volumes 11, 12, 16, 18, 21, 43, 45, 47, and 48, and in the five Volumes of the Calendar of Maryland State Papers. Unfortunately, all of the St. Mary's County men recorded on these muster rolls could not be identified due to the fact that many of the same family names are found in the several Southern Counties. More of these individuals can probably be identified through the use of the Revolutionary War pension records at the U.S. National Archives in Washington, D.C. However, that is beyond the scope of this book.

Researchers definitely should not accept this record as the final word but resort to the basic records at the Hall of Records in Annapolis where there is doubt or further verification seem desirable. Also there are unpublished militia lists at the Maryland Historical Society in Baltimore and compilation of other Revolutionary War data by Margaret Roberts Hodges at the Daughters of the American Revolution Library in Washington, D.C., which might be consulted.

This book is an effort to contain in a single handy volume all of the County Revolutionary records in chronological order throughout the war period which not only gives a complete picture of the tremendous effort and sacrifices made by the people to maintain their liberties but also provides a list of approximately 2000 individuals, both military and civil, who participated in this battle for freedom.

It is evident that every able-bodied man between the ages of 16 and 50 did his duty when it is realized that the total population of the County was only about 8000 during this period. And many of these men responded to the call not once but several times. Casualties were high and it is unfortunate that casualty lists as such were not maintained or if they were, are no longer extant, so the names of many of our men who died on the battlefields or in the prison ships are unknown and few will ever be identified. For example, it seems safe to assume that every man of the Flying Camp Company of St. Mary's of July 28, 1776, died in battle or on a British prison ship where there is only one reference after his name, which was the record of his enlistment. None of these men should be forgotten for they compiled a truly magnificent record, fighting against overwhelming odds over a period of seven long years. It is right and just that we honor them in our 200th year of independence.

Edwin W. Beitzell
February 22, 1975

LIST OF ILLUSTRATIONS

INTRODUCTION

ST. MARY'S COUNTY, MARYLAND IN THE AMERICAN REVOLUTION
CALENDAR OF EVENTS

As the relations between the English Colonies in America and Great Britain deteriorated in the 1770's, a Congress or Convention as it was called, met for the first time in Annapolis, Maryland on June 22, 1774, and organized with Matthew Tilghman as chairman. At no time in the history of Maryland did a representative body meet characterised by greater wisdom, truer patriotism, and more lofty unselfishness of purpose. Clearly declaring their real motives and aims, they resolved upon a general system of non-intercourse and appointed deputies to a Congress of all the Colonies to insure unity of action.

The General Congress met in Philadelphia in September, 1774 and agreed upon a definite plan of action. Public meetings to ratify this policy were held in all the Counties of Maryland, committees chosen to carry it out, and delegates elected to a second Convention which met in November, and before it the deputies to the Congress laid the report of their proceedings. This Convention passed a series of resolutions approving the action of the Congress and providing more specifically for carrying out the non-importation policy, and especially for the organization and drill of the militia, and the purchase of arms and ammunition.

The Convention met again in April 1775, and during this session the news arrived of the battle of Lexington. After its adjournment, the battle of Bunker Hill was fought and open war had begun.

As so large a body as the Convention could not remain continuously in session, it appointed a certain number of its members a standing Executive Committee with the title of Council of Safety, which was the permanent administrative body for all matters and measures connected with the policy of resistance within the limits provided in its constitution. It was assisted by a Committee of Observation in each County, who kept the Council constantly advised and carried out its orders.

Archives of Maryland, Vol. 11, Preface v, vi.

ST. MARY'S COUNTY, MARYLAND IN THE AMERICAN REVOLUTION
CALENDAR OF EVENTS

August 1774

The officials of St. Mary's County, Maryland, turned away from the public landing in St. Mary's River, Capt. George Chapman, Master of the British Brigantine, Mary and Jane, with his load of tea, on which they refused to pay the tax.

McSherry, History of Maryland, p. 173; Scharf, History of Maryland, Vol. 2, p. 159.

April 24 - May 3, 1775

Convention of Maryland, members attending from St. Mary's County:
John Reeder, Jr.
Richard Barnes
John Allen Thomas
Calendar of Maryland State Papers No. 4, Part 1, p. 1 (Item 3).

July 22, 1775

Committee of Observation, St. Mary's County
Certificate of election held at the Court House in Leonard Town on May 12 to choose Deputies to represent St. Mary's County in the Convention of Maryland:
John Reeder, Jr.
Richard Barnes
John Allen Thomas
Jeremiah Jordan
Signed by Timothy Bowes, Clerk
Calendar of Maryland State Papers Vol. 4, Part 1 (Item 7)

July 26 - August 14, 1775

Revolutionary Convention held in Annapolis.
Delegates from St. Mary's County were as shown above.
Proclamation issued by the Delegates

THE MARYLAND CONVENTION 1775
ASSOCIATION OF THE FREEMEN OF MARYLAND
July 26, 1775

The long premeditated and now avowed design of the British Government to raise a revenue from the property of the colonists without their consent on the gift, grant and disposition of the Commons of Great Britain; the arbitrary and vindictive statutes passed under color of punishing a riot, to subdue by military force, and by famine, the Massachusetts Bay; the unlimited power assumed by parliament to alter the charter of that province, and the constitution of all the colonies, thereby destroying the essential securities of the lives, liberties and properties of the colonists; the commencement of hosilities by the ministerial forces, and the cruel prosecution of the war against the people of the Massachusetts Bay, followed by General Gage's proclamation, declaring almost the whole of the Inhabitants of the united colonies, by name or description, rebels and traitors are sufficient causes to arm a free people in defence of their liberty, and to justify resistance, no longer dictated by prudence merely, but by necessity, and leave no alternative but base submission or manly opposition to uncontroulable tyranny. The Congress chose the latter, and for the express purpose of securing and defending the united colonies, and preserving them in safety, against all attempts to carry the above-mentioned acts into execution by force of arms.

Resolved, that the said colonies be immediately put into a state of defence, and now supports, at the joint expence, an army to restrain the further violence, and repel the future attacks of a disappointed and exasperated enemy.

We therefore inhabitants of the Province of Maryland, firmly persuaded that it is necessary and justifiable to repel force by force, do approve of the opposition by arms to the British troops, employed to enforce obediance to the late acts and statutes of the British parliament for raising a revenue in America, and altering and changing the Charter and Constitution of the Mass- achusetts Bay, and for destroying the essential securities for the lives, liberties and properties of the subjects in the united colonies. And we do unite and associate, as one band, and firmly and solemnly engage and pledge ourselves to each other, and to America, that we will to the utmost of our power, promote and support the present opposition, carrying on, as well by arms, as by the continental association, restraining our commerce.

And as in these times of public danger, and until a reconciliation with Great Britain, on constitutional principles is effected (an event we most ardently wish may soon take place) the energy of government may be greatly impaired, so that even zeal unrestrained, may be productive of anarchy and confusion; we do in like manner unite, associate, and solemnly engage in maintenance of good order, and the public peace, to support the civil power in the due execution of the laws, so far as may be consistent with the present plan of opposition; and to defend with our utmost power all persons from every species of outrage to themselves or their property, and to prevent any punishment from being inflicted on any offend- ers, other than such, as shall be adjudged by the civil magistrate, continental congress, our convention, council of safety or committees of observation.

                Signed by: Matthew Tilghman, Chairman
                            John Reeder Junr.
                            Richard Barnes
                            Jeremiah Jordan
                            John Allen Thomas
representing St. Mary's County, and by 106 others representing the several other counties of Maryland.
Archives of Maryland Vol. 11, p. 66, 67.

During this Convention St. Mary's County agreed to form two Companies of Minute Men (every able bodied Freeman between the ages of 16 and 50 years of age, with a few exceptions, had to enroll in a Company of Militia), each of which Companies to consist of one Captain, two Lieutentants, one Ensign, four Sergeants, four Corporals, one Drummer, one Fifer and 68 privates - the Companies of St. Mary's, Charles and Prince George's Counties to form one Battalion and to each Battalion there be one Colonel and one Lieutentant Colonel, two Majors, one Quarter Master and one Adjutant appointed and commissioned. A Committee of Observation composed of 24 members was formed in St. Mary's County. Also formed was a General Committee for St. Mary's County with John Reeder, Jr. as Chairman and Timothy Bowes as Clerk.
        Archives of Maryland Vol. 11, p. 3, 5, 17, 18, 27, 41, 43, 44;
        Calendar of Maryland State Papers No. 5, p. 29, (Item 224).

July 22, 1775
        Trial of Archibald Campbell and Wm. Lilburn, factors in Leonardtown and St. Inigoes for violation of the 6th Resolve of the Provincial Convention held in Annapolis Dec. 8, 1774, which prohibited the export of provisions of any kind, etc., from the colony. Trial conducted by the General Committee of St. Mary's County, John Reeder, Jr., presiding, Timothy Bowes, Clerk. Found guilty.
        Archives of Maryland Vol. 11, p. 41-44.

July 29, 1775
John Allen Thomas, a delegate from St. Mary's County in attendance at the Maryland Convention of July 26 - August 14, 1775.
Archives of Maryland, Vol. 11, p. 5.

August 3, 1775
Proceedings of the Maryland Convention
Upon reading the Petition of Archibald Campbell and William Lilburn and considering the Resolution of the Committee of St. Mary's County, Resolved, that the said Archibald Campbell and William Lilburn have not been guilty of a breach of the Resolve of the late Convention and therefore that no further proceedings be had against them.
Archives of Maryland Vol. 11, p. 9.

September 12, 1775
Jeremiah Jordan, John Allen Thomas, Richard Barnes, George Plater and John Reeder, Jr., elected Delegates to the Provincial Convention. Attested by Timothy Bowes, Clerk, November 30, 1775.
Calendar of Maryland State Papers No. 5, p. 26 (Item 203).

December 7, 1775
Convention of Maryland, St. Mary's County Members:
Jeremiah Jordan
John Allen Thomas
Richard Barnes
George Plater
John Reeder, Jr.
Calendar of Maryland State Papers No. 5, p. 29 (Item 224).

January 2, 1776
5th Independent Maryland Company, St. Mary's County Officers elected by the Convention, January 2, 1776:
John Allen Thomas, Captain
John Steward, 1st Lieutenant
John Davidson, 2nd Lieutenant
Henry Neale, 3rd Lieutenant
(The roll of the Company men is missing)
Archives of Maryland, Vol. 18, p. 25.

January 3, 1776
Richard Watts, Pvt., enlisted in Capt. Thomas Ewing's Company (4th) on 1/3/1776. He appears in the 1st. Reg. on 12/10/1776 and in the 3rd. Reg. in 1778.
Archives of Maryland Vol. 18, p. 11, 173, 291.

January 12, 1776
Ballot to determine the rank of Colonels, statewide. In St. Mary's County, Jeremiah Jordan ranked 6 and Richard Barnes 21.
Calendar of Maryland State Papers, No. 5, p. 34 (Item 257).

January 23, 1776
Council of Safety (1775-1777) ordered that the Committee of Observation for Charles County send 2 1/2 barrels of powder and 1000 pounds weight of lead under the care of a Commissioned Officer of the Militia to the Committee of Observation for St. Mary's County, half a barrel of said powder for Capt. John Allen Thomas' Company of regular Troops, and the residue for the two Battalions of Militia in that County.
Archives of Maryland Vol. 11, p. 106.

January 24, 1776
    John Lemmon (Lemon) enlisted in the 1st. Co. of Matrosses in the Province of Maryland.
    Archives of Maryland Vol. 18, p. 563.

January 27, 1776
    Council of Safety-Col. George Plater, Richard Barnes and Hanson Briscoe of St. Mary's County to collect all the gold and silver coin that can be procured in the County to comply with the resolves of the Continental Congress.
    Archives of Maryland, Vol. 11, p. 132.

January 29, 1776
    Richard Carberry, Pvt. enlisted in Capt. Thomas Ewing's Company (4th) Regular Troops.
    Archives of Maryland Vol. 18, p. 12.

February 10, 1776
    Council of Safety requests that the Committee of Observation of St. Mary's County send to Annapolis all Gun-Locks in the County belonging to the Province.
    Also ordered the Treasurer of the Western Shore pay to Capt. John Allen Thomas 200£ Currency on acct. of his Company.
    Archives of Maryland Vol. 11, p. 148.

February 23, 1776
    Richard Barnes, Leonardtown to Council of Safety
    As directed by the Committee of St. Mary's County, is sending 7 gunlocks by Henry Neale; also sending gold to be exchanged for paper money; Lt. Philip Reed of the Leonardtown Company in the 21st. Battalion has resigned; recommends Ensign Bennet Combs in his place and James Williams as Ensign.
    Archives of Maryland Vol. 11, p. 181.

February 24, 1776
    John Allen Thomas to the Council of Safety
    Requests the Council to order 1st. Lt. John Stewart and the men he has enlisted to Leonardtown; he has failed to obey Thomas' orders to that effect; his own men are there supported by Benjamin (?) Ford; wants a horse for the use of the Company; the bearer, Henry Neale, will deliver his account for 7 gunlocks sent by the Committee and 6 purchased; 2nd. Lt. John Davidson reports a servant in Baltimore is a good fifer and is valued at about 15£ .
    Archives of Maryland Vol. 11, p. 184.

March 5, 1776
    George Plater of Sotterley sends 224 £, 1s. 3d. in gold collected in St. Mary's County to the Council of Safety as requested. It included 106 Guineas, 23 half Guineas, 5 half Johannes, 1 two Pistole Piece and 1 half Pistole.
    Archives of Maryland Vol. 11, p. 202.

March 7, 1776
    Commissions issued to Bennet Combs, appointed 2nd. Lieutenant and James Williams, Ensign of a Company of Militia in St. Mary's County.
    Archives of Maryland Vol. 11, p. 205.

March 8, 1776
    Report to the Council of Safety by John Allen Thomas
    Three armed vessels are near the mouth of the Patuxent; have taken a vessel laden with flour; arms and supplies are needed; sending Lt. John Steward for arms; part of his men are stationed on the Patuxent and the rest on the Potomac; Mr. Ford and Mr. Neale are handling provisions for the troops; recommends Robert Chesley and

Henry Carberry as Cadets; requests a seine for each division so men can catch fish, and a frying pan for each mess.
Archives of Maryland Vol. 11, p. 221, 228.

March 9, 1776
Letter from the Virginia Committee to the Council of Safety proposing the erection of beacons or signals in the Potomac River for communicating intelligence of the approach of enemies up the river in a more speedy manner than can be done by land and requesting that Maryland Commissioners be appointed to cooperate in effecting it.
Archives of Maryland Vol. 11, p. 228.

March 10, 1776
Ben Burroughs, Pvt. enlisted in Capt. Pat. Sims Company (2nd) and Charles Burroughs, Pvt. enlisted in the same Company on March 11, 1776.
Archives of Maryland Vol. 18, p. 8.

March 14, 1776
Council of Safety ordered that Capt. John Allen Thomas' Independent Company be stationed at Leonardtown.
Archives of Maryland Vol. 11, p. 245.

March 18, 1776
Capt. John Allen Thomas, Mouth of Patuxent to Council of Safety
Has received Council's letter of March 12; had not previously heard of order to keep troops in Leonardtown; this would have saved men much fatigue as on March 5 they marched to the Mouth of Patuxent and last Thursday to Point Lookout where the enemy were reported about to land; if he is only to defend Leonardtown he wants positive instructions as only thus could he justify to the public his failure to go to meet an invasion; needs money as he has used all his own he could scrape together; will transmit his accounts as soon as John Stewart returns; has 50 men stationed at Mrs. Carroll's; the rest, unarmed are at Leonardtown.
Calendar of Maryland State Papers No. 5, p. 40, (Item 301).

March 19, 1776
Council of Safety ordered George Plater, Esq. and Brig. Gen'l. John Dent to meet with the Virginia Committee of Safety on erecting Beacons on the Potomac River.
Archives of Maryland Vol. 11, p. 262, 263, 264, 286, 291.

March 23, 1776
Capt. John Allen Thomas is refused permission by the Council of Safety to purchase a Virginia Pilot Boat for conveying troops to and from Calvert and St. Mary's Counties, etc.
Archives of Maryland Vol. 11, p. 276.

Council of Safety to the Maryland Deputies.
".... a flying report by Charles Landsdale this Day, that they (British-Men-of-War) were lately seen at the mouth of Potowmack..."
Archives of Maryland Vol. 11, p. 277.

March 28, 1776
Lt. John Thomas Boucher of the Ship Defence resigns his commission to command the Virginia Potomac Fleet.
Archives of Maryland Vol. 11, p. 293, 294.

April 2, 1776
Capt. John Allen Thomas, in a letter of March 18, objected to being obliged to keep his force in Leonardtown; needs to watch both the Patuxent and Potomac Rivers;

Council of Safety makes a "tart" reply; he shouldn't "divide the Company"; however, will consider another plan if the Committee of Observation should be of that opinion; sent 150 Ł. by Lt. Steward.
Archives of Maryland Vol. 11, p. 303, 304.

April 6, 1776
James Adams, Pvt. enlisted in Capt. Patk. Sims' Company (2nd).
Archives of Maryland Vol. 18, p. 7.

April 12, 1776
Council of Safety ordered Treasurer of the Western Shore pay to Mr. Athanasius Ford 143 Ł.1s.5d. for subsistence for Capt. John Allen Thomas Independent Company. Also pay Capt. Thomas 61 Ł.5s.11d. being the balance of his General Account.
Archives of Maryland Vol. 11, p. 328, 332.

April 19, 1776
Lt. Uriah Forrest should be given 300 Ł. to pay soldiers.
Calendar of Maryland State Papers No. 4, Part 2, p. 33 (Item 203).

April 22, 1776
Council ordered the Commissary of Stores deliver to Capt. John Allen Thomas for Capt. Rezin Beall's Independent Company 29 Musquets, 4 Rifles, Powder Horns, Pouches and Bullet Moulds, 6 Musquet Bullet Moulds, 300 Gun Flints, 100 Gun Slings, 62 Cartouch Boxes and Belts, 104 Hats and 5 Bolts of Osnaburgs.
Archives of Maryland Vol. 11, p. 367.

Capt. John Allen Thomas has Leave to procure leathern Caps for his Independent Company instead of Hats. Also ordered delivery to Capt. Thomas 13 Musquets, 4 Rifles, 6 Musquet Bullet Moulds, 4 Rifle ditto and 5 1/2 Bolts of Osnaburgs. Capt. Thomas also requested to purchase all the Buck Shot he can procure in St. Mary's County. 1 Barrel and 10 Kegs of Gun Powder and 600 lbs. of lead ordered sent to the St. Mary's County Committee of Observation.
Archives of Maryland, Vol. 11, p. 367, 368.

April 23, 1776
Council of Safety orders Treasurer of Western Shore to pay Capt. John Allen Thomas 28 Ł.14s. and 5 d. being balance of his general acct. to Apr. 3 - also pay him 394 Ł. 1s. 8d. on Acct. of his Company. Ordered Mr. Athanasius Ford of St. Mary's Co. pay Capt. Thomas 27 Ł. 7s. & 6d. for money paid him over & above just amount of his Acct. Ordered Commissary of Stores to deliver to Capt. Thomas 1/2 a Ream of Cartridge paper and 10 pieces of Check.
Archives of Maryland Vol. 11, p. 371.

April 30, 1776
Report of John Dent and George Plater - have met with the Commissioners from Virginia for erecting Beacons on the Potomac River & have fixed the number of stations for the same to the number of twenty, whereof 13 are in Maryland, one in Prince George's, nine in Charles and 3 in St. Mary's averaging about 5 miles from each other. Also agreed upon the form of the Alarm Post which is to be a kind of Iron Grate suspended by a chain on the end of a sweep fixed with a Swivel so as to be turned agreeable to the wind.
Archives of Maryland Vol. 11, p. 394.

May 20, 1776
Council of Safety ordered Treasurer of the Western Shore to pay Col George Plater for the use of John Mason 2 Ł.13s.6d. for shot sold to Capt. J. A. Thomas.

Also pay Col. Richard Barnes 31 Ł. 9s. 2d. for pay & subsistence of a Company of his Battalion on Duty on late alarm.
Archives of Maryland, Vol. 11, p. 431.

May 25, 1776
George Plater, Esq. took oath as a member of the Council of Safety and again qualified and took the oath on July 16, 1776.
Archives of Maryland Vol. 11, p. 449; Vol. 12, p. 53.

May 27, 1776 - March 20, 1777
Hon. George Plater of St. Mary's County qualified as a member of the Council of Safety and took the prescribed oath. Mr. Plater requested (May 28, 1776) to have a Chart of Smith's Creek in St. Mary's County made immediately, with the Soundings into the River and the Altitude of the banks on each side of the said Creek. Mr. Richard Barnes was appointed in the place of Mr. Plater to join with Brig. Gen'l. Dent in erecting Beacons on the Potomac River.
Archives of Maryland, Vol. 11, p. 449.

June 3, 1776
Letter from the Council of Safety to Richard Barnes and Capt. John Allen Thomas informing them that a British Man of War may be daily expected in the Bay.
Archives of Maryland, Vol. 11, p. 461.

June 15, 1776
Letter to Col. George Plater from George Cook giving the channel soundings etc. in Smith Creek and reporting that Lord Dunmore's fleet is expected up the Bay.
Archives of Maryland, Vol. 11, p. 493.

June 18, 1776
Council of Safety ordered Treasurer of the Western Shore pay to George Plater, Esq. 37 Ł. 17s. 2d. 3f. on account of Capt. John Allen Thomas' Company and on June 19, 1776 to pay Plater 8 Ł. 4s. 6d. for expenses incurred in erecting Beacons in the Potomac River.
Archives of Maryland, Vol. 11, p. 497, 499.

June 19, 1776
Council of Safety ordered that in case Col. Joshua Beall has not already sent the Musquets made by John Yost for the use of this Province to Captains Rezin Beall and John Allen Thomas, Capt. Barton Lucas be requested to send the same in a Wagon to be procured for that Purpose.
Archives of Maryland, Vol. 11, p. 500.

June 20, 1776
Council of Safety issued commissions to John Mackall, appointed Captain Thomas Jenkins 1st Lieut., Bennet Tarlton 2nd Lt. and Philip Evans, Ensign of a Company of Militia in St. Mary's County.
Archives of Maryland, Vol. 11, p. 504.

June 21, 1776
Convention of Maryland. List of Members, St. Mary's County
Jeremiah Jordan
Richard Barnes
George Plater
John Reeder
Anthanasius Ford
Calendar of Maryland State Papers, No. 4, Part 1, p. 28 (Item 157).

June 24, 1776
Council of Safety ordered Capt. John Allen Thomas to march his Independent

Company to Cedar Point or Susquehanna in the lower part of St. Mary's County and guard the shores from thence to the Potomac River to prevent any servants, negroes or others from going on board the British Ship of War Fowey. (The Fowey, under a flag of truce, was in Annapolis to take off Governor Robert Eden).
    Archives of Maryland, Vol. 11, 511.

June 25, 1776
    Council ordered Treasurer of the Western Shore pay to Thomas Briscoe 15 shillings for going express on Acct. of No. Carolina Prisoners.
    Archives of Maryland Vol. 4, p. 515.

June 28, 1776
    Resolution by the Convention of Maryland appointing George Plater......
to visit Somerset County and take necessary measures to unite it with other Counties
......
    Calendar of Maryland State Papers No. 4, Part 1, p. 33 (Item 186).

June 29, 1776
    Council of Safety ordered that the Treasurer of the Western Shore pay
to

Uriah Forrest	Capt. St. Mary's Co.	69 £. 15s.
Wm. Bond	1st Lt. Do	46 £. 10s.
Moses Tabbs	2nd Lt. Do	46£. 10s.
Edward Mattingly	Ensign Do	37£. 5s.

    Archives of Maryland, Vol. 11, p. 534.

July 1, 1776
    Proceedings of the Committee of observation, St. Mary's County
    Present: Col. Abraham Barnes, Chairman, Capt. Edward Abell, Maj. Samuel Abell, Capt. Gerard Bond, Maj. James Eden, Maj. Ignatius Fenwick, Capt. Vernon Hebb, Wilfred Neale, Col. John Hatton Read, Nicholas L. Sewall, Capt. John Smith, William Taylor, Henry Tubman, Daniel Wolstenholme, "Collector of his Majesty's Customs on North Potomack", having obtained a warrant from his Majesty's Board of Treasury to return to Great Britain because of his ill health, is granted a passport to leave the Province.
    Calendar of Maryland State Papers No. 4, Part 2, p. 52 (Item 337).

July 3, 1776
    Convention of Maryland - Resolution directing that "a new Convention be elected for the express purpose of forming a new government"; four representatives are to be chosen for each county ....
    Judges of the election in St. Mary's County
            Abraham Barnes
            Hugh Hopewell
            Henry Tubman
    Calendar of Maryland State Papers, No. 4, Part 1, p. 35 (Item 203).

St. Mary's County

Capt. Uriah Forrest	2nd. Lt. Moses Tabbs
1st. Lt. Wm. Bond	Ensign Edward Mattingly

    A List of men enrolled by Capt. Uriah Forrest, Lieut. Wm. Bond, Lieut. Moses Tabbs and Ensign Mattingly, to compose one company in Col. Thomas Ewing's Battalion for the Flying Camp. Mustered, examined and passed July 28th, 1776 by Ign. Fenwick, Jr.

George Armstrong	Thos. Shircliff	William Rock	Wm. Adams
Chas. Llewellin	Jo Bradshaw	Jere Allstone	Robt. McClannon
Ign. Simms, Jr.	James Bramhall	(Allstan)	(McClelland)
Sam'l. H. Briscoe	Thos. Davie	Alex Shanks	Jo. Adams

Wm. J. Hager	Luke Cusick	Ign. Knott	Wm. Hendry
John Maddox	Jesse Herbert	Thos. Bridgitt	John Christopher
John McKoy	Thos. Martin	Wm. Moles	Richard Hindmore
(McKay)	Richard Bullock	Joseph Long	Joseph Alvey
Edw. Spalding	Jesse Jordan	John Bond, Jr.	Ign. Watkin
Geo. Elms	Wm. Hebb	Moses Adams	(Wathen)
Edw. Marshall	Joshua Ellis	John Baker	John Fields
Fran Watkin	Gabriel Williams	Enoch Sanders	Richard Weakley
(Wathen?)	John Moore	John Price, Jr.	(Weaklin)
Edward White	Richard Gardiner	Henry Horn Carter	John C. Watkin
John Bramhall	Sam'l. Jordan	Wm. Howard	(Wathen)
Austin Howard	James Jordan	Wm. Burnett	John Hughes
Matthew Shanks	Chas. Bond	Thos. Cook, Jr.	Thos. Cahill
Charles Jones	Justinian Weeden	Enoch Adams	John Holland
Wm. Ennis	(Wheeden)	Richard Morris	John Compton
Thos. Bartcly	Wm. Cheseldine	Wm. Johnstone	Thos. Biggs
Elias Bailey	Reubin Craig	(Johnson or Johnston)	Rich. E. Catton
Robert Shanks	Thos. Wood	Wm. Carpenter, Jr.	(Gadden)
Jesse Dennis	Wm. Coode	Richard Kerbey	Joseph Johnstone
James Tear	Joseph Dailey	Thos. Haywood	(Johnson or Johnston?)
James Melton	Jesse Tennison	Thos. Files	John Graves

Enlisted by Lieut Wm. Bond, July 3rd, 1776. Reviewed and passed by John H. Briscoe, July 12th, 1776.

Gerard Cheseldine

Archives of Maryland, Vol. 18, p. 30.

July 5, 1776

Council of Safety ordered that the Commissary of Stores at Annapolis deliver to Capt. J. A. Thomas 50 musquets, one set of large bullet molds & 3 bolts of Oznabgs and 60 yards of country linen. Ordered that Capt. Rezin Beall be requested to deliver to Capt. J. A. Thomas six of the rifles lately sent him by the Council of Safety and also that he and Capt. Thomas immediately send all the spare musquets now in his possession under the direction of Capt. Thomas to the public Magazine at Annapolis. Ordered that the Commissary of stores at Annapolis deliver to Lieut. Adams for the use of Capt. Rezin Beall 6 ps. Check & 2 bolts Oznabgs. Ordered that the Western Shore Treasurer pay to Capt. J. A. Thomas 20 L.16s. Curry.for making 104 hunting shirts.

Archives of Maryland, Vol. 11, p. 551.

July 6, 1776

Convention of Maryland

Order directing Col. William Smallwood and his battalion and the independent companies in Talbot, Kent, Queen Anne's and St. Mary's Counties to proceed to Philadelphia and there be subject to the orders of Congress....

Calendar of Maryland State Papers No. 4, Part 1, p. 41 (Item 234)

Capt. John Allen Thomas being ordered by the Honorable Convention with his Company to Philadelphia, the good people of this Province are requested to give him every assistance in their power on his march, and to furnish him with carts &c, which may be proper, all necessary expenses will be defrayed by the Council of Safety. Ordered that Capt. Rezin Beall immediately furnish out of his Company as many musquets with bayonets as will completely arm Capt. John Allen Thomas' Company.

Council of Safety to Capt. Rezin Beall - as Capt. Thomas is directed by the Honorable Convention to march immediately with his Company to the Northward, and as 'tis proper his men should be as completely armed as possible, we have ordered that you furnish him with such of the guns with bayonets belonging to your

Company as may be sufficient for that purpose. He will leave with you what of his guns have not got bayonets - we desire to have a particular state of the arms of your Company after Capt. Thomas may have delivered you his that we may immediately order you a proper supply from here to make up the deficiency if there should be any wanting.

Archives of Maryland, Vol. 11, p. 554, 556.

July 6, 1776 - November 11, 1776
George Plater of St. Mary's County appointed as a member of the Council of Safety.

Manual, State of Maryland, 1973-1974, p. 811.

July 9, 1776
Council of Safety ordered Capt. John Allen Thomas to furnish a Roll of the Troops of his Battalion which will march to Phila. with an account of their arms, accoutrements, camp utensils and baggage.

Archives of Maryland, Vol. 12, p. 16.

July 10, 1776
A List of Ships in Lord Dunmore's Fleet
Roebuck a forty four gun ship - Commodore Hammond, Commander
Fowey a twenty gun ship   Montague   "
Otter a ten gun Sloop of War   Squires   "
Dunmore a frigate built Ship mounting 4 Sixpounders on one side
William a Ship with 2 four pounders of a side, a part of the 14th Regt. on board
Anna a Ship barricaded with a part of the 14th Regt. on board
Dun Luce a Ship occupied by the Queens Loyals, a Regt. of Ds. raising
Grace a Ship belonging to & occupied by Mr. Fleming and family
Levant a Store Ship on which Gov. Robt. Eden has taken a passage
Brigantine Fincastle belonging to and occupied by Niel Jamieson
Brigt. Dolphin belonging to and occupied by Hector McAlester
Brigt. Maria occupied by John Allason and family
    Do   Fanny   "   "   Doctor McCaa & family
    Do   Betsy   "   "   Capt. Boynoe   "   "
    Do   Do   "   "   Dr. Coakley   "   "   , sometimes wt. negroes
    Do   -   "   "   Mr. Feener   "   "
A Spanish Snow, Prize Master, Super Cargoe, Capt. & Crew on board
Brigt. Helena belonging to Roger Steuart, occupied as Prison for Prisoners
    Do   William & Charles from Barbadoes, on board 300 Hhds. R & 100
            Do Sugar sent in by the Governor of Barbadoes for Sir Peter Parker
Snow Unicorn, on board of which is Black Smith Shop
Brigt. Hammond, occupied by Mr. John Hunter & Mr. Sprowles family
Schooner Thomas, occupied by William Calderhead & family
    Do   Charlotte   "   "   "   Hargisdes   "   "
Sloop Campbell   "   "   Mr. Farmer   "   "
    Do   Peace & Plenty belonging to and occupied by Mr. Eilbeck
    Do   Lady Augusta   "   "   "   "   " Capt. Lowes
    Do   Lady Gower, a Tender, John Wilkie, Commander
    Do   Lady Stanly, "   "   Willm. Younghusband "
Sloop Lady Susan a Tender Briger Goodrich, Commander
Schooner Gaze   "   "   belonging to the Roebuck
Sloop Fincastle of 12 guns belonging to the Otter
    Do Lady Gage a Tender belonging to the Fowey
Seven Sloops occupied by Messrs. Spedden & Goodriches familys
Two Schooners   "   "   John Brown & Family
Ship Logan belonging to & occupied by Mr. Logan & family
Sloop John Grymes occupied by said Grymes & some Dragoons
Most of the other Vessels are Small Craft and occupied by Trades people & negroes,
    vessels that are not fit to go to Sea

MARYLAND'S ROW GALLEYS

It was realized that to build a Navy comparable to that of Great Britain was impossible. Instead hundreds of Privateers were commissioned, a few Ships were built and row galleys (which also were equpped with sails) were utilized to protect the coastal and inland waterways, as will be seen in the Calendar entries.

Row galley construction was begun in Maryland in June 1776. Archibald Buchanan, of Baltimore, at the suggestion of Henry Sewall of St. Mary's County, was awarded a contract to build two of these crafts. George Wells of Baltimore also contracted to build two and Stephen Steward, who had a boat yard in Annapolis, together with Samuel Galloway, was given a contract to build five of these vessels. Likewise, Thomas Smyth, of Chestertown built one or more, so the Colony had a fleet of about a dozen of these craft. Galleys also were built by the neighboring Colonies of Pennsylvania and Virginia and they were used extensively on Lake Champlain.

We are indebted to Mr. Howard I. Chapelle for the sketches of the galley, Washington, shown below, which appear in his fine book The History of The American Sailing Ships. Mr. William B. Kerkam, Jr., a Navy buff of Washington, D.C. was kind enough to arrange for the reproductions.

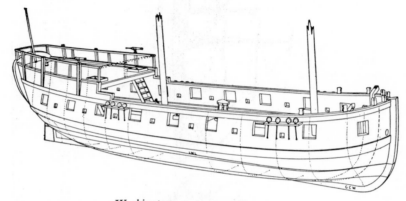

CONTINENTAL GALLEY *Washington.*

Washington, LAKE CHAMPLAIN GALLEY, 1776.

These craft ranged from 45 to 90 feet in length, with a beam of 16 to 20, drawing 8 to 10 feet of water and were equipped with 14 to 20 sweeps or oars. They were armed with 8 to 12 guns from 4 to 18 pounders and usually had as many swivels. They were in action as far out as the Capes of Virginia. The Galleys, Conqueror, Baltimore, and Independence were under the Command of Capt. George Cook of St. Mary's County and were used extensively in the waters surrounding the County.

Archives of Maryland Vol. 11, p. 227, 458, 462, 477, 541; Vol. 12, p. 17, 31, 141, 157, 207, 263, 460, 485, 515, 556; Vol. 16, p. 6, 7, 58, 81, 125, 127, 130, 132, 134, 260, 288, 333, 422, 442.

See Text, page 19, 32, 36, 40, 41, 42

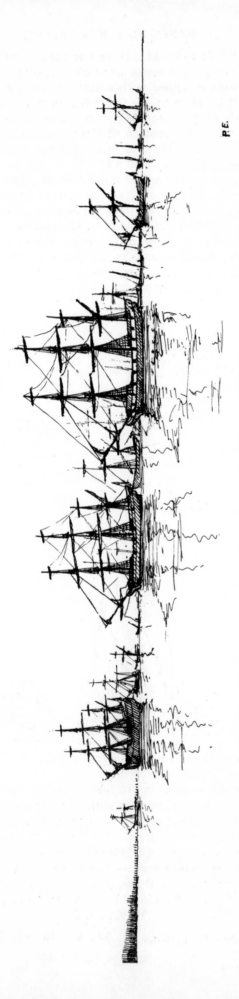

P.E.

LORD DUNMORE'S FLEET, AS IT MUST HAVE APPEARED, OFF ST. GEORGE'S ISLAND, JULY 12, 1776.
by Peter Egeli, St. Mary's County, MD

From the book, Life on the Potomac River

The Lively, frigate cruising of the Capes.
> Archives of Maryland, Vol. 12, p. 24, 25. Calendar of Maryland State
> Papers No. 4, Part 1, p. 43 (Item 248).

July 12, 1776
> Letter to Capt. Richard Chew, Saturday morning 7 O'clock

Dr. Sir.

I this moment recd by Express a line from Collo. Somervill acquainting me that there are forty Sail of Square Rig'd Vessells as far up the Bay as Point Lookout. We have ordered the Captains of our Battalion to call their Companies together immediately and have their Guns put in the best order they will admit of. Like for them to be ready to march at a moments warning. Capt. Parran's Company is under Arms, have herd (sic) the whole of the militia of St. Maries is in Arms. If the Vessel (sic) come up farther, which I make no doubt they will, Barbara begs that Mrs. Chew will come down here. I am in grate haste, then conclude by Subscribing myself.

> Your Most Obedient Servant, Joseph Wilkinson
>> Archives of Maryland, Vol. 12, p. 39.

July 13, 1776
> Richard Barnes to the Council of Safety   St. Inigoes 13th July 1776

Gentn. I recd. information on Friday the 12th July that there was arrived a considerable number of Ships and small Vessels between Smiths Point & Point Lookout on which I ordered five Companys of Militia to repare (sic) there as fast as possible and immediately set out to the Point myself in order to git further information. On my arrival there I found about forty Sail of Vessels - they were then about twenty five miles off the Point in the Bay, where they continued till in the night. In the morning about fifty eight Sail were discovered opposite Smiths Creek in Potomack & eight in the Bay, on which I gave orders to call the Companys of my Battalion immediately to march to Potomack in order to prevent their landing in the District of the 21st. Battn. We have had two small vessels drove on shore from the Fleet, on board of one of them was three whites & two Negroes, three of which now have the Small Pox on them. On(e) of the white men informed us the Fleet was Dunmore's, and that Govr. Eden was on board the Foey & that he heard it surmised that they intended to take possession of St. George's Island, since which the Foey and her Tender have come to in St. Mary's River and I don't doubt but the greatest part if not all of the Fleet will be there in the morning. We have between two and three hundred of our Militia Stationed in different places, and I have just sent off an express to Colo Jordan to supply me with one or two hundred men of his Battalion if possible. From the above affair I think it would be proper (if) Captn. Beall's Company from Drum Point should be ordered here and their place there supplyed with the Militia of the Coty. I should be glad of your advice and assistance. I should have wrote you more particularly but have been marching from place to place from the morning till now, which is twelve o'clock in the night, and am much tiard (sic). Mr. Hugh Hopewell has promised to hire an express in Calvert to carry this to you, should therefore be glad you would pay him.

> I remain Gentn Your hble Servt.   Richd Barnes
>> Archives of Maryland, Vol. 12, p. 43, 44.

> John Allen Thomas to the Council of Safety. Agreed to pay John David 30s. a day for a vessel to transport his company to Annapolis.
>> Archives of Maryland Vol. 12, p. 186; Calendar of Maryland State Papers, No. 4
>> Part 2 (Item 348).

July 14, 1776
> Alex Somervill to the Council of Safety   5 oclock Sunday Calvert County

Gentlemen. About one o'clock yesterday morning by express from Capt. Beall, I received information that there were forty sail of vessels off Point Look Out (Eight of which were Square Rigged) & requesting some Assistance from our Militia (and to get the other part in Readiness in case they should proceed up the Bay) Colo. Mackall not being in the County, I gave such Orders as I thought might put us in the best posture of Defence: the Six Upper Companys were to hold themselves in readiness to march on the shortest notice & with Part of the rest I went to Drum Point. About 4 o'clock a firing of Cannon &c was heard (Supposed to be in Potowmack) which is confirmed this morning by Mr. Hugh Hopewell Junr who was down near where the firing was; and brought the Inclosed Letter from Colo. Barnes: who also requested the Assistance of Captn Beall & his men. Mr. Hopewell came to Drum Point this morning abt nine oclock & Captn Beall with all the men he had there, set out about half past Ten; leaving that Post in the Charge of our Militia......The Ships of War, Tenders &c was this morning lying off between St. Mary's River & Point Look Out & it is reported by some Desserters from thence that they intend to Land on St. George's Island .... Colo Barnes could not get an Express to carry his Letter to you in St. Mary's, therefore sent it this way....I am Gent Your Mo: obedt Hbl Servt

Alex Somervill

Archives of Maryland, Vol. 12, p. 45; Calendar of Maryland State Papers, Vol. 4, Part 1, p. 43 (Item 250).

July 15, 1776

Council of Safety ordered the Treasurer of the Western Shore to pay 38₤. 5s. for Leathern Caps furnished Capt. Thomas' Company.

Council of Safety to Lt. Col. Alexander Somervill

Sir. We received yours...and one also from Col. Richard Barnes informing us that Lord Dunmore and the Fleet were within the mouth of Potowmack and... intended to take Possession...of St. Georges Island but as their designs are uncertain we think you had better give notice to your Battalion to keep themselves in readiness to march to oppose any attempt they may make to Land in your County and likewise to assist in any neighbouring County. Capt. Beall will have orders from us to remain in St. Mary's County with Colonel Barnes to watch the motions of the Enemy....

Council to Captain Rezin Beall

....You will stay in St. Mary's County so long as you apprehend the Enemy may have any design of Landing there or making any attempt to distress or plunder the Inhabitants, if they should move from thence.....you will follow them with all dispatch....

Council to Brigadier General John Dent

....We think it expedient that in this emergency you should yourself take the Command (in St. Mary's County) and remain with them till you hear further from us – as the militia for the Flying Camp are not in readiness. We conceive it will not interfere with your duty as Brigadier of those Corps, and your presence will be much wanted at this time in your District. Capt. Beall with his Independent Company is now in St. Mary's County....He and his Company will likewise be subject to your Command....

Council to Colonel Richard Barnes

We have yours of the 13th and are glad you sent for Capt. Beall's Company.... we have wrote to Brigadier Dent to have all the Militia in his District kept in readiness to march to your assistance....he will also take on him the Command of the Independent Company – you will on all occasions send us up Notice of the Motions of the Enemy and we shall order you every assistance in our power.

Council to Captain John Allen Thomas

We have just received intelligence that makes it necessary for us to stop your proceeding up the Bay with your Company; we therefore desire you will immediately return with it to Annapolis.

Colonel Jeremiah Jordan to the Council

Gentlemen: St. Mary's County July 15th 1776

This (is) to inform you that there is now lying off the mouth of St. Mary's River between seventy and eighty sail of vessels. I am now at Leonard Town on my way down with part of the 6th Battalion under my command, where I received an Express from Colo. Barnes (who is now at St. Inigoes Neck with the lower Battalion) informing me that this morning Ten Boats full of men landed on St. George's Island and had

IN CONGRESS, JULY 4, 1776.

The unanimous Declaration of the thirteen united States of America.

[Facsimile of the handwritten Declaration of Independence text and signatures]

DECLARATION OF INDEPENDENCE

The Declaration of Independence was adopted by the Continental Congress, in Philadelphia, on July 4, 1776. John Hancock was president of the Congress and Charles Thompson was secretary. A copy of the Declaration, engrossed on parchment, was signed by Members of Congress on and after August 2, 1776. On January 18, 1777, Congress ordered that "authenticated copies, with the names of the Members of Congress subscribed the same, be sent to each of the United States, and that they be desired to have same put upon record." Authenticated copies were printed in broadside form in Baltimore, where the Continental Congress was then in session.

On July 16, 1776 the Council of Safety in Annapolis wrote to the Committee of Observation of St. Mary's County as follows: "Gentlemen: Inclosed we send you the Declaration of Independence and the letter that accompanied it from Congress to the Convention, Requesting that it should be proclaimed in our Colony. We transmit the Declaration to you that you may proclaim it in your County in the manner you Judge most proper for the Information of the people."

IN HONOR OF
MARYLAND'S FOVR HVNDRED
WHO ON THIS BATTLE-FIELD
AVGVST 27ᵗʰ 1776
SAVED THE AMERICAN ARMY

GOOD GOD! WHAT BRAVE FELLOWS
I MVST THIS DAY, LOSE
GEORGE WASHINGTON

Maryland's 400 was composed of men from
the Southern Counties and the Eastern Shore.
(See Text, page 23, 26 and 27)

Courtesy of Mrs. Jane Schwertfager

returned for more. I expect to be opposite the Island some time this night and shall endeavour to get the best intelligence I can of their numbers and give the earliest notice. We shall want more powder and lead and also flints if they are to be had. Major Eden by whom this goes will inform you more fully. The Committee (of Observation) for this County sat this day and have detained Capt. (Uriah) Forrest's Company until they hear from you. I am Gentlemen: Your Mo: obedt Servt

Jeremiah Jordan

Enclosed are Capt. Forrest's & Lieut. Bond's enrollments, the other two officers have completed theirs, but have not returned them to Capt. Forrest....

Archives of Maryland, Vol. 12, p. 47, 48, 49, 50, 51.

July 14, 1776

Council ordered Treasurer of the Western Shore pay to George Plater, Esqr. 14 £.2s.8d. for expenses attending his Journey to Somerset County.

Archives of Maryland, Vol. 12, p. 62.

July 16, 1776

The Honble George Plater Esq. a member of the Council (of Safety) attended and was qualified before Mr. Jenifer by taking the Oath prescribed by the Convention.

The Council of Safety to the Committee of Observation of St. Mary's County.

Gentlemen: Inclosed we send you the Declaration of Independence and the letter that accompanied it from Congress to the Convention, Requesting that it should be proclaimed in our Colony. We transmit the Declaration to you that you may proclaim it in your County in the manner you Judge most proper for the Information of the People.

Instructions for obtaining Firelocks, Blankets, etc. for troops raised in the County for the Flying Camp. Can pay as much as 4 £.10s. for Muskets with a steel Ramrod and Bayonet.

Archives of Maryland, Vol. 12, p. 53, 55, 57.

July 17, 1776

Council of Safety to Captain David Crawford

Sir. This is to advise you that we are ordering some Ammunition to St. Mary's County; you are therefore desired to prepare a Waggon with all expedition to be ready to receive it as soon as the Cart sent from hence may arrive with you, which we think will be this Evening or tomorrow morning and to forward it under a Guard of Eight Men and an Officer to Leonard Town in said County. We trust you will use all diligence and give the greatest dispatch to this necessary business.

Council to Brig. Gen'l. John Dent

Sir. We received a letter from Colo. Jordan last night advising that some of Dunmore's party had landed on St. George's and that the Boats were gone off to the Vessels...for more...we request you will communicate to us by the return of the Express all the Information you can collect...We have countermanded the orders given Captains Thomas and Hindman to march to Philadelphia and expect them here to Day or Tomorrow, upon receiving intelligence from you we shall be able to form an opinion whether it will be necessary they should be ordered to your assistance. Powder, Lead and Flints are sent off this Morning to Leonard Town and we hope will arrive there to morrow night or on Friday morning. We approve the Committee's detaining Capt. Forrest's Company, and think it would be best if the Militia will part with their Guns that the Company should be armed with them and immediately be subject to your orders.

Council to Thomas Smyth, Esq.

...We are sorry we cannot comply with other requests you have made.... in Kent (County) Our Province is actually Invaded by Lord Dunmore with his whole Fleet who are now come into Potowmack and are landing at St. George's Island, our own Battalion and Independent Companies are marched off to the eastward....

Col. Jeremiah Jordon to the Council of Safety

St. Mary's County, St. George's River July 17, 1776

Gentlemen. I arrived down here on the 15th Inst. with about one hundred of the Militia, where I found Capt. Beall with part of his Company and one Company of Colo. Barne's

Battalion. About daybreak yesterday we were visited by a Row Galley or Row Gondola carrying 5 Swivels on each side and a six pounder in her head and another in her stern, they rowed along side our centinals and not a man to be seen and instantly began a very heavy firing which lasted about one hour but without doing any execution, altho their shot reached the ground on every spot where the men were stationed. In the evening she returned again and engaged us again for upwards of two hours, and at the same time the troops landed from the ships in St. George's Island to the amount of about 300 pushed down to the point opposite to us with swivels and musquetry and kept up a heavy fire from which Capt. Beall was dangerously wounded in the shoulder with a ball (as he says from a rifle) which has rendered him incapable of duty.

I shall endeavour to keep the post we are at at present if possible, if not shall retreat to the woods about half a mile.

From a report we had given us yesterday they are constructing another vessel like the above and that they intend attacking us on the Potowmac side. I think from all appearances the Fleet will continue some time, if so, some Cannon and Swivels, will be absolutely necessary to dislodge the men they have landed on the Island. With what assistance we can give in this quarter I think 500 of the Militia of the Upper Battalion will be full enough to oppose the enemy. We have now at different posts about 600 men.

For further particulars refer you to Mr. Hopewell by whom this goes express, he also will inform you the difficulties we labour under in getting provisions for the men without money to pay for it immediately. Ł. 300 I think would be sufficient. Col. Barnes with his Battalion is on the other side of the river, watching the motions of the enemy there.

I am Gentlemen Your most obedt Servt   Jeremiah Jordan
Alex Somerville to the Council

Gentlemen. You will be informed by Mr. Hopewell that the enemy hath landed on St. George's Island that Capt. Beall is wounded- That they want men in St. Mary's. I shall proceed down to their assistance with about fifty of the best men I can get that are now stationed at Drum Point and shall leave orders for as many more to follow unless ordered otherwise by you....

Archives of Maryland, Vol. 12, p. 63, 64, 65, 66.

July 18, 1776

Council of Safety ordered that three 4 pounders mounted on Carriages with their necessary Apparatus and a sufficient Quantity of powder and ball be sent down to St. Mary's County, and that Major Thomas Price be requested to provide the necessary Carriages to transport same with all convenient Speed.

Ordered that the Treasurer of the Western Shore pay to Mr. Hugh Hopewell 300 Pounds for the use of the Commanding Officer in St. Mary's County to supply the Militia on duty there with Provisions.

Ordered that the Commanding Officer in St. Mary's County take under his Charge the Schooner lately taken from the Enemy unlade her and put her to what use he may think best for the public service; likewise the Sloop which is now aground if it can be done with safety.

Ordered that Major Price immediately proceed to St. Mary's County and take command of the regular Troops and Militia.

Ordered that all persons between Annapolis and St. Mary's County be requested to give their Aid and Assistance in getting down the Cannon, Ammunition, etc. to St. George's Island in the County aforesaid.

To the Commanding Officer, St. Mary's

....Some Powder and Ball we dispatched to you yesterday....immediately send you for Field Pieces &c...by Mr. Hopewell 300 Pounds...concerned to hear that Capt. Beall is wounded, but hope it is not dangerous, and as we understand you have several Surgeons with you, trust he will soon do well.

Cunningham's Examination (a captured prisoner)

Summary Dunmore's ship damaged at Gwinn's Island and some men killed and wounded. Small pox and gaol fever among the negroes - 500 died and were buried on Gwinn Island - about 300 troops in the fleet of 72 ships - many small boats - all were

soldiers that landed on St. George's Island. Gov. Eden on the Fowey - has nothing to do with the fleet. Capt. Hammond and Lord Dunmore at variance. The fleet is after wood and water. Tenders are cruising in the Bay. There were 20 men in the Gondolas, 10 on each side. Tenders have taken cattle. Marines and sailors would desert. Fowey within musket shot of the shore - gave number of guns on several ships.
Archives of Maryland, Vol. 12, p. 71, 72, 73, 74.

July 19, 1776

Council of Safety ordered that Capt. (John Allen) Thomas immediately proceed with his Company to St. Mary's County and put himself under the Direction of the Commanding Officer there.

Ordered that the Commissary of Stores furnish each non commissioned Officer and Private of Capt. Thomas' Company with 23 Rounds of Cartridge with Ball.

Ordered that the Contractor for provisions furnish Capt. Thomas' Company with two Day's Rations.

Ordered that the Defence's small Tender convoy Capt. Thomas' Company to the Mouth of Patuxent in St. Mary's County.

Council to Hon. John Page Esqr. Pres. of the Council of Virginia.

Sir. Your favour communicating the intelligence that the Enemies Fleet had been drawn from their Station and their Forces obliged to abandon Gwynn's Island came safe to hand....They have since arrived in Potowmack and Landed some Men on St. Georges Island....where they have thrown up Entrenchments. We are making preparations to dislodge them as soon as possible.....

Council to the Deputies for Maryland in Congress

Report of Lord Dunmore's invasion and the action in St. Mary's County to date.

Report of Gen'l. John Dent to Council from St. Mary's River

Gentn. On my arrival at this place on the 16th Inst. I found there had been an engagement with the Enemy with no other loss but the misfortune of Capt. Rezin Beall being badly wounded....By four Deserters who came over to us yesterday we are informed the mate or midshipman of the Roe Buck was killed in action. By the best information the Enemy have not more than 50 Regulars of the 14th Regiment, about 150 Tories and 100 Negroes that bare arms, all of whom are landed every morning and embarked in the evening under cover of the Fleet, which continues in the mouth of St. Mary's River opposite the lower end of St. George's Island. Our strength at present is about 400 Militia exclusive of the Independent and Captn. Forrest's Company... (ordered) to our assistance three full companies of Militia from Col. Hawkins Battalion ....shall discharge an equal number of....those now on duty. The Fleet.... of eighty sail is now reduced to little more than half that number, many of the Tenders and Square Rigged vessels having gone to Virginia...where a pretty constant Cannonade has been kept up...told by Deserters that fleet intend only to wood and water on the Island, burn all or most of their small craft and proceed to Sea. Had we a few great guns at a place called Cherry Fields Point...we might annoy the fleet so as to oblige them to quit....Capt. Forrest's Company has relieved an equal number of the Militia who readily parted with their arms such as they were.
Archives of Maryland, Vol. 12, 77, 78, 80, 83, 84.

July 20, 21, 1776

Gen'l. John Dent to the Council of Safety

St. George's Head Quarters 20th July 1776

Gent. From the accts. given me by several deserters that the Fleet entered up Potomack River to water and from the motions of the Roebuck, five other ships and a sloop, I have the greatest reason to believe they are now on their way for that purpose. Nanjemoy, we suppose to be the place of their Destination. I have by letter informed the Committee of Correspondence....and shall endeavour to watch their motions and prevent their Depredations with all my Might. There was a brisk and severe Cannonade from two or three tenders and a row galley of Smith's Creek about six o'clock this morning the consequence of which I have not yet heard.

Council to Brig. Gen'l Dent, July 21, 1776

...approve action....have ordered Major Price down with 3 Field Pieces and one 9 pounder with Capt. Thomas' Independent Company....These will enable the

Major and you to speak more properly with the Row Gally...continue to watch movements of enemy - wish to be informed of type of deserters. Soldiers, Sailors, Tories or Prisoners taken by them.

Archives of Maryland, Vol. 12, p. 87, 90.

July 23, 1776

Council of Safety ordered that as soon as the Enemy which are now in Patowmack River may leave the Colony of Maryland, or there appears to the Commanding Officer at St. Georges in St. Mary's County no further Occasion for detaining the fifth independent Company now there, that Capt. John Allen Thomas march the said Company to the northward and join the Troops already sent from hence.

Report of Maj. Thomas Price to the Council.

...arrived at this place (Upper Camp, St. George's) the 21st Inst. with one of the four Pounders, the other two I left at Leonard Town...After inspecting this Camp....went over to the Lower Camp commanded by Colo. (Richard) Barnes....think a nine pounder could reach the Fowey from one of the points, tho I doubt our doing her much damage...rest of the fleet lay outside of her - ordered other two pieces of Cannon to the Lower Camp, including the nine pounder....will intrench as near the Fowey as possible...have several Deserters with small pox - the shores are full of dead bodies, chiefly negroes....has held up passage of Mr. Daniel Wolstenholm to England, (approved by St. Mary's County Committee of Observation) until approved by the Council...The Fowey and Otter with about fifty sail of vessels still here...

Lengthy Report concerning Mr. Wolstenholme's (the King's Collector of Customs) request for passage to England.

St. Mary's County Committee of Observation
Coll. Abraham Barnes, Chairman

Major James Eden	Colo. Jno. H. Read
Major Samuel Abell	Maj. Ignatius Fenwick
Capt. John Smith	Mr. Wilfred Neale
Capt. Edward Abell	Mr. William Taylor
Capt. Gerrard Bond	Mr. Henry Tubman
Capt. Vernon Hebb	Mr. Nicholas L. Sewall

Timothy Bowes, Clerk

Archives of Maryland, Vol. 12, p. 97, 98 - 104.

Maryland Deputies to the Council of Safety

Philadelphia, July 23rd 1776

Gentlemen. Yesterday's Post brought us your Letter of the 19th Inst. The copies of the Letters of Colonels Barnes and Jordan you omitted to enclose. We hope the necessity of recalling the Captains Thomas and Hindman will soon be removed and that they will be permitted to march to the flying camp as soon as possible. It is of the last Consequence to collect a sufficient force to oppose the british Army which may be hourly expected at Staten Island. General Washington has not above 15,000 Troops. Two Battalions of the Virginia Regulars are ordered to N. York, four Battalions in this province and two more in New Jersey are ordered to reinforce the flying Camp.....We have no intelligence from New York since the 19th. Lord Howe's fleet not then arrived....

Brig. Gen'l. John Dent to the Council of Safety

Protests the appointment of Major Thomas Price to the command (in St. Mary's County) in his place.

Archives of Maryland, Vol. 12, p. 105, 107', 111.

July 25, 1776

Brig. Gen'l. Thomas Johnson to the Council of Safety

.....there are many of the Enemy's Ships in Potowmack, yet there are but few men in them; those sickly and die fast. The Fowey and Otter with about fifty sail of Vessels still at Saint Georges. The Roebuck with three Ships and a few small Vessels are as high up Potowmack as Mattawoman.....

Major Thomas Price from the Council

You will make use of all or part of the Cannon as you see cause, taking care not to waste Powder.... You should be particularly cautious in taking care to secure Deserters, some of them you may depend upon it are Spies: the Negro you mention that escaped from the Guard may have been sent on purpose to seduce the Slaves in the Neighbourhood....

The Council to Col. Richard Barnes

....received a letter from Major Price in which Mr. Wolstenholme's affair was mentioned. The Council of Safety thereupon passed a General Order to all the Commitees of Observation and Military Commanders not to suffer any person whatever to go out of the Province for the present....The suffering Gentlemen to go off on Board the Men of War or Tenders or any other Vessel that may have communication with them is attended with great danger to the Colony - every means of intelligence must be cut off if possible.

Archives of Maryland, Vol. 12, p. 114, 115.

July 26, 1776

Council of Safety to the Maryland Deputies in Congress

The Letters from Colonel Barnes and Jordan were not inclosed in our last from inattention, we now send them...Dunmore's Fleet have separated; the Fowey and the Otter with a number of Vessels haveing Tory Families on board remain in the mouth of Saint Mary's River; the Roebuck and Six or Seven other Vessels have moved up the River Potowmack as high as Quantico in Virginia where they stopt to take in water. There are some flying reports of their having landed at Mr. William Brent's and burnt his Houses, which are confirmed this day by Charles Landsdale. He says 'tis feared they are landing on Colonel Smallwood's Estate....As soon as the Regulars are replaced that have and are about to march to the Northward, we shall use our endeavours to compleat the remaining Battalions...and send them forward either in Battalions or Companys as they get ready....On Tuesday last we gave orders to Capt. Thomas to march with his men to Philadelphia as soon as the Commanding Officer below thinks he can be spared....we have ordered Capt. Hindman to move forward although we apprehend the Eastern Shore will be weakened thereby....we feel for the State of New York, but cannot help feeling also for Maryland and shall endeavour....to give every assistance in our power to them and to the Common cause without exposing ourselves to destruction. Since the march of our Regulars we are truly in a defenceless state... Maj. Thomas Price to General Lewis and the Council

St. George's Camp July 26th 1776

Sir. The enemy comes on St. George's Island in the day time to get water and wood and in the evening retire on board their ships: they have no manner of Fortification on the Island. The Fleet lays from the North East side of St. Georges River a Bout a mile....The Island lays from the main about a hundred yards. The water at low tide about knee deep where we threw up a small Intrenchment. There are three pieces of Cannon on Cherry field point (about a mile from the Fowey) one a nine pounder, one a four, the other three. I have another on the South West side of the river the narrowest water between the land and main is a four pounder. I have about 400 men (half of which are well armed, the other but poorly) placed on each side St. George's River. I have good reason to think with the force I have I can prevent the Enemy's landing or plundering the Inhabitants. I yesterday morning sent 100 on the Island about half after two o'clock. They marched silently through the Island till day appear'd and then lay hid 'till they came from the ships to water, the advanced party being rather eager was too soon discovered and the whole Enemy ran to their boats, my people then pursuing them with all speed and firing on them as they were getting into their boats when our people say that they killed three or four that they saw fall and several wounded and one taken prisoner. The Fowey then fired on them and compelled them to retire after destroying their water casks and filling up a well, the best on the Island....they returned to the main without loss. By the best advice I can get from the Prisoners and many deserters the whole fleet does not intend to stay here longer than those up Potowmack comes down which they expect every day. Capt. Beal who was wounded in the first engagement is recovering fast.

N.B. I yesterday sent under a small guard for Annapolis one Prisoner taken yesterday and three deserters, one of them an officer of Dunmores who made his escape....

Col. Richard Barnes to the Council   Camp at Cherry Fields 26th July 1776

        Gentn. I am informed Colo. Kent that was approved by the Convention to command the Defence declines the acceptance of the Command I shall therefore take the liberty to recommend Captn. George Cooke....(he) has served on board the English Navy for seven years and has been in several engagements....Colo. Plater is well acquainted with (him).....

        Archives of Maryland, Vol. 12, p. 119, 120, 122, 123, 124, 125.

July 27, 1776

Col. Alex. Somerville to the Council of Safety   Calvert County July 27th 1776

        Gentlemen. I received orders from Collo. Mackall (who is now at St. Georges) yesterday to send a company of our Militia to St. Mary's to relieve the Company now stationed there, which I shall do without loss of time.....

        B. Mackall to the Council

        I left the Camp at St. George's yesterday & Major Price desired me to send to the Council, attended by a Subaltern officer, Mr. Braithwait, who deserted from the Fleet Thursday night and brought with him two trunks which shall be sent up to you as soon as Mr. Middletons boat returns from the mouth of Potowmack, where she is waiting upon the Defence.

        Archives of Maryland, Vol. 12, p. 131, 133.

July 29, 1776

        Capt. John Allen Thomas to Col. George Plater

                      Head Quarters St. George 29th July 1776

        Dear Sir. Yesterday the Roebuck with the Fleet under her convoy arrived here from their cruizen up the River, they were watched all the way down by two Row Gallies from Alexandria, they will be here this evening and I expect to night we shall engage the Fleet. The Roebuck stood down the Bay and is now out of sight. The Defence made her appearance yesterday morning but on the Foey's warping out thought it prudent to stand down again. We are preparing all the boats we can get to assist in boarding all such vessels as are not armed and I am in hopes we shall be able to give a good account of them. I most sincerely wish the Business over, the place is exceedingly disagreeable, not a drop of water but what is brought near three miles together with the uncomfortable tents that we have. I am afraid will make us all sick, near half both of mine and Capt. Beall's Company are down. The militia do every duty so exceeding ill and the service is so very unknown to them that the whole Burthen lies upon the few regulars that are here. I went on the Island yesterday morning a little before day with a party of forty men but could fine none of the Enemy there...nearly half the Fleet have gone and the rest will go in a few days....Whenever they go, I shall proceed to Annapolis on my way to the Northward and shall be extremely obliged to you if you will have the Tents, Knapsacks, Havresacks, Camp Kettles and Canteens completed for my company ready at Annapolis....If the Tents are large they will hold eight men so...I shall want fifteen tents for the whole Company....shall necessarily be delayed here a few days to get on board the Cannon and in procuring vessels to transport us.... P.S. I forgot to mention that we yesterday morning opened our Battery which played as 'tis thought with success on the Fowey. Numbers of dead bodies come on shore every day, that we are poisoned with the stench. J.A.T.

        Major Thomas Price to the Council of Safety

Gentlemen   Upper Camp St. Georges July 29th 1776

        The day before yesterday in the Evening the Roebuck and other Ships returned down the river and came too about 5 miles from this place at two o'Clock yesterday morning. I recd. a line from Captn. Nicholson Acquainting me that he intended to Attack the Fleet at Day break. I immeaditly dispatched an officer with orders if Possible to speak to Captn. Nicholson and let him know the Ships had returned down the river and where then within Nine or Ten Miles of the fleet and that I did not think it Prudent to Attack them. Colo. Barnes had dispatched an officer some time before The one I sent Got over to his Camp but neither of them could come up with Captn. Nicholson. I Immeaditly on rect. of the Letter Ordered the Troops under Arms and dispatched Captn. Thomas with about forty on the Island to Alarm the Enemy on that

Quarter. Major Eden with about the same number on the Point with a four Pounder and I took the remainder 25 in Number on board of Two Boats and Cannoes & went down St. Georges River as near the Enemy as we Could with Safety where I left them under Command of Lieut Addams with Orders if there should be any Confusion in the fleet to Push up with their Boats to Cherry field Point where I would be. I then went a Cross to the Point where our People from the Lower Camp had been at work all night and by the time the sun was rising Mounted the two Largest Cannon about an Hour after we Espied the Defence making up for the fleet. The Fowey which lay aft a mile from the Battery did not see her or seemed to take no notice of her for more than an Hour when we Noticed boats goeing a Head of her as we suppose to Carryout her Anker in Order to whey her out and in a Short time we observed her halling out when I immeaditly Ordered the Cannon to be fired at her. We fired four times from the nine pounder & two from the four one of which the nine we think huld her the other struck a boat laying at her Stern with I Beleave Men in her. I saw them a very little before, the Fowey all the time halling out. By this time Observed the Defence put about and stand down the River. I Beleave she must have seen the Roebuck who was seen some time after standing down after her the Fowey giveing Chase a very little while before Upon the whole the Enemy Appears to be a Good Deal Alarmed and I am in hopes will leave this in a Short time. Captn Boucher came to Camp last night - he left two Roe Gallys about 15 miles above this place. I furnished him with a Boat and some hands to goe Back by Water, he Expects to be down with the Gally this Evening. I am Collecting all the Boats and Cannoes to give him all the assistance in my Power. The Remainder of the Militia here must be Discharged tomorrow night. I expected to have had a fresh recrute of them by this time - shall be very week, not less than Twenty of the regulars down with fevers at this time. There will be great Difficulty in getting the Cannon back by Land - should think it best to have them Carried by Water if Vessels can be had as soon as the Enemy goes of (f). Enclosed you have Governor Edens Answer to Mr. Wolstenholms letter which was brought to Captn. Forrest who I Ordered to that station in Place of Captn. Mackall who I could not so well depend upon. You also have Enclosed Captn. Forrests Letter to me and Mr. Wolstenholms Answer to Governor Eden. This is a Shocking Country, every thing scarce, Water we are Oblidged to hall near Three Miles, no Liquor but bad Whisky to Drink - every Body fatigued and Tired of the Place - if the Enemy Continue here must certainly have fresh Troops. I had almost forgot to Inform you that the Nine Pound Cannon turns out Extraordinary Good, Perhaps none Better, we all here are much pleased with her.

   I am Gentlemen   Your most Obedt. Servt. Thos. Price
   Archives of Maryland, Vol. 12, p. 136, 137, 138, 139.

   Upon application of Mr. (Henry) Sewell, by the desire of Mr. Cowen to him, we agreed if it were agreeable to the Council of Safety to undertake the building of two or three Gundaleus to begin upon immediately....Archd Buchanan
   Archives of Maryland, Vol. 12, p. 137.

July 30, 1776
   Council of Safety ordered that Capt. Peter Mantz immediately march to Leonard Town in St. Mary's County and be stationed in that County to supply the place of Capt. John Allen Thomas' Company who are to march to the Northward. Also Ordered that he take such Station in said County as may be directed by Major Thomas Price, or in his Absence by the Committee of Observation for said County. And further Ordered that the said Capt. Mantz and his Company be furnished with Rations by the Contractor at the public Expence and that he remain in St. Mary's County until the further Order of this Board.
   Council of Safety to Major Thomas Price
   Confirmation of orders to Capt. Mantz above. Cannon to be brought from the mouth of the Patuxent by water if the passage appears safe - otherwise by land.
   Archives of Maryland, Vol. 12, p. 140, 142.

July 31, 1776
   Council of Safety to Major Thomas Price
   Captn. Mantz, who commands a Company of the Frederick Battalion well

armed and accoutred this day marches to relieve Captn. Thomas & his Company, whom you may thereupon order up to this place on his way to the camp to the Northward.... Captn. Mantz will occupy the posts and places where Captn. Thomas' Company were stationed......The officers dispatched by you to give Captn. Nicholson notice not being able to overtake him had very near occasioned a loss of the Defence, she was becalmed & obliged to come to an anchor Tide agt. her; the english Fleet had a wind which brought them down Potowmack within three miles of her.....when fortunately a Breeze sprung up which enabled her to escape....it is unsafe at this period of Time to permit Mr. Wolstenholme to depart this Province....
Archives of Maryland, Vol. 12, p. 148, 149.

July - 1776
Deposition of Capt. George Cook - swears before Jacob Young that in July 1776 he was a resident of St. Mary's County when his negro servant Charles ran away; with Charles was a Negro owned by John Mackall of St. Mary's County; Cook believes Negroes joined Lord Dunmore's Army; George Biscoe saw Charles on an English frigate.
Calendar of Maryland State Papers No. 5, p. 54 (Item 398).

-- 1776
Applications for Marine Service
St. Mary's County: Jesse Jordan, William Lee, Charles Chilton
Applications for Sea Service
St. Mary's County: Robert Chesley, Henry Carbury (Carberry), Jesse Jordan, William Lee, Charles Chilton.
Calendar of Maryland State Papers No. 5, p. 70 (Items 522, 523).

August 2, 1776
Council of Safety to the Maryland Deputies in Congress
....Since our last we have received two letters from Major Price, copies of which are inclosed, from them you will learn the situation of the Enemy below, our pilot boat came up last night & informs they are not yet gone off, several vessels are dismasted and on shore at the point of St. George's island with intention to burn them; Middleton thinks they are going off down the Bay and we hope soon to be able to write you to that effect.....
Archives of Maryland, Vol. 12, p. 161, 162.

August 5, 1776
Council of Safety to Messrs. Vanbibber & Harrison
....Dunmore's fleet is gone off from the mouth of Potowmack very sickly and in great distress....
Archives of Maryland, Vol. 12, p. 172.

Council ordered Treasurer of the Western Shore pay to Hugh Hopewell 8 ℔. for Expresses.
Archives of Maryland Vol. 12, p. 170.

August 7, 1776
Council ordered the Commissary of Stores deliver to Capt. Thomas 18 Camp Kettles and 104 Canteens.
Commissions issued to: John Davidson, app't'd. 1st. Lieut; Henry Neale, app't'd. 2nd Lieut.; Robert Chesley, app't'd. 3rd Lieut of Capt. Thomas' Independent Company of regular Troops.

Council of Safety to Captn. James Nicholson
Sir. We have some powder and small arms arrived at great Wiccomico in Virginia - we want your small tender to go up that river for them and the ship Defence to go down below the mouth of Potowmack to protect her....

St. Mary's County Committee of Observance to Council

Unhappy with Capt. Mantz and (h)is Company - request they be replaced with part of Capt. Beall's Company now stationed at Port Tobacco. Similar letter from Capt. Mantz requesting transfer.

Archives of Maryland, Vol. 12, p. 180, 184, 185.

August 9, 1776

Council of Safety ordered that Capt. Peter Mantz march immediately from St. Mary's County to Annapolis on his way to Philadelphia....Ordered that Capt. Uriah Forrest remain in St. Mary's County....until further orders.

Council to St. Mary's Committee of Observation

Confirms orders to Capt. Mantz and Capt. Forrest

Council to Maryland Deputies in Congress

Gentn. We have the pleasure to inform you that the enemy's fleet left Potowmack River on Friday last (August 9) and is gone off down the Bay; they had collected a number of small vessels which they had dismasted and left on the point of St. George's Island with intention to set fire to them, but a high Tide floated them off and they were driven on Shore near our Guard who have taken possession of them and have found sundry goods and other effects on board to the value of three or four hundred Pounds currency; some of the Hulks may be repaired and made fit for service - they burnt some other small vessels, and from appearances expect they are gone down to the capes.....

Captn. (John Allen) Thomas is on the way to Philadelphia....

Archives of Maryland, Vol. 12, p. 189, 190, 191.

August 11, 1776

John Allen Thomas to the Council of Safety

Arrived here (Head of Elk) after tedious passage of four days; applied for Provisions but Col. Henry Hollingsworth could not comply because he had no orders from the Council; has procured beef and bread and will start out tomorrow; a general order authorizing Hollingsworth to supply troops that come here would expedite matters greatly.

Calendar of Maryland State Papers No. 4, Part 2, p. 74 (Item 481);
Archives of Maryland, Vol. 12, p. 194, 195.

August 12, 1776

Council of Safety to Colo. Thomas Ewing

....Captn. Forrest we have ordered to remain in St. Mary's County to supply the place of Thomas' Independent Company - he will be obliged to borrow arms from the militia.....

Archives of Maryland, Vol. 12, p. 197.

August 13, 1776

Thomas Stone, Delegate to the Continental Congress to the Council

Gentn. I am very glad to be informed that Ld. Dunmore and his fleet have quitted the Bay and am hopeful this circumstance will induce your militia to lend Assistance to the neighbours with more alacrity than could be expected while an Enemy was hovering on their Coast....Capt. Thomas is arrived with his company.... Genl. Washington is not so strong as he could wish. Upon these movements of the Enemy, he ordered a reinforcement of 2,000 from Jersey to York-the Maryland Battalion was immediately sent to him.

Archives of Maryland, Vol. 12, p. 199, 200.

August 14, 1776

Capt. Uriah Forrest commissioned for the Flying Camp.
Archives of Maryland, Vol. 12, p. 201.

H. Hollingsworth to the Council of Safety

....The troops as they arrive (will be) provided with waggons at Elk to carry the baggage &c to Xteen, whare shallops are provided or if not there at Newport or Wilmington...whare there is Baraks....provisions, shallops and Waggons (will be provided) to forward them to Chester....so that by this method of proceeding the Troops will make the march from Elk to Philadelphia in Three days (one day of 18 and two of 15 miles)....Capt. (John) Alin Thomas was with me who highly approved the mode of proceeding....

Archives of Maryland Vol. 12, p. 203.

August 14, 1776 - November 11, 1776

Members of the Convention which Framed the First State Constitution were: St. Mary's County - Richard Barnes; Ignatius Fenwick; George Plater; Jeremiah Jordan.

Manual, State of Maryland 1973-1974, p. 811.

August 15, 1776

Council ordered Treasurer of the Western Shore pay to Wm. Bellwood 11 Ł.10s. for Boat Hire. Also pay George Gough 11 Ł. 7s. 6p. and Wm. Thomas 12 Ł. 5s. for Boat Hire.

Archives of Maryland Vol. 12, p. 205.

August 16, 1776

Council of Safety to Tentmakers

As all the Troops belonging to this Province are directed to March immediately to the Northward, and as they will be greatly distressed for Tents unless we can be supplied with Tenting Linnen from you, we earnestly beg you will send us what you can with the utmost dispatch.

Council to Maryland Deputies

We received yours of the 13th and have seen what you wrote to Major Jenifer on the State of Publick Affairs in Consequence of a Resolve of the Convention. We have given orders to all the Independent Companies, four in number to march. Col. Carvel Hall and Col. Ewing, and six or seven Companies of the Eastern Shore have like orders to March, so that with Griffith's Battalion, we shall have near 4000 men with you in a short time - this exceeds our proportion for the flying Camp but we are sending all we have that can be armed and equipped and the people of New York, for whom we have great affection, can have no more than our all...We depend in case of Invasion on being supported powerfully by our neighbours in Pennsylvania, New York & the Jerseys, besides having part of our own Troops sent back.....These Companies are not fully armed and equipped but we hope soon to Collect enough.

List of the Troops from Maryland

Smallwood's Battalion, 9 Companies 76 each	684
Capt. Veazey 100, Capt. Hindman 100, Capt. Thomas 100	300
Capt. Beall 100, Capt. Gunby 100	200
Capt. Woolford 100, Capt. Watkins 100	200
Griffith's Battalion 9 Companies 90 men each	810
Col. Carvell Hall's ditto ditto	810
3 Companies of Col. Ewing's	270
7 Companies of Eastern Shore Battalion	644
	3,918

the remaining Companies of Ewing's and the Eastern Shore Battalion must borrow Arms from the Militia to do duty here, they can get Arms on no other terms.

Council to Mr. John Gordon, Baltimore Town

As all the Troops belonging to the Province are directed to march immediately to the Northward, we beg you will work Day and Night in furnishing the Knapsacks and Havresacks you have engaged to make, as they cannot march without them.

Archives of Maryland, Vol. 12, p. 211, 212, 213.

August 17, 1776

Council of Safety ordered the Treasurer of the Western Shore to pay Capt. Jno. Thomas for use of Capt. Edmund Plowden 53 Ł. 7s. 10p, for his Company on duty.

Archives of Maryland, Vol. 12, p. 215.

August 18, 1776
    Col. Thomas Ewing to the Council of Safety
    ....I should be glad to know what companys your Honors intend to give me in place of Captain's Forrest, Tillard & Bowie. I should at the same time esteem it a favor to be permitted to have them Companys with me...
    Yesterday forwarded three companies...to Head of Elk on their way to Phila-delphia under the command of Major (James) Eden....arrived at camp N. Harlem on September 18....and since....Capt. Uriah Forrest....has arrived (October 13, 1776) ....enemy has landed 4,000 troops at Kingsbridge, N.Y....
    Archives of Maryland, Vol. 12, p. 219, 347, 348.

August 19, 1776
    Council of Safety to Col. Thomas Ewing
    Sir. We received yours of the 18th and observe your Complaint which arises not from us but a very different cause, we mean your Companies not being Armed.... Capt. Forrest and Capt. Brooks have no Armes but what they have Borrowed or can borrow of the Militia, we have therefore ordered them to their Stations in Calvert and St. Mary's to supply the place of Capt. Beall and Capt. Thomas.....As soon as they get arms we shall order them to March immediately.
    Archives of Maryland, Vol. 12, p. 221.

August 20, 1776
    Council of Safety ordered Treasurer to pay Colo. Rd. Barnes 311 Ł, 6s, 10p., half penny for Pay of his Battalion.
    Archives of Maryland, Vol. 12, p. 223.

August 22, 23, 1776
    Council of Safety ordered Treasurer to pay Major Ignatius Fenwick 131 Ł.,6s, 7p. for militia on duty.
    Ordered Treasurer to pay Captn. Uriah Forrest 64 Ł.14s.7p. for subsistence of his Company. Also pay for use of Dr. H. Reeder 10 Ł, 9s, 6p for attending Captn. Thomas' Company and for use of Elias Smith 2 Ł,6s,8p for Barracks for Captn. J. A. Thomas' Company. Also ordered that Treasurer pay to Captn. Forrest for use of Henry Sewell 33s for Traveling Expences for part of the Artillery Company going to St. George's and for use of Dr. Robinson 5 Ł, 6s,6p for attendance of his Company, and for use of Francis Brooke 20s for services at the camp at St. Georges.
    Archives of Maryland, Vol. 12, p. 232.

August 23, 1776
    Aaron Abell and Cuthbert Abell enlisted in Capt. John Brooke's Co. of Calvert County Militia.
    Archives of Maryland, Vol. 18, p. 34.

August 26, 27, 1776
    Council of Safety ordered the Treasurer to pay Major Philip Fenwick 119 Ł.2s6p. for militia on duty.
    John Hanson Briscoe appointed Surgeon to the seven Independent Companies. Dan'l. Jenifer appointed Surgeon Assistant to Dr. Briscoe.
    Treasurer order to pay Doctr. Briscoe 20 Ł. to purchase a Sett of Surgical Instruments.
    Battle of Long Island - see Col. Smallwoods report of Oct. 12, 1776.
    Archives of Maryland, Vol. 12, p. 240, 241, 242.

August 31, 1776
    Council of Safety ordered Treasurer to pay to Colo. Jeremiah Jordan 353 Ł. 7s.1p for militia on duty.
    Treasurer ordered to pay Jas. Boyd 8 Ł, 2s, 6p for Bayonets.
    Treasurer ordered to pay Timothy Bowes 2 Ł, 13s for Amt. of his Acct.
    Archives of Maryland, Vol. 12, p. 250.

August 29, 30, 1776

      Council ordered Treasurer pay to Wm. Bellwood 5 Ł. for Boat Hire.
      Also pay Hugh Hopewell 12 Ł. 15s & Wm. Thomas 4 Ł.10s. for Boatage.
      Archives of Maryland, Vol. 12, p. 247.

Sept. 2, 3, 1776

      Council of Safety ordered that Captain's Forrest & Brooke immediately with their Companies to the City of Annapolis on their way to the Flying Camp.
      Ordered Treasure to pay Dan'l. Jenifer, Junr. 9 Ł.7s.6p. for his medical attendance at St. George's Camp.
      Council ordered Treasurer pay to Wm. Bellwood 5 Ł. for Boatage for the Flying Camp.
      Archives of Maryland, Vol. 12, p. 253, 255.

Sept. 4, 1776

      Capt. John Allen Thomas to the Council of Safety - Harlem 4th Sept. , 1776
      Informs the Council that many of his men sick and fifteen to twenty extremely ill - only two surgeons here from the Province and one very sick - nearly 200 men unfit for duty.
      Archives of Maryland, Vol. 12, p. 256, 257.

Sept. 5, 6, 1776

      Council of Safety ordered Treasurer pay to Capt. Edwd. Abell 113 Ł.15s.10p. for his Compy. of Militia on duty.
      Treasurer ordered to pay Jno. H. Briscoe 7 Ł. 19s. for Bal. of his acct.
      Archives of Maryland, Vol. 12, p. 257, 259.

Sept. 9, 10, 1776

      Council of Safety ordered Treasurer pay to Captn. Uriah Forrest 334 Ł.15s.9p. for pay and subsist. of his Company. Also pay to said Forrest for use of Belwood & Parran 5 Ł. 5s. for Boatage.
      Treasurer ordered to pay Henry Sewell 8 Ł.6s.11p. for subsist of Flying Camp.
      Archives of Maryland, Vol.12, p. 262, 263.

Sept. 12, 1776

      Council of Safety ordered that Sam'l. Messersmith be requested to deliver to Captn. Forrest all the guns which were left in his custody to be repaired by Captn. Hammond.
      Council to Hopkins
      To Mr. Gerrerd Hopkins Deputy Commissary
      Sir. We this Day gave an order to Capt. Forrest to receive from you 100 Camp Kettles. We must request that they be put on Board the Defence's Tender and that by the same vessell you'd send some Cannon Shott.....and also 86 Canteens with as many Priming Wires and Brushes.
      Archives of Maryland, Vol. 12, p. 266, 267.

Sept. 13, 1776

      Ordered that James Boyd of St. Mary's County contract with the Council of Safety for making musquets compleatly fitted in the usual manner at 4 Ł..5.. each, the Council engaging to take any quantity of him & find Powder for their Proof.
      Council to Cooke
      To Capt. George Cooke, St. Mary's County
      Sir. We have the pleasure to inform you that you were yesterday appointed Commander of the Ship Defence now lying at Annapolis, bound out on a Cruise....
      Archives of Maryland, Vol. 12, p. 269, 270.

Sept. 16, 1776

      Barton Tabbs appointed Surgeon Assistant to Doctr. Briscoe of the Seven

Independent Companies.
    Council ordered Treasurer pay to Barton Tabbs 7 Ł.1s.6p. for medical
Attendance at St. George's Camp.
    Archives of Maryland, Vol. 12, p. 273, 274.

Sept. 17, 18, 1776
    Council of Safety ordered Treasurer pay to Colo. Richd. Barnes 145 Ł.17s.3p.
for militia duty. Also pay Capt. Uriah Forrest for use of Abn. Barnes of Belwood &
C Chesley 19 Ł.3s.4p. for Amt. of Acct. Pay to Colo. Jeremiah Jordon 79 Ł.6s.2p.
for Militia Acct. and 3 Ł.13s.6p. for repairing Guns.
    Archives of Maryland, Vol. 12, p. 276, 277, 279, 280.

September 19, 1776
    List of St. Mary's County Sailors on the Ship Defence.
    George Cook,Commander   Michael Craig, Serjt. Marines
    Henry Carberry, Seaman   William Howard, Carpenter's Crew
    William Piercy, Yeoman   Joseph Dunbar, Ship Steward
    Thomas Howard, Seaman   Francis Herbert, Seaman
    William Herbert, Seaman   Thomas Moore, Seaman
    William King, Seaman   Abell Mason, Seaman
    Joseph Jones, Seaman   Benjamin Thompson, Seaman
    Hoshier Cole, Seaman   Basil Smith, Seaman
    Patrick Cole, Seaman   John Davis, Seaman
    William Morris, Serjt. Marines   James Brown, Cabin Boy
    Vachel Yates, Serjt. Marines   James Armstrong, Pvt. Marines
    John Lemmon, Pvt. Marines   James Smith, Pvt. Marines
    Wm. Davis, Pvt. Marines
        Archives of Maryland, Vol. 18, p. 606, 607.

Sept. 20, 1776
    Council ordered Treasurer pay to Capt. Uriah Forrest 161 Ł.1s.10p. for Acct.
of his Compy. Also pay to Colo. Ricd. Barnes 16 Ł.1s.6p. for Amt. of Acct. and
4 Ł.8s.4p. for sundries furnished Captn. Forrest's Company.
    Ordered that Capt. Vernon Hebb and Mr. Timothy Bowes or either of them dis-
pose for use of this state such Part of the Captures lately made out of Dunmore's
Fleet that may be deemed perishable or wasting.
    Archives of Maryland, Vol. 12, p. 287.

Sept. 23, 24, 1776
    Cooke to Council   Potowmack Ship Defence Sept. 23rd, 1776
    Gentlemen. I have thought it necessary to send the Tender up as her mainmast
head is sprung and is under the necessity of keeping Mr. Middleton as a Pilot to carry
the ship down the bay. I have endeavoured to get one at Smith's Creek but could not.
I am informed by Commodore Boucher that he was chased by the Fowey (on the 14th)
off our Capes. I shall use every proper method in my power for the safety of our ship.
I have the pleasure to inform you that the greatest Harmony subsists amongst the
whole Ship's crew and all in high spirits and good health. I shall inform you fully of
our State by the return of Mr. Middleton.
                    I have the honor to be Gent
                Your most obedt Hble Servt   George Cooke
    Several letters of Capt. Cooke - lost an anchor while anchored off Point
Lookout - called on Commodore Boucher of the Congress or Capt. Brooke of the Liberty
to help recover.
    Archives of Maryland, Vol. 12, p. 296, 297, 298.

Sept. 28, 1776
    Council to Read   Colo. John Hatton Read of St. Mary's Coty.
    Sir. We do not address this letter to Colo. Barnes because we expect he will
be at the Convention. We request you would assist Mr. Middleton in getting a nine

pounder on board his boat, and also in getting up a small anchor lost by the Defence.
Archives of Maryland, Vol. 12, p. 307.

Oct. 2, 1776
Council of Safety to Colo. Wm. Smallwood

Sir. We are desirous of having a particular account of the Troops at present under your command, as well regulars as militia, distinguishing those that are effective from those that are sick, wounded or prisoners; also a List of those that have been killed. We have heretofore wrote about sending us an Inventory of arms and other stores belonging to this State to which we refer and repeat our request that you would comply therewith. We are surprised you have never wrote us a Line since you left Annapolis, and more especially since the Battle on Long Island. We are much pleased to hear the great character the Marylanders have acquired & heartly wish you health and good success.
Archives of Maryland, Vol. 12, p. 316.

Oct. 4, 5, 1776
Cook to Council
Ship of Warr Defence at Sea Octob 4th, 1776
Has captured as Prizes a Snow from Glasgow and a Sloop from St. Augustine.
Ordered Treasurer pay to Wm. Thomas 24 Ł. for attending as Adjutant to the 25th Battalion of Militia.
Archives of Maryland, Vol. 12, p. 319, 320, 321.

October 10, 1776
Council to Dr. Neale

Sir. Inclosed you have a Commission for an Assistant Surgeons office in Col. Smallwood's Battalion now encamped near New York. You are desired immediately to join the Battalion. Dr. Francis Neale Oct. 10th 1776.
Archives of Maryland, Vol. 12, p. 332, 335.

October 12, 1776
Report of the Battle of Long Island, August 27, 1776, by Col. Wm. Smallwood

Summary. Regrets delay in reporting – since arrival in New York it has been the fate of this Corps to be generally stationed at Advanced Posts and to act as a covering Party which must expose Troops to extraordinary Duty and Hazard not to mention the extraordinary Vigilance and Attention in the Commandant – on the 26th, the Maryland and Delaware Troops which composed part of Lord Sterling's Brigade were ordered over – he was ordered by General Washington to attend a court martial and got over early the next morning – found our Regiments engaged – Lord Sterling having marched them off before Day to take possession of the woods and difficult passes between our lines and the enemy's encampment, but the Enemy overnight had stole a March, having gotten through those passes, met and surrounded our Troops – became necessary to retreat over a Marsh and Creek – General Washington ordered me to march down a New England Regiment and Captn. Thomas' Company to support and cover the retreat – the fire was very heavy on both sides – Thomas' men contributed much in bringing over the troops – have enclosed a List of the Killed & Missing amounting to 256 officers inclusive – notwithstanding the Maryland Troops had but one days respite, they were ordered on the Advanced Post at Fort Putnam and remained to cover the retreat on the 29th, which was happily completed under cover of a thick fog. On the retreat below Fort Washington on Sept. 15, General Washington expressly sent and drew our Regiment from its Brigade to march down towards New York and cover the retreat.
Archives of Maryland, Vol. 15, p. 338-343.
For another account of the Battle of Long Island, see Chronicles of St. Mary's, Vol. 1, No. 2; McSherry, and Scharf, History of Maryland.

George Washington Custis, adopted son of General George Washington, in a letter to the Reverend Charles White, D.D. pays a glowing tribute to the untiring and

patriotic efforts of Father John Carroll in the Revolution and goes on to say, "The famed regiment of Smallwood, composed of the flower of the Maryland youth , both Catholic and Protestant, was recruited principally in the lower Counties and the Eastern Shore. The Tenth Legion in the American Army marched into Philadelphia in 1776, eleven hundred strong, was cut to pieces at the Battle of Long Island, Gallantly struggling for victory against an overwhelming foe, and at the close of the memorable campaign of '76 at the Battle of Princeton, mustered sixty men commanded by the late Governor Stone, then a Captain; the prison ship and the grave had all the rest."
American Catholic Historical Researches, Vol. 17, p. 162.

Oct. 13, 1776
Col. Thomas Ewing to the Council of Safety
Camp N. Harlem 13th Octo, 1776
Honble Sirs. I arrived here the 18th ult. where I found the three companies I forwarded from Baltimore under the care of Major (James) Eden, Capt. Posey, Young and Low....The next day, we were joined by Capt. Hanson and Magruder, the 22nd by Capt. Tillard and Bowie and the 1st inst. by Capt. (Uriah) Forrest so that I have 8 companies here and am in dayly expectation of Capt. Brook's compy which will compleat my battalion....By the last return I had 237 privates sick, besides officers owing to our lying on the cold ground without straw or plank...medicine very scarce... Numbers of soldiers are without blankets....The three first companies have gained great honor under the command of the Major.....
Archives of Maryland, Vol. 12, p. 347, 348.

Oct. 17, 1776
Council of Safety to Vernon Hebb & Timothy Bowes
Gentn. We take the liberty of inclosing you a resolve of the Convention, which we should be much obliged if you would execute. We are informed that some of the vessels may easily be got up to Mr. Stephen Steward's Shipyard to be repaired. We should be glad if you will have them fitted with Jury masts for that purpose as soon as possible and procure hands for them, all the sails belonging to them, or any others, that came on shore may be sent with them. Those vessels that cannot be raised and fitted out, you will have disposed of in the best manner....

Lengthy report from Gen'l. Wm. Smallwood to the Council of Safety relative to the Maryland troops under his command.
Archives of Maryland, Vol. 12, p. 357 -363.

October 19, 1776
Council ordered Treasurer of Western Shore pay to Bennett Riley (Ryley) 1 £.12s. for Am't. Acct.
Archives of Maryland, Vol. 12, p. 368.

Oct. 21, 1776
Whereas, Information hath been lodged before this Board (Council of Safety) by Mr. Timothy Bowes that a certain John Francis Taney of St. Mary's County had detained in his possession 3 pieces of Sprig Lawn, the property of this state.... the said Taney to deliver....or appear before this Board....
Likewise, Dr. Brehon of St. Mary's County deliver to Timothy Bowes all Books of Physic or of any other kind ...taken on board of any of the Captures at St. George's Island....
Archives of Maryland, Vol. 12, p. 388, 389.

Oct. 25, 1776
Vernon Hebb and Timothy Bowes appointed to take the Deposition of any Witnesses relative to a Sloop sunk by Dunmore's Fleet near St. George's Island and the sails and other Things taken from and out of her by Wm. Richardson and transmit the same, when taken, to the Council of Safety.
Archives of Maryland, Vol. 12, p. 401.

October 29, 1776
        Council of Safety ordered Western Shore Treasurer pay to Jenifer Taylor for use of Thomas Keimer 9Ł.11s. and also pay for use of Ignatius Taylor 32 Ł.10s.2p...
        Archives of Maryland Vol. 12, p. 408.

October 30, 1776
        Report to the Council of Safety and also to Hon. Geo. Plater from Capt. Geo. Cook of the Ship Defence - has captured this day a small schooner with Rum, Sugar, Coffee, Limes, etc.
        Archives of Maryland, Vol. 12, p. 410, 411, 412.

November 2, 1776
        Council of Safety ordered Treasurer to pay to Colo. Jeremiah Jordon for use of Thomas Hobb & Wm. Thomas 10 Ł. 13s.6p.
        Maj. M. Gist reports to Council from White Plains that 5 Officers killed and 3 wounded, including Gen'l. Smallwood and 38 privates killed and wounded.
        Archives of Maryland, Vol. 12, p. 416, 418.

Nov. 4, 1776
        Hebb and Bowes to the Council of Safety
                                                Leonard Town, November 4th, 1776
        Gentlemen. Agreeable to the requisition of your Honble Board, we examined into the state and condition of the vessels drifted on shore or made Captures of from Lord Dunmore's Fleet and are of opinion that of the following vessels lying at Kitts Point (To wit)-
        1 very large Pilot Boat
        1 Schooner of about 1400 Bushs Burthen
        1 Sloop of about 2000 Bushs (do wth some Rigging)
        The Sloop only in a condition to be removed and in order to do that, it will be necessary to send hands down with an anchor and cable, no hands to be hired here.
        At Cherry Fields
        1 Sloop about 1400 Bushs Burthen
        1 Schooner of About 1200 Bushs Do, much repairs necessary before either can be removed.....   We are, Gentlmn yr very hbl Servts
                                        Vernon Hebb
                                        Timothy Bowes
        Archives of Maryland, Vol. 12, p. 421.

November 8, 1776
        Convention of Maryland - Text of the Constitution of Maryland adopted; to introduce the new government an election is to be held for Electors of the Senate on November 25 and the Electors chosen are to meet on December 9; the elections for Delegates and for Sheriffs are to be held December 8 in the same manner as before; the General Assembly is to meet February 10, 1777 and elect the Governor and Council; elections in the counties are to be held in the Courthouses.....
        Judges of elections in St. Mary's County are to be:
                                        Abraham Barnes
                                        Hugh Hopewell
                                        Henry Tubman
        Calendar of Maryland State Papers No. 4, Part 1, p. 55 (Item 321)

November 11, 1776
        Council of Safety ordered Treasurer pay to George Plater, Esq. 20 Ł.6s. for 29 day's attendance in Council of Safety.
        Archives of Maryland, Vol. 12, p. 438.

November 16, 1776
        Vernon Hebb and Timothy Bowes are authorized to sell all the Vessels with their Tackle, Apparel and furniture belonging to the State lying in or near St. Mary's River, drifted on shore or made captures from Lord Dunmore's Fleet.

SOTTERLEY
1727

Home of Honorable George Plater

TUDOR HALL
c. 1754

Home of Abraham and Richard Barnes

Pictures courtesy of The Maryland Historic Trust

PORTO BELLO
c. 1745

Home of Vernon Hebb

MULBERRY FIELDS
c. 1767

Home of William Somerville

Pictures courtesy of The Maryland Historic Trust

Archives of Maryland, Vol. 12, p. 452.

November 22, 1776
John Pratt of Capt. (John Allen) Thomas' Company being an Invalid ordered that he be discharged from the Service. Council of Safety also ordered that the Paymaster discharge the pay of the said John Pratt from the 8th of October to this Day.
Archives of Maryland, Vol. 12, p. 471.

December 1, 1776
George Cook to the Council of Safety.
....As soon as the Tender is fit to be sent to Potomack, I shall send her off with Instructions to call at Annapolis, and take Mr. Middleton with them to endeavour to find our anchor....
Archives of Maryland, Vol. 12, p. 497.

December 5, 6, 1776
Council of Safety ordered that the paymaster pay John Gardner of Capt. John Allen Thomas' Company for four months & an half's Service and that the said John Gardner be discharged from the Service.
Council to the Maryland Delegates
....You have heard no doubt of the arrival of the ship Defence, she has taken five Prizes none of any great value....
Archives of Maryland, Vol. 12, p. 507, 510.

Dec. 6, 1776
William McWilliams, Pvt. enlisted in the 5th Reg. Md. Line and was discharged 12/6/1779
Archives of Maryland Vol. 18, p. 227.

December 7, 1776
Council ordered Treasurer of Western Shore pay to Ignatius Taylor for the use of Nicholas Sewall 20s.
Archives of Marylnd, Vol. 12, p. 511.

December 10, 1776
Joseph Mattingly Pvt. enlisted in 1st Reg. Md. Line, and re-enlisted in the 7th Reg. 2/31/1780 and discharged 2/1/1783.
Archives of Maryland Vol. 18, p. 136, 234, 389, 438, 512, 546.

George Armstrong Lieut. in 3rd. Md. Reg.
Archives of Maryland, Vol. 18, p. 79.

Nicholson Watkins Corpl. enlisted 1st. Reg. Md. Line, Discharged 12/27/1779.
Archives of Maryland, Vol. 18, p. 173.

Joseph Ford, Capt. in the 1st Md. Reg. resigned, no date.
Archives of Maryland, Vol. 18, p. 108.

December 14, 1776
Commission issued to Thomas McWilliams appointed Captain of Marines on Board the Sloop Molly, Thomas Conway Commander.
Council ordered the Treasurer pay to Capt. Uriah Forrest 150 ₺. on the Flying Camp Account.
Council to Capt. Ign. Taylor...There is a man on board Capt. Conway's Sloop who has small Pox. He belongs to St. Mary's County and has a desire to return there but lest he may spread the Infection the greatest care ought to be taken....
Archives of Maryland, Vol. 12, p. 527, 528.

December 15, 1776

....we have ordered Captn. Cooke to proceed with all the men that can be spared from the Defence to Phila. and there to receive the orders of Congress....
(departed with 60-70 men on the 17th)
Archives of Maryland, Vol. 12, p. 531, 537, 539.

December 23, 1776

Mr. Enock Fenwick Senr. was appointed Inspector at Coles Warehouse on St. Cuthbert's Creek, St. Mary's County.

Colo. Abraham Barnes. Sir. Information has been made to us that Mr. Sam'l. Abell of St. Mary's Co. being lately chosen Sheriff of said County declined to act as Inspector, which office he has for some time past exercised. Should this be the case, Mr. Abell must make a written resignation of his office of Inspector to the Committee and you will then deliver the inclosed Commission to Mr. Enoch Fenwicke Senr and transmit us an Acct of such proceedings.
Archives of Maryland, Vol. 12, p. 547, 548.

January 1, 1777

Council of Safety ordered Treasurer pay to Philip Key 94 Ł.11s.9d.
Archives of Maryland, Vol. 16, p. 3.

AAron Spalding, Pvt. enlisted in the 2nd. Reg. Md. Line and was made Sergt. May 1780 and served until 11/15/1783.
Archives of Maryland, Vol. 18, p. 161, 356, 462, 494, 554.

January 9, 1777

Council to Capt. George Cooke.

....(we) further submit to your consideration if it would not be well to send your Tender to the mouth of the Potomac....you may by this step forward the Enlistment.
Archives of Maryland, Vol. 16, p. 29, 30.

January 10, 1777

Henry Spalding, Pvt enlisted in the 2nd. Reg. Md. Line, discharged 1/10/1780
Benjamin Thompson, Pvt enlisted in the 2nd. Reg. Md. Line, listed as a Deserter (A.W.O.L.) 6/10/1778, discharged 1/10/1780
Jeremiah Tarlton enlisted in the 1st Reg. Md. Line, promoted to Corpl. 6/1/1778 and to the Invalid Corps 1/10/1780
Archives of Maryland,Vol. 18, p. 162, 169, 251, 416, 473, 509, 558.

January 15, 1777

John Blair, Pvt. enlisted in the 3rd. Reg. Md. Line for 3 years, Capt.-Lieut. George Armstrong's Company
Archives of Maryland, Vol. 18, p. 298.

January 16, 1777

Council to Jesse Hollingsworth.

....we intend loading the ship entirely with Tob. and as we expect the price to be very high at Baltimore Town, and as we can purchase cheaper on Potomack, we propose to send the ship around to that river where we hope to get her lading of long dull tobacco at 20s. or 25s. pr Ct....
Archives of Maryland, Vol. 16, p. 55.

January 17, 1777

Barton Tabbs who studied under Dr. John Bond is recommended as a surgeon in a regiment.
Calendar of Maryland State Papers No. 5, p. 74 (Item 556).

January 20, 21, 1777

Council of Safety ordered the Treasurer pay to Capt. John Steward One thousand Dollars by order and for use of General Smallwood - same to Capt. Benjamin Ford for same.

Thomas Contee to the Council

I have enquired something about Tobacco on Potomack, am informed 22s. and 6d. has been offered and Tobacco comes in slow - my acquaintance thinks it may be had at 25s. and 5 s. for cask....

Archives of Maryland, Vol. 16, p. 63, 66, 67.

January 24, 1777

Council ordered Treasurer pay to Doctr. John Hanson Briscoe 5 Ł.14s. also the farther Sum of 30 Ł.

Archives of Maryland, Vol. 16, p. 72.

February 3, 1777

Dr. Barton Tabbs to Dan'l. of St. Thomas Jenifer Esq. The soldiers in Lawrance's Barracks are breaking out fast with the Small Pox....I think it will be the best way to move them to the poor House and inoculate them immediately....

Council of Safety ordered Treasurer pay to Clement Sewell 5Ł. 2s. 2d.

Archives of Maryland, Vol. 16, p. 112, 114.

Volunteers as Matrosses for the duration of the war - signatures include William Coode (Coe), Joshua Coode (Cord), Ignatius Gough (Gauf), Aaron Spalding.

Calendar of Maryland State Papers No. 5, p. 76 (Item 574).

February 8, 11, 1777

Council of Safety to Robert Harrison

....We have now several vessels ready to send to you....but when they will depart from hence is uncertain as there are a number of British Ships of War in our Bay....

Ordered the Treasurer pay to Doctr. B. Tabbs 30 Ł. for two months pay as Surgeon to the Regulars.

Resolve of Congress

Resolved, That it is recommended to the Council of Safety of Maryland to prevent the sailing of all provision vessels while the Enemy's ships of war infest the Bay, as there is the greatest reason to fear they cannot avoid falling into the possession of the Enemy

By order of Congress
John Hancock, Prest.

Archives of Maryland, Vol. 16, p. 128, 130, 131.

Richard Hindmore in the 3rd. Reg. Md. Line, died 2/11/1777

Archives of Maryland, Vol. 18, p. 281.

February 15, 1777

Council of Safety ordered Treasurer pay to John Davidson 40 Ł.10s. Also pay to Maj. Uriah Forrest $1,000.00

Archives of Maryland, Vol. 16, p. 138.

February 17, 20, 1777

British Fleet on way to Chesapeake Bay

Pay to Maj. Forrest $1,000.00

Pay to Capt. John Davidson 175 Ł. for clothing for soldiers of Capt. J. A. Thomas' late Company.

Archives of Maryland, Vol. 16, p. 141, 142, 147.

February 21, 1777

Robt. Morris to Danl. of St. Thos. Jenifer

...I had a concern of 140 bbls Powder lately taken by the Men of War in the Bay...

Archives of Maryland, Vol. 16, p. 150.

February 24, 1777
Council ordered Treasurer pay to Doctr.John Hanson Briscoe 5 Ł.14s. and also the further Sum of 30 Ł.
Archives of Maryland , Vol. 16, p. 72.

February 27, 1777
Capt. John David Appointed Captain of the Row Galley, Conqueror.
Archives of Maryland, Vol. 16, p. 153.

March 3, 4, 1777
Smallwood to Jenifer
....I have just received Intelligence that the Phenix and her Tenders are now at Anchor in the Middle of the Bay opposite Hoopers Straights and that Callalo returned to Smith's Island....the Enemy's having rec'd a reinforcement in New Jersey which has occasioned Congress to issue a Resolve requiring the Troops raised on the Continental Establishment in the several States to march....
Council to Vernon Hebb & Timothy Bowes
As there are many persons bringing accounts here about the Articles which you had the management & sale of which accounts we conceive you to be better acquainted with than we possibly can be, we therefore desire that you will examine, adjust & pay all those Accounts out of the money in your hands & if that should prove not sufficient you are to draw on us.
Archives of Maryland, Vol. 16, p. 159, 160.

March 4, 1777
Jacob Gray, Pvt. enlisted in 2nd Reg. Md. Line.
Archives of Maryland, Vol. 18, p. 112.

Clement Sewall, Pvt. enlisted in the 1st. Reg. Md. Line, promoted to Sergt. 9/14/1777.
Archives of Maryland, Vol. 18, p. 160.

March 5, 1777
Council ordered Western Shore Treasurer pay to Capt. John David 246 Ł.15s.3d. and also the further sum of 50 Ł.
Archives of Maryland, Vol. 16, p. 162.

Joseph Bullock member of crew of Sloop Molly, discharged 5/10/1777.
Archives of Maryland, Vol. 18, p. 608.

March 10, 1777
Peter Carberry, Pvt. First enlisted in Capt. Moore's Co. March 10, 1777 and was sent as a Recrutt to Chestertown. In 4th Co. 3rd. Reg. Md. Line August 28, 1781. In 3rd Battn. Jan 1, 1782. In Lieut. Lynn's Co. Northern Detachment in 1783, after reinlisting in the Maryland Line. Received pay from 8/1/1780 to 1/1/1781. Invalided from the Md. Line 11/15/1783.
Archives of Maryland, Vol. 18, p. 345, 394, 453, 509, 529, 601, 603.

March 17, 1777
Joseph Lee Bullock, Pvt. in Col. Grayson's Reg.
Archives of Maryland, Vol. 18, p. 602.

March 18, 1777
John Allen Thomas to the Council
Objects to stationing his men at Leonardtown-too far away from the Patuxent and Point Lookout - is maintaining 50 men at each location - the rest not having any kind of arms are at Leonardtown.
Archives of Maryland, Vol. 16, p. 182,1183 .

March 20, 1777
        Council ordered Treasurer to pay Col. Geo. Plater 31 ₤.10s. for 45 days of attendance at Council.
        Archives of Maryland, Vol. 16, p. 184.

April 2, 1777
        Charles Wallace Howard designated by the Council of Maryland (former Council of Safety) to receive the blankets collected for the troops in the Southern Counties, including St. Marys County.
        The British are expected to invade Maryland via "the head of Elk".
        Archives of Maryland, Vol. 16, p. 196, 197.

        James Roach is commissioned to collect blankets in Newtown Hundred, St. Mary's County.
        Calendar of Maryland State Papers No. 5, p. 86 (Item 656).

April 4, 1777
        Council of Maryland ordered Treasurer pay to Captn. John Davidson 14 ₤.14s. for amount of his Acct. for board of Troops at Annapolis. Also pay Col Jeremiah Jordan for the use of James Boyd 4 ₤.7s.3d. and Caleb Sesson 30 ₤. as Adjutant of his Battalion.
        Archives of Maryland, Vol. 16, p. 199, 209.

        Cuthbert Jones, Drummer, in 3rd. Reg. Md. Line made a Pvt. 4/2/1778 and discharged 4/4/1780.
        Archives of Maryland, Vol. 18, p. 127, 384, 409.

April 5, 1777
        Council of Maryland to Capt. John David.
        We expected you would by this Time, have been down with the Conqueror; if any new Difficulties, advise us; we presume the Galley is at least so far fitted as that she may be worked about the Bay to exercise the Men; if she is you are to come to Annapolis for Orders.
        Archives of Maryland, Vol. 16, p. 201.

April 10, 1777
        Dr. Barton Tabbs, Surgeon, 7th. Reg. Md. Line resigned 10/3/1779.
        Archives of Maryland, Vol. 18, p. 252, 291, 621.

April 11, 1777
        Council to Capt. John David
        You are hereby desired to bring the Conqueror to Annapolis immediately. The Acoutriments you want will probably be procured as soon if you were here as if you remain at Baltimore.
        Archives of Maryland, Vol. 16, p. 207.

April 16, 1777
        Joseph Long, Pvt. enlisted in the 6th. Reg. Md. Line, served to 11/15/1783.
        Archives of Maryland, Vol. 18, p. 224, 349, 358, 440, 498, 544.

April 17, 1777
        Council ordered Treasurer pay to Capt. John Davidson 5 ₤.10s. for Blankets.
        Archives of Md. Vol. 16, p. 217.

April 21, 1777
        Stephen Tarlton commissioned as Coroner of St. Mary's County. Commission signed by Gov. Thomas Johnson.
        Calendar of Maryland State Papers No. 5, p. 90 (Item 694).

        Maryland raising seven Battalions of Troops for General Washington.
        Archives of Maryland, Vol. 16, p. 223.

April 23, 1777
        Council ordered Treasurer pay to Capt. John David 100 Ł. on acct., and the Commissary of Stores deliver to him 43 pr. of Trowsers, 15 pr. of shoes, 24 shirts, 2 hatts, 6 jackets and one piece of Russia drab.
        Archives of Maryland, Vol. 16, p. 224.

        John Allen Thomas, St. Mary's County to Gov. Thomas Johnson
        The bearer, Henry Massey, was a soldier but "is desirous of entering on Board the Defence"; Capt. George Cook knows him and would be glad to have him.
        Calendar of Maryland State Papers No. 4, Part 2, p. 154 (Item 1005).

April 28, 1777
        Council ordered Treasurer pay to Dr. Barton Tabbs 72 Ł.10s. per his account.
        Archives of Maryland, Vol. 16, p. 231.

April 29, 1777
        Gov. Thomas Johnson to Gov. Patrick Henry
        ....according to the last Accounts from Philadelphia nine Men of War within or about the Capes of the Bay have been too successful in their Depredations on the American Trade. As soon as we can get any of our Row Gallies ready they will be ordered down in such a Situation that they may be easily collected to take Advantage of a Calm and with Orders to act in Concert with yours, it is our idea that in a Calm an Attack might be decisive against a Man of War...
        Archives of Maryland, Vol. 16, p. 232, 233, 238.

        Capt. Uriah Forrest to Col Nathaniel Ramsey
        Commissions promised officers of the 3rd. Regiment have not been received; Col. Mordecai Gist has Col. Ramsey's, and Major Uriah Forrest was commissioned twice; orders can be sent by Capt. Benjamin Brookes; pay from Dec. 10, 1776 should be drawn in Philadelphia.
        Calendar of Maryland State Papers No. 4, Part 1, p. 72 (Item 416).

May 1, 1777
        Richard Evans, Pvt. in 6th. Reg. Md. Line, discharged 5/1/1780.
        Archives of Maryland, Vol. 18, p. 203.

May 3, 1777
        Major Uriah Forrest and his men march through Philadelphia.
        Archives of Maryland, Vol. 16, p. 239.

May 11, 1777
        Capt. George Cook on the Defence, Patuxent River to Gov. Thomas Johnson
        Four recruits have been gotten and others promised since anchored in Mouth of Patuxent; will sail to St. Mary's River for 2 or 3 days and then to Yeocomico River where recruits are expected; 13 have been sick since leaving Annapolis; only 3 or 4 on board are seamen, except Officers; is sure will have his quota soon but there will be few seamen; will return to Annapolis as soon as quota is filled.
        Calendar of Maryland State Papers No. 4, Part 2, p. 157 (Item 1027).

May 17, 1777
        Council ordered Treasurer pay to Capt. John David 269 Ł.19s.5d...
        Archives of Maryland, Vol. 16, p. 258.

        Mordecai Gist to Gov. Johnson
        Major (Uriah) Forrest says Officers of the Battalion are much dissatisfied that they have not received their Commissions...
        Archives of Maryland, Vol. 16, p. 260.

May 19, 1777

Ignatius Simms, Pvt. enlisted in 1st. Reg. Md. Line, died 7/17/79.
Archives of Maryland, Vol. 18, p. 160.

May 25, 1777

James Roach declines Commission to collect blankets at Newtown because the small pox has rendered him incapable of executing it.
Calendar of Maryland State Papers No. 5, p. 102 (Item 787).

Benjamin Cheshire appears as a Marine on the ship Defence and served until 12/31/1777. On Apr. 6, 1778 he enlisted in the 3rd. Reg. Md. Line for the duration of the War and the record is noted "run off" However, he was transferred to the Invalid Corps on 2/7/1780 from the 3rd. Reg.
Archives of Maryland, Vol. 18, p. 329, 623, 655.

May 30, 1777

List of Men belonging on board the Ship of War Defence
George Cook, esqr. Commander - includes names of Henry Barnes, Mackey Biscoe, John Coode (Coard), Joseph Fowler, Clement and Thomas Garner, Thomas Hopewell, Jeremiah Jordon, Christopher Leigh (Lee), William Leigh, Walter Lilburn and others.
Calendar of Maryland State Papers No. 5, p. 104 (Item 801).

May 31, 1777

Council to Capt. John David
You are to proceed with the Conqueror to this Place (Annapolis) with all Dispatch, fitted as well as you can and apply to Capt. Walker for his Men to go with you...
Archives of Maryland, Vol. 16, p. 269.

June 3, 1777

Council to J. Hollingsworth
....The exorbitant Prices of every Thing makes the utmost Frugality necessary; Capt. (John) David had a Hogshead of Whiskey lately...a small Allowance of Spirit must do and that of the cheapest kind, the Public cannot afford Rum at 40/ or 45/ a Gallon for the Row Gallies, nor will it do to frequent the Markets for Beef at 15d. or 18d. per lb., the Prices we hear it is at in Baltimore.
Archives of Maryland, Vol. 16, p. 272.

June 4, 1777

Commissions to John Reeder, Junr
    Henry Greenfield Sothoron
    Richard Barnes
    Henry Reeder
    Vernon Hebb
appointed Justices of the Orphans Court of St. Mary's County.

June 12, 1777

Council to S. Steward
Capt. (John) David sends his Boat for his square Sails, he also wants the Swivel Balls, the four Pound and double headed Shot which are at your Yard. You'll please to send them, we want to fit Capt. David for Action.
Archives of Maryland, Vol. 16, p. 288.

Richard Barnes, Leonardtown to Gov. Thomas Johnson
Called his Battalion together as directed but 38 privates were all that enrolled at the Meeting; more may be enlisted from among those absent, especially if strong measures are taken by the legislature.
Calendar of Maryland State Papers No. 4, Part 2, p. 171 (Item 1116).

June 14, 1777
      James Bright, Pvt. 5th. Reg. Md. Line, discharged by Col. Uriah Forrest 5/14/1780.
      Archives of Maryland Vol. 18, p. 184.

      Council ordered Commissary of Stores deliver to Capt (John) David 24 pr. shoes, 40 pr. Trowsers, 24 shirts 8 Hatts, one Jacket, 6 Bolts of Canvass, No. 7 and 6 Bolts, ditto No. 4 and that the Armourer deliver to him 1000 Weight of Cannon Powder, one Ct. wt. of Musqt. ditto, 50 wt. of Musqt. Ball and 15 Musqts with Cartouch Boxes.
      Archives of Maryland Vol. 16, p. 289.

June 16, 1777
      Council to Capt. (John) David
      As you inform us that the Conqueror is now fit for Service, we are desirous that her Efforts may be exerted to clear the North Channel of the Capes of the armed Vessels which we are informed have lately infested it. We presume you are stronger than any of them. We learn the Frigate, Virginia lies in York River, wherefore you will first go there, advise with Capt. (James) Nicholson as to your Plan, from him get Assistance in Men, if necessary and act in Concert with any force that he may have the Direction of. We expect that some of the Virginia Galleys may probably join you....
      Archives of Maryland Vol. 16, p. 290.

June 20, 1777
      Certificate of Jeremiah Jordan certifies that Stephen Tarlton has qualified as Coroner of St. Mary's County.
      Calendar of Maryland State Papers No. 4, Part 3, p. 109 (Item 839).

July 1, 1777
      Commission issued to Richard Barnes, appointing him Lieutenant of Militia (Head) for St. Mary's County.
      Archives of Maryland Vol. 16, p. 303.

July 9, 1777
      Vachel Yates, 1st. Lieut. of Marines, served from Feby. 23.
      Archives of Maryland Vol. 16, p. 313.

July 11, 1777
      Council ordered Commissary of Provisions deliver to Capt. (John) David 10 barrels Beef, 5 Bbls Pork & 1000 lb Bread.
      Archives of Maryland Vol. 16, p. 317.

July 12, 1777
      Council to Capt. John David
      You will proceed with the Conqueror to York River... for the Arms and other goods belonging to this State...
      Archives of Maryland Vol. 16, p. 318.

July 28, 1777
      John Christopher, Pvt. enlisted in the 2nd. Reg. Md. Line. Shown as a Prisoner of War 8/16/1780 - 11/1/1780.
      Archives of Maryland Vol.18, p. 92.

July 29, 1777
      Council to Capt. John David
      ....ordered to return to the York River for the residue of the Arms, and also some Gunlocks, Tin, etc., and to deliver to Annapolis.
      Archives of Maryland Vol. 16, p. 320.

July 30, 1777
     Council ordered Treasurer pay to Thomas McWilliams 73 ₤.2s.6d. Balance
of his Acct.
     Archives of Maryland Vol. 16, p. 321.

August 5, 1777
     Council ordered Treasurer pay to Capt. John David 440 ₤.14s.9d. Bal. of
his Acct.
     Archives of Maryland Vol. 16, p. 326.

August 7, 1777
     Thomas Brewer, Sergt. 2nd. Reg. Md. Line discharged 6/1/1780.
     Archives of Maryland Vol. 18, p. 82.

August 10, 1777
John Jordan, Pvt. enlisted in 5th. Reg. Md. Line, transferred to Q.M. Oct. 1780.
     Archives of Maryland Vol. 18, p.218.

August 21, 1777
     British passed Annapolis in Armada of 260 ships. On the 25th had landed and
reached as far as the Cecil County Court House on the way to Philadelphia.
     Archives of Maryland Vol. 16, p. 340, 344.

August 23, 1777
     Gov. Thomas Johnson to I. Craycroft.

                                        Annapolis Augt. 23d. 1774
     I have directed Ignatius Craycroft of St. Marys County to purchase a Number
of Black Cattle for the Public Use, they will be wanted for the support of the Militia
who is to march. Our Treasury now being removed I cannot supply him with Cash, but
what he purchases will be honestly paid for. You are to purchase what Beef Cattle
you can in St. Mary's County and to reinforce General Washington. As you purchase
on the Water Side have them drove into the Country and when you get a good clever
Drove, send them along the Elk Ridge Landing so that you may avoid the Rivers....
     Archives of Maryland Vol. 16, p. 342.

August 26, 1777
     Commissions issued to:
                    Jeremiah Jordan Col.
                    John Reeder   Lt. Col.
                    John Allen Thomas   Major

Charles Jordan Capt.   Gerard Bond Capt.
John Eden   1st. Lt.   John Shanks   1st. Lt.
Samuel Maddox 2nd. Lt.   Clement Gardiner   2nd. Lt.
Meveral Lock   Ensign   Stephen Tarlton   Ensign

John Thomas   Capt.   Thomas Attaway Reeder   Capt
Francis Millard 1st. Lt.   John Breem   1st. Lt.
William Thomas 2nd Lt   John Cartwright 2nd Lt
Clement Power   Engisgn   Zachariah Hammett   Ensign

John Mills   Capt   James Roach   Capt
Thomas Nicholls 1s Lt.   James Rapier   1st Lt
William Walton   2nd Lt.   William Rapier 2nd. Lt.
Henry Swann   Ensign   Joseph Woodward   Ensign

Edmund Plowden   Capt   William Kilgour   Capt
William Spink   1st Lt   John Edwards   1st Lt
Joseph Stone   2nd Lt   Benjamin Edwards   2nd Lt
Wilfred Reswick Ensign   John Johnson Sothoron   Ensign

                    William Bond   Capt
                    Edward Mattingly   1st Lt.
                    Jonathan Edwards   2nd Lt
                    William Cartwright   Ensign
Belonging to the Upper Battalion in St. Mary's County

Ignatius Fenwick   Col
Vernon Hebb   Lt. Col
Ignatius Taylor, Major

John Armstrong   Capt
Alexander Watts   1st Lt.
Ignatius Combs   2nd Lt
George Howel Leigh   Ensign

John Horn Abell   Capt
Robert Armstrong   1st Lt
William Bennett   2nd Lt
Benja. Williams   Ensign

John Smith   Capt.
Zachariah Forrest   1st Lt
Zephaniah Forrest   2nd Lt
John Smith   Ensign

Ignatius Abell   Capt
Enoch Abell   1st Lt
Barton Abell   2nd Lt
John Mills   Ensign

John Greenwell   Capt.
Philip Fenwick   1st Lt
Bennett Combs   2nd Lt
James Williams   Ensign

John Mackall   Capt
Thomas Jenkins   1st Lt
Benjamin Morgan   2nd Lt
Philip Evans   Ensign

Saml. Jenifer   Capt
John Abell   1st Lt
Richard King   2nd Lt
George Aisquith   Ensign

Hugh Hopewell   Capt
John Aisquith   1st Lt
John Chesley   2nd Lt
Robert Jarboe   Ensign

William Barton Smoot   Capt
George Gaither   1st Lt
Joseph Langley   2nd Lt.
Joshua Tarlton   Ensign

belonging to the Lower Battalion of Militia in St. Mary's County.
Archives of Maryland, Vol. 16, p. 345, 346.

August 30, 1777

Council of Maryland

....The Militia who have been called in having generally left their Arms behind them and there not being public Arms enough to furnish the whole of the Militia who ought at this Time of Invasion to be in Service. The Militia Officers are requested to borrow or purchase for the use of the public all the effective Arms they can and to forward them to such places as they may conveniently be ordered into the hands of the marching Militia and all persons who have effective Arms are desired to furnish their Arms either on Loan or Sale and they may depend on being paid the Value of their Arms lent in case of Loss.

Th. Johnson

Archives of Maryland, Vol. 16, p. 351.

September 1, 1777

Council to Lt. Richard Barnes

We shall in all Probability have more Militia than we can arm. We are therefore desirous, as Your County is so remote and the People may be wanted at Home, that none should immediately march from thence. Possibly those who first go may want to be relieved. You will therefore get your Militia settled in the best Manner you can and have two Companies of each Battalion ready to march in Case they should be ordered. We do not hear of any capital move yet of our Enemies; Genl. Washington's Van is in their Neighbourhood and Report makes us out full strong enough for them.

Archives of Maryland, Vol. 16, p. 357.

September 4, 1777

Richard Barnes, Leonardtown to Gov. Thomas Johnson

Johnson's instructions to stop the militia arrived just in time as four companies were about to march this week; the Lower Battalion was much averse to losing any of its men because the returns of able-bodied men are erroneous and there are hardly more men in the County than are needed to defend it; the whole affair has been made

especially disagreeable by the number of poor men who have been begging to be re-
leased from duty to take care of their many small children and prevent their crops
from being lost.
        Calendar of Maryland State Papers No. 4, Part 2, p. 199 (Item 1272).

September 6, 1777
        Benjamin Rumsey to Gov. Johnson
        ....Two Deserters....say one Half of the Fleet is to go into Delaware Bay and
the other to fall down to York River, that the Ships had no Soldiers on Board, having
landed 13,000 under Gen'l. Howe (to March on Phila.) That half the Fleet in Delaware
was to assist the operations of the Army and the Residue to receive them here in case
of a disaster. They say the 64 Gun Ships have but 350 sailors to navigate them and
64 Marines that they design to plunder the unarmed part of our Coasts of Provision
of which they are in want....that the negroes were received on board the merchant
vessels of which there were several in the Fleet who boasted they would make their
Fortunes by selling them in the West Indies....I congratulate your Excellency....on
the affair of Bennington (and) the Raising the Seige of Fort Stanwix....
        Archives of Maryland, Vol. 16, p. 365.

September 8, 1777
        Council ordered the Treasurer pay to Ignatius Craycraft 650 Ł. on Account he
being employed to purchase Cattle for the Public.
        Archives of Maryland, Vol. 16, p. 366.

September 12, 1777
        Council ordered Treasurer pay to Thomas Nichols 16 Ł.18s. per Account passed.
        Archives of Maryland Vol. 16, p. 374.

September 15, 1777
        Richard Barnes, Leonardtown to Gov. Thomas Johnson
        Ignatius Craycraft has delivered Johnson's letter reporting on the "Affair to the
Northward"; "God grant Washington may give Howe a compleat drubbing before he
returns down this way", as this is the worst-armed part of the State and the Negroes
in the lower part of the County are becoming very insolent, one company is stationed
at the mouth of the Patuxent and another will be sent to Point Lookout; will be glad to
advise Craycraft in the purchase of cattle.
        Calendar of State Papers No. 4, Part 2, p. 204 (Item 1300).

September 17, 1777
        Council ordered Treasurer pay to John Allen Thomas 23 Ł.10s.6d. per
Acct. passed.
        Archives of Maryland, Vol. 16, p. 377.

October 3, 1777
        Council of Maryland
        ....we shall order a Detachment of our Matrosses (Bombardiers) from hence
(Annapolis) with two Field Pieces and have to Day ordered 10 Companies of Militia
from St. Mary's, Charles and Calvert to relieve the Militia at Camp.....

        Council to Richard Barnes, Esq. Lt of St. Mary's County
        It is quite uncertain whether it may not be necessary to keep up a Body of our
Militia at Camp and the Time of those who are not there being nearly expired, we request you will immediately order the first & second Classes of the Militia in your
County to march, they will do well to take each of them a Blankett, we have none with
which we can supply them and such as can, a Gun. The Arms, Tents, Camp Kettles
and Accoutriments in the Use of those now at Camp will be put into Hands of those
who are to supply their Places; but probably, as is too common, some of the Arms may
be carried away and others abused so as not to be immediately servicable. Through
Baltimore Town will be the best Rout and we shall be glad that an Officer from each

Company should come to us here by the Time the Militia get to Marlbro. We wish all Expedition to be used as eventually it may be necessary to form a large Body of Militia, or, what is indeed to be wished, our Affairs maybe in such a Situation as to allow us to dismiss them on their Way.

Archives of Maryland, Vol. 16, p. 390, 391.

October 10, 1777

Samuel Chase to Gov. Johnson   York Town (Pa) Fryday Evening

I wrote to you this Morning the best Accounts, I could obtain of the Battle of the 4th. Inst....Major Forrest had his thigh broke by a Musquet Ball....our Loss is between 6 & 700, killed, wounded and missing....

Archives of Maryland, Vol. 16, p. 395, 396.

October 11, 17, 18, 1777

Council ordered Treasurer pay to Ignatius Craycroft 673 ₤.7s.8d. balance due him for Cattle purchased for the State. Ordered Treasurer pay to Lt. Col. Samuel Hanson 500 ₤. for use of the Marching Militia from St. Mary's, Charles and Calvert Counties and Capt. Joseph Ford 200 ₤. for recruiting to be charged to the First Maryland Regiment and to be accounted for.

Archives of Maryland, Vol. 16, p. 397.399.

October 14, 1777

George Elms, Fifer, in the 6th Reg. Md. Line, discharged 11/1/1780.

Archives of Maryland Vol. 18, p. 203, 469, 510.

October 16, 1777

Richard Barnes to Gov. Thomas Johnson

Intended to march the militia from St. Mary's County last Monday but has had difficulty getting enough men to make up the necessary companies; the companies from the Upper Battalion were inadequate in number and poorly Clothed; in the Lower Battalion only 30 privates marched out of two companies of 71 privates each; Supplied Capt John Thomas with 51 ₤. Lt. John Shanks with 51 ₤. and Lt. Philip Fenwick with 42 ₤. for the use of their respective Companies.

Calendar of Maryland State Papers No. 4, Part 2, p. 213 (Item 1351).

November 7, 1777

Council ordered Treasurer pay to Nicholas Lewis Sewall 3 ₤.10s. Amt of Acct passed.

Archives of Maryland, Vol. 16, p. 411.

November 20, 1777

Council ordered Treasurer pay to Capt. John David 544 ₤.16s.6d. due to the Crew of the Galley Conqueror.

Archives of Maryland Vol. 16, p. 418.

November 22, 1777

Council ordered Treasurer pay to Ignatius Fenwick 100 ₤. to Ship hands &c for the Lydia to be charged in Account.

Council to Capt. George Cook

By the General Orders of this Day, the three Galleys, Conqueror, Baltimore and Independence are to be under your Command as Chief or Principal Officer and you are to proceed with them to the sound between the Islands and the Main of the Eastern Shore and there check or distress the Enemy all you can.....

Archives of Maryland, Vol. 16, p. 422.

November 26, 27, 1777

Council ordered Treasurer pay to Colo. Richard Barnes 334 ₤. 8p. due per Acct.

John Allen Thomas appointed Collector of Cloathing (in St. Mary's County)

agreeable to an Act of the present Session of Assembly intitled "An Act to procure Cloathing for the Quota of this State of the American Army".
Archives of Maryland, Vol. 16, p. 425, 426.

December 2, 1777
Capt. Joseph Ford applies for appointment as recruiting officer for St. Mary's County.
Calendar of Maryland State Papers No. 4, Part 3, p. 17 (Item 105).

December 3, 1777
Council ordered Treasurer pay to Capt. Joseph Ford $1,000.00 per General Order from Colo. Stone.
Archives of Maryland, Vol. 16, p. 430.

December 9, 1777
Council to Lt. Francis Ware, Charles County
In Consequence of the Intelligence received of some British Ships of War having gone up Patowmack we have sent a Waggon down with Arms &c which we request you will distribute as you will see best for the Public Service. We hope you will take the necessary Steps to prevent the Enemy from committing Ravages on the inhabitants by placing Guards at suitable Stations. You are also to endeavor to obstruct all Intercourse and if the Service should require it, that you will take the Command of the Prince George County Militia.....
The Council sent: 60 Musquets with Bayonets
47 Cartridge Boxes with fix'd Ammunition
43 Bayonet Belts
250 Flints
Archives of Maryland, Vol. 16, p. 431, 432.

December 14, 1777
Capt. George Cook, St. Mary's River, to Gov. Thomas Johnson
As Commander of the galleys Conqueror, Baltimore and Independence he arrived in Tangier Sound on Nov. 26....cruised the Sound often but the enemy had sailed down the Chesapeake Bay before he arrived; on Dec. 8, he anchored in the Bay above the mouth of St. Jerome Creek; on the 9th, he bore towards Point Lookout; he heard the Phoenix with 40 guns and the Emerald with 32 guns and 2 tenders were in the Potomac; on the 10th, early, Cook "beat up" the river above St. George Island and anchored in St. Mary's River; he wrote Col. Richard Barnes...believes the enemy has at least 8 ships in the Bay; heard from Barnes that the enemy ships are as low as Nanjemoy and should be down soon.
Calendar of Maryland State Papers No. 4, Part 2, p. 224 (Item 1426).

December 19, 1777
Council ordered Treasurer pay to John Mills 1 Ł.11s.6d. due him...
Archives of Maryland, Vol. 16, p. 438.

December 20, 1777
Council ordered Treasurer pay to Athenasius Ford 11 Ł.2s.4d. due to a party of St. Mary's County Militia commanded by John Greenwell, Jr...
Archives of Maryland, Vol. 16, p. 438.

December 21, 22, 1777
Council to Colo. Richard Barnes
By the Defence's Tender, we send you 100 Stand of Arms with Orders to land them at Hopewell's as it appears to us the most convenient Place to which we can, with Prudence trust them. Governor Henry has advised us that he has ordered two of the best Virginia Gallies up to Potowmack to act in Concert with ours.

December 20, 22, 1777
Col. Richard Barnes Leonardtown, to Gov. Thomas Johnson

Enemy ships are in the Potomac and have landed on Blackistone Island, taking all the stock; they were prevented from landing on "Priest Town" (Priest Point) by the Militia; Capt. George Cook is near Blackistone Island, failed in several attempts to get near them; the Virginia galley, Safeguard, has joined him; he can prevent further damage by the enemy - needs provisions; one man dead on the Conqueror and two sick and one man died on the Independence last night (22nd) and four sick.
Calendar of Maryland State Papers No. 4, Part 2, p. 224 (Item 1426).

Council to Capt. George Cook
This by the Defence's Tender who goes down with 100 Musquets to be lodged at Hopewell's for Colo. Barnes and some Provisions for the Gallies. The Skipper has Orders to call in St. Jerom's to learn your situation and that of the Enemy before he goes into Patowmack. By a Letter from Gov. Henry we are informed he has ordered two of the best of the Virginia Gallies to Patowmack to act in Concert with ours. We hope they have joined you before this Time.

Council to Ware and Barnes
A Report prevails and it has reached us in several Ways that many People on Patowmack and particularly between Cedar Point and Wiccomico have been exchanging Provisions with the Men of War for Salt and other Articles. Whatever temporary Convenience may result to Individuals from such a Practice, none can be ignorant how contrary it is to their Duty as Subjects to this State, or not foresee the pernicious Consequences. We therefore request your utmost Vigilance to put a Stop to all Kinds of Intercourse between the People and the Men of War. It is said the Ships are ballasted with Salt, which if true, proves the Intention of their going up Patowmack and if they are treated as half Friends we may expect enough of their Company.

Order of Council
The General Assembly having passed a Resolution for the Sale of the Ship Defence and allowing Liberty to any of the Marines to enter the Matross Companies or on board the Gallies. The Commanding Officer on board the Defence is to discharge any of the men who inlist with Capt. Campbell or enter on the Gallies.....

Council to Capt. G. Cook
We yesterday sent off the Defence's Tender with 100 small Arms for Colo. Barnes....Mr. Vanbibber tells us he has a Quantity of Cordage, amongst it some Cables at Fredericksburg in Virginia....If you think it will be safe, we would have you send the Tender on this Business....We are in Hopes, before this Time, you have been joined by two Gallies from Virginia and that you have been able at least to prevent the infamous Intercourse with the Men of War....
Archives of Maryland, Vol. 16, p. 439, 440, 441.

December 29, 1777   Headquarters Valley Forge
General George Washington to Governor Thomas Johnson
Sir: Gen'l Smallwood will, by this Conveyance, transmit you a Return of Seven of the Maryland Regiments. The eight, which was composed of part of the German Battalion and part of Rawlin's is in the same situation in point of numbers. By this you will discover how deficient, how exceedingly short they are of the complement of Men....
...Should we have a respectable force to commence an early Campaign, before the Enemy are reinforced I trust we shall have an opportunity of striking a favorable and happy stroke....we may rest assured that Britain will strain every nerve to send from home and abroad, as early as possible, all the Troops it shall be in her power to raise or procure.....We had in Camp on the 23d instant, by a Field Return then taken, not less than 2898 men unfit for duty by reason of their being bare footed and otherwise naked...
We have taken post here for the Winter, as a place best calculated to cover the Country from the Ravages of the Enemy and are busily employed in erecting Huts for the Troops. This circumstance renders it the more material that the supplies

should be greater and more immediate than if the men were in warm comfortable Houses....
> Archives of Maryland, Vol. 16, p. 448, 449.

----1777
> List of Probable St. Mary's County Sailors on the Ship Defence

*James Armstrong, Marine
George Bennett May 19 - July 23, 1777
*Mackie Biscoe May 19-June 1, 1777
Nathaniel Bond Midshipman & Purser
  4/15-12/31/1777
James Briscoe, Marine 10/23-12/31/1777
*Benjamin Cheshire, Marine 5/25 -
  12/31/1777
James Clarke, Marine 7/1-12/31/1777
*George Cooke, Lieut. 9/12-11/15/1776
          Capt. 11/15/1776-12/31/1777
*John Davis, Corpl. of Marines, 1777
Wm. Davis, Marine, 1777
Joseph Dorsey, Marine 10/23-12/31/1777
Richard Dorsey, Midshipman 1777
*Joseph Dunbar,Cooper 1/11-12/31/1777
Robt. Evans 8/1-10/31/1777
*Richard Fenwick, Marine 10/23-12/31/1777
Joseph Fowler(Boy) 5/19-12/31/1777
Clement Gardiner, Marine 5/22-12/31/1777
Thomas Gardiner 5/22-7/7/1777
*Joshua Gibson 5/22-12/31/1777
John Goldsborough, Marine 10/23-
  11/15/1777
Stephen Goldsborough, Marine 10/23-
  11/15/1777
*John Hall, Third Mate 1777
*Stephen Hall, Mate   1777
Wm. Hall 5/26-7/28/1777
Francis Herbert, Boatswain Mate 1777
*Thomas Hopewell, Midshipman
  5/15-12/31/1777
*Thomas Howard,Midshipman
  2/2-12/31/1777
*Wm. Howard, Carpenter's Mate
  8/15-12/31/1777
*Wm. Howard, Marine   1777

Sam'l. Jordan, Corpl of Marines
  10/22-12/31/1777
*Jeremiah Jordan 1/23-12/31/1777
*John Jordan, Sgt. of Marines
  1/23-12/31/1777
*Christopher Leigh, Marine
  5/20-12/31/1777
*William Leigh, Surgeon's Mate 1777
John Lemmon, Marine   1777
*Walter Lilburn 5/22-11/24/1777
Henry Lusby, Midshipman 10/15 - 11/13
  Lt. of Marines 11/13-12/31/1777
Robert McCleland, Marine
  6/26-12/31/1777
John Maddox, Marine 6/3-10/15/1777
*Henry Lee Massey, Mishipman
  5/10-12/31/1777
*Abell Mason, Ordinary Seaman 1777
*Enoch Medley, Seaman 10/23-12/31/1777
Jonathan Mills 5/22-7/23/1777
*Thomas Moore, Ordinary Seaman 1777
*John Moore, Marine 5/10-12/31/1777
Wm. Morris, Lieut. of Marines 1777
*Wm. Piercy, Midshipman 1/13-12/31/1777
*Robt. Swailes, Marine 10/23-12/31/1777
Geo. Thompson 1/11-3/1/1877
Revel Wharton 1777
*Richard Yates, Boatswain's Mate
  4/28-12/8/1777
*Vachel Yates, Sgt. of Marines & Lieut.
  of Marines 2/15-10/15/1777
  Capt. of Marines 10/15-12/15/1777

> Archives of Maryland, Vol. 18, p. 654-661.

* Known to be St. Mary's Countians

January 1778-1781
> George Plater of St. Mary's County, a Delegate to the Continental Congress.
> Manual, State of Maryland 1973-1974, p. 841.

January 1, 1778
> Council ordered Treasurer pay to Ignatius Gough (Goff) 46 ₤.7s.1d. due him per Account and discharged him from the Artillery, having the spleen and having been in the Hospital for several months.
> Archives of Maryland, Vol. 16, p. 453.

> John H. Briscoe, Sergt. resigned from the 2nd. Reg. Md. Line.
> Archives of Maryland Vol. 18, p. 82.

January 5, 1778
>   Council ordered Treasurer pay to Capt. Joseph Ford $500.00 to be expended in
Bounties to Recruits to be charged to the 1st. Maryland Continental Regiment.
>   Archives of Maryland Vol. 16, p. 454.

January 9, 1778
>   Council ordered Treasurer pay to Joseph Dunbar 8 Ł. 17s.
>   Archives of Maryland Vol. 16, p. 463.

January 13, 1778
>   Capt. George Cook to Gov. Thomas Johnson
>   Requests jobs for the officers who belonged to the Defence; especially re-
commends Vachel Yates and Henry Lusby, his two Lieutenants and his Clerk, now ill.
>   Calendar of Maryland State Papers No. 4, Part 2, p. 231 (Item 1467).

January 16, 17, 1778
>   Commission issued by the Council of Maryland to Zachariah Forrest, appointed
Sheriff of St. Mary's County in the room of James Mills who resigned.
>   Ordered that Treasurer pay to Capt. Ignatius Fenwick 350 Ł. on Account of the
Ship, Lydia....
>   Archives of Maryland Vol. 16, p. 468.

January 18, 1778
>   Richard Barnes to Gov. Thomas Johnson
>   Has the Governor's letter informing him of James Mills resignation as Sheriff
of St. Mary's County; has since learned from Maj. (John Allen) Thomas that
Zachariah Forrest has the appointment, which he had expected would be hard to fill
as it pays too little; will try to get pork for the Militia and flour and bread, which are
more difficult; Timothy Bowes has paid him some of the money for the vessels goods
"rec'd from Dunmore's Fleet"; the rest he can get from Col. Vernon Hebb.
>   Calendar of Maryland State Papers No. 4, Part 2, p. 231 (Item 1470)

January 27, 1778
>   Council Circular to St. Mary's and other Southern Counties
>   We desire you will forward without Delay, the Cloathing you have procured for
the Army to Annapolis and that you will continue your utmost Exertions in buying &
collecting what farther may be in your Power.
>   Archives of Maryland, Vol. 16, p. 475.

January 30, 1778
>   Council to Capt. Ignatius Fenwick
>   Yours of the 18th is just come to Hand. The Galley left this some Days past
to meet your Vessel, according to appointment, with the Stores required. We would
have you proceed to meet the Galley. We shall be under Difficulties in sending hands
from hence & hope you will be able to procure them. We shall, in a few Days send
to you at Smith's Creek where we hope you will be.
>   Archives of Maryland, Vol. 16, p. 480.

February 6, 1778
>   Council ordered Treasurer pay to Richard Clarke 100 Ł.1s.6d. for work done
on the Galley Independence and 21 Ł.12s.6d. for work done on the Galley Conqueror...
>   Archives of Maryland Vol. 16, p. 484.

February 8, 9, 10, 1778
>   Vernon Hebb, St. Mary's County to Col. Richard Barnes   Leonardtown

Reports two British Frigates at the mouth of the Patuxent River. (John?) Smoot and _____ Walls have been ordered out.

Proclamation by John Lewis Gideoin, Commander of....the Richmond and Senior Officer of his Majesty's Ships in St. Mary's River, "If the duty of His Majesty's Ships is not interfered with; he will not land men or destroy houses. Encloses a proclamation to Hebb "to prevent the inhabitants being uneasy"; two Americans are on the Richmond; they are being sent and an equal number of prisoners should be returned, "if you have any prisoners in your possession". Col. Richard Barnes advised Hebb he has no prisoners and thinks none are in the country.

Col. Vernon Hebb, Porto Bello to Capt. Richard Barnes
Ships have retreated to St.George's Island; twenty or thirty guns are needed to pursue captors of Capt. Ignatius Fenwick. Capt. Smith's brig may be the next victim of the enemy; no Communication shall be permitted to the Enemy.

Richard Barnes to Gov. Thomas Johnson
Capt. Fenwick was taken by the enemy; Capt. (John) David tried to prevent the capture in St. Mary's river but could not; Mr. Medley is to be paid for the "express"; arms sent to Hopewell are "a parcel of refused things" and a vessel should come take them back to Annapolis; "no part of this State (is) so badly Armed as we are; Cols. Jordon and Reeder and Maj. Thomas dislike the arms sent; Col. Hebb will have thirty of the best by morning.
Calendar of Maryland State Papers No. 4, Part 3, p. 20 (Items 133-138).

February 12, 13, 19, 1778
Council to Colo. Sam'l. Smith
....We have just received Advice that there are two men of War in Patowmack and that they have taken the State Ship Lydia.

Council to R. Barnes
We received yours of the 10th last night. Nothing is left in our Power with Respect to Capt. (Ignatius) Fenwick but to endeavour to get him and his people back again. We have got Prisoners enough taken in Merchant Vessels to exchange for the Lydia's Crew but they are at a Distance from hence and it will be several Days before they can be sent down. If the Men of War are not already gone down, we request you to send Fenwick and the Crew on Shore for whom we will send a like Number of Prisoners of equal Rank on board the Man of War and you are impowered to pledge our Faith for the Performance or if the Capt. will not send them on Shore, to desire his Promise that they shall not be sent away 'til we have an Opportunity of sending a Flag with Prisoners in Exchange. We do not know the number or Rank of Fenwicks People on Board, if you can ascertain them please to advise us. Capt. (John) David's Galley wants heaving down and several Things to be done to her, we wish her to come up as soon as she can with Safety. The Arms we sent we designed should be and thought were effective....

Council to Capt. David
As Capt. Fenwick has fallen into the Enemy's Hands we imagine your stay in Patowmack will be of no Service and therefore desire, as soon as you think you safely may, you will proceed up to Annapolis to get the Galley fitted, but if the Men of War continue in Patowmack and Colo. Barnes should think your Stay usefull, on which you are to advise with him, we would have you continue whilst the Men of War remain in Patowmack.

Council to Capt. Fenwick
We had an Account of the Capture of the Lydia and supposed you had fallen into the Hands of the Enemy. We shall be glad to see you up as you propose. There can be no Justice or Colour for the Claim of the Sailors to the Things saved; those we would have sent to us by Capt. David or, if he cannot bring them, have secured. We do not know what Contracts you made with the Seamen, from what passed, we expected you would be obliged to give River Pay; if so we think them entitled to their Wages or

if they had not contracted, they will be entitled for the Time they were in our Service, wherefore we would have, unless they contracted for the Voyage and had their Advance, and were not by Contract, excluded from River Pay, to settle their Accounts and pay up to the Time of the Capture.

Archives of Maryland, Vol. 16, p. 492, 493, 494, 511.

Note

It is uncertain from the records just what happened to the Lydia and Capt. Fenwick and his crew. From the foregoing, apparently Capt. Fenwick was becalmed, caught at anchor or gradually overhauled and he and his crew escaped in small boats, taking some of the armaments, stores, etc., and presumably they beached or scuttled the Lydia. In any event he escaped the British and was issued Letters of Marque on Jan. 11, 1779 for the Maryland Brigantine, Sally, a privateer of 14 Guns and a crew of 30 seamen. After the War, he made his home at "River View" on Canoe Neck Creek in St. Clement's Bay, St. Mary's County.

Naval Records of the American Revolution 1775-1788, p. 451; Life on the Potomac River, p. 20.

February 13, 1778

Council to Richard Barnes

....Capt. (John) David's Galley (Conqueror) wants heaving down and several things to be done to her. We wish her to come up from St. Mary's River as soon as she can with Safety...

Archives of Maryland Vol. 16, p. 493.

February 14, 1778

Council of Maryland to Gov. Henry of Virginia

.....The number of Men of War in the Bay and their activity confirms us in opinion that Communication by Water will be too uncertain to rely on...when the Enemy discover the Army draws its Supplies through the Bay, the Number of Men of War will be increased; urges use of Gallies (with those of Maryland) to force the British ships to keep together; The Enemy took a fine Tobacco Ship in Patowmack the other Day....

Archives of Maryland, Vol. 16, p. 498, 499.

February 17, 1778

John Allen Thomas, St. Mary's City to Gov. Thomas Johnson

Repeats his request of February 3 for two prisoners from the Frederick Gaol, a weaver and a shoemaker; can send them down by a wagon expected in early March; the ships of war in the Potomac have gone down the Bay; they took Capt. (Ignatius) Fenwick.

Calendar of Maryland State Papers No. 4, Part 2, p. 236 (Item 1495).

February 18, 1778

Council of Maryland to Hon. Horatio Gates, Pres. of the Board of War

....Several People on Patowmack River who have Fisheries there would willingly contract for considerable quantities of salted Shad perhaps 4 or 5 Thousand Barrels.

Archives of Maryland, Vol. 16, p. 506.

February - 1778

Bishop Benedict Fenwick reported that in 1778, the General Monk, a British Sloop of War fired a ball through old St. Inigoes Manor House on the St. Mary's River, which narrowly missed Rev. John Lewis, S.J. The patch in the brick wall could be seen until the Manor House burned in 1872.

Woodstock Letters, Vol. 10, p. 90.

Jesse Greenwell, Pvt. 4th Reg. Md. Line died of wounds.

Archives of Maryland Vol. 18, p. 115.

February or March, 1778
        Subscribers to the Oath of Allegiance, St. Mary's County
        See Appendix A for a list of 1,166 names of all males eighteen years and over
who took the oath of allegiance in St. Mary's Co. The list is arranged alphabetically
and also includes the names of the officials who administered the oath.
        The taking of this oath was considered treason against the Crown of England
and was an overt act of resistance on the part of the subject. It qualifies descendents
of the various individuals for membership in several patriotic societies.
        Chronicles of St. Mary's Vol. 4, No. 7

        Father Joseph Mosely, S.J. of St. Mary's County reported "every Catholic
took the oath of allegiance in due time under my direction, not one excepted, and I,
as soon as I understood the cordial concurrence and consent of the clergy, took the
earliest opportunity to pledge my fidelity and allegiance to the state".
        Woodstock Letters, Vol. 42, p. 145.

March 2, 1778
        Richard Barnes to the House of Delegates
        Cannot attend sessions of the House of Delegates until next week.
        Calendar of Maryland State Papers No. 5, p. 120 (Item 892).

March 9, 1778
        Council of Maryland to B. Matthews
        We just now are informed that a Ship, a Brig and Seven Sloops were yesterday
beating up the Bay and in the evening were as high as Patuxent....
        Archives of Maryland, Vol. 16, p. 531.

March 14, 1778
        Philip Ford, Gerard Cecil (Sissel) and James Thompson of St. Mary's County
took the Oath of Fidelity and Support of the State (in Annapolis, before the Council)
        Archives of Maryland Vol. 16, p. 536.

March 17, 1778
        Richard Yates enlisted in the 2nd. Reg. Md. Line, died 9/15/1778.
        Archives of Maryland Vol. 18, p. 180.

March 25, 1778
        Capt. John Thomas of St. Mary's County appointed by the Council of Maryland
as an Agent for Purchasing Provisions for the Army in said County.
        Archives of Maryland, Vol. 16, p. 551.

March 27, 1778
        Council of Maryland ordered Treasurer pay to Athanasius Ford 80 Ł.16s. to
be delivered over to Capt. John Greenwell for the use of Part of the 21st Battalion of
Militia under his command whilst in actual service....
        Archives of Maryland, Vol. 16, p. 554.

March 31, 1778
        George Piercy of St. Mary's County....took the Oath of Fidelity and Support
to this State....
        Archives of Maryland, Vol. 16, p. 559.

April 2, 1778
        Council of Maryland ordered Treasurer pay to Richard Barnes Esq. 88 Ł.10s.3d.
due to himself & 21 Ł.13s.10d. and 26 Ł.1s.7d. due to W. B. Smoot's Company of
Militia per Accounts passed by the Committee of Claims.
        Archives of Maryland, Vol. 21, p. 4.

        Justinian Jordan Sergt. in 3rd. Reg. Md. Line.
        Archives of Maryland Vol. 18, p. 127, 298.

April 3, 1778
    Council ordered Treasurer pay to Edward Abell 86 Ł.2s.9d. due...
    Archives of Maryland Vol. 21, p. 6.

April 4, 1778
    John Davidson is mentioned as Captain of the 2nd. Md. Reg.
    Archives of Maryland Vol. 21, p. 8, 567.

    John McKay, Pvt. enlisted in the 5th Reg. Md. Line, discharged 11/1/1780.
    Archives of Maryland, Vol. 18, p. 227, 352, 394, 485.

    Thomas Biggs, Pvt. enlisted in the 2nd. Reg. Md. Line, discharged 4/3/1779.
    Archives of Maryland Vol. 18, p. 83.

April 5, 1778
    James Daffin, Corpl. enlisted in the 4th. Reg. Md. Line, discharged 4/5/1781.
    Archives of Maryland Vol. 18, p. 105, 359, 531.

April 9, 1778
    Council of Maryland ordered Treasurer pay to Capt. John Thomas $1400.00 out
of the money remitted by Congress for the Purchase of Provisions.
    Archives of Maryland, Vol. 21, p. 22.

    Basil Brown, Pvt. in the 3rd. Reg. Md. Line, discharged 11/1/1780.
    In the 1st. Co. 1st. Battn. Md. Line 1/1/1782, discharged 11/15/1783.
    Archives of Maryland Vol. 18, p. 86, 296, 357, 430, 496, 524.

April 13, 1778
    Council ordered Treasurer pay to...John Mackall 15 Ł.16s. per Acct...
    Archives of Maryland Vol.. 21, p. 33.

April 16, 1778
    Council issued Commissions to:

        Alexander Hawkins Watts, Capt.
        John Reeder, Junr. 1st. Lieut.
        George Combs   2nd. Lieut.
        Robert Greaves   Ensign

        William Bennett   1st. Lieut.
        Benjamin Williams 2nd. Lieut.
        William Holton,   Ensign

of Capt. John H. Abell's Company and William Herbert, Ensign of Capt. John Mackall's
Company belonging to the Lower Battalion of Militia in St. Mary's County.
    Archives of Maryland, Vol. 21, p. 37.

    Edmond Barton Cecil (Cissell) enlisted in the 3rd. Reg. Md. Line. Promoted
to Corpl. in July 1780 and discharged 11/1/1780. Re-enlisted and died 1/13/1782.
    Archives of Maryland Vol. 18, p. 96, 329, 449, 527.

April 20, 1778
    William Spalding of James, Pvt. enlisted in the 3rd. Reg. Md. Line, dis-
charged February 1779.
    Archives of Maryland Vol. 18, p. 164.

April 22, 1778
    Nicholas Milburn, Pvt. enlisted in the 6th Reg. Md. Line and served throughout
the War, discharged 11/15/1783.
    Archives of Maryland Vol. 18, p. 228, 347, 353, 440, 487, 547.

April 24, 1778
        Justinian Bullock, Pvt. enlisted in the 3rd. Reg. Md. Line, dead, date unknown
        John Bullock, Pvt. enlisted in the 3rd. Reg. Md. Line, discharged in April
or May 1780.
        Archives of Maryland Vol. 18, p. 86, 87, 329.

        Thomas Green Alvey enlisted in the 3rd. Reg. Md. Line, was wounded and
furloughed. Made Corpl. 2/1/1779.
        Traverse Alvey, Pvt. enlisted in the 3rd. Reg. Md. Line, discharged 11/1/1780.
        Archives of Maryland, Vol. 18, p. 79.

April 26, 1778
        John and William Rock, Pvts. enlisted in the 3rd. Reg. Md. Line and were
discharged 5/2/1781.
        Archives of Maryland Vol. 18, p. 157, 298, 329, 552.

        Bennett Chesser, Pvt. enlisted in the 3rd. Reg. Md. Line 4/26/1778 for the
duration of the War. He was transferred to the Invalid Corp. January 1780 and discharged on pension 7/10/1783.
        Archives of Maryland Vol. 18, p. 96, 298.

April 27, 1778
        John Farding (Farden), Pvt. enlisted in the 3rd. Reg. Md. Line, "struck off"
November 1780.
        Archives of Maryland Vol. 18, p. 109.

        Randolph French, Pvt. enlisted in the 3rd. Reg. Md. Line, discharged in
February, 1779. Stephen French, Pvt. enlisted in the 2nd. Reg. Md. Line May 25, 1778,
discharged 4/3/1779.
        Archives of Maryland Vol. 18, p. 109.

April 28, 1778
        John Sprague, Pvt. enlisted in the 3rd. Reg. Md. Line, died 3/6/1779.
        Archives of Maryland Vol. 18, p. 164.

        Elias Smith, Pvt. enlisted in the 6th. Reg. Md. Line, was discharged
1/1/1780 and re-enlisted.
        Archives of Maryland Vol. 18, p. 247.

April 29, 1778
        Jeremiah Scrabler (Scraher, Scriables?) Pvt. enlisted in the 3rd. Reg. Md.
Line, died 10/14/1778.
        Archives of Maryland Vol. 18, p. 164, 329.

April 30, 1778
        William Slye, Pvt. enlisted in the 7th. Reg. Md. Line, made Corpl. July 1780.
Missing 8/16/1780, prisoner of war. Discharged 4/30/1781.
        Archives of Maryland Vol. 18, p. 249, 555, 617.

        John Trueman (Truman) Pvt. enlisted in the 3rd. Reg. Md. Line, was promoted
to Sergt. in 1780 and shortly thereafter on 1/26/1780 was commissioned an Ensign
in the 3rd. Reg. and Lieut. on 3/16/1781. He was a prisoner of war in 1782 and
invalided out of the service. In 1790 he was on pension at half pay.
        Archives of Maryland Vol. 18, p. 170, 298, 329, 363, 378, 478, 522, 627;
                        Vol. 43, p. 69; Vol. 48, p. 521.

May 1, 1778
        Council of Maryland to County Lieutenants
        You are earnestly requested to deliver over to some Recruiting Officer in the
Continental Service all the Recruits and Substitutes already furnished and which may

be furnished...in Order to have them marched without Delay to Wilmington or such other Post as the Commander in Chief may think proper, first equipping them with what Necessaries they may require from the Stock of the Purchaser of Clothing in your County may have on hand....Recruits & Substitutes from St. Mary's County.....to receive Deficiency of Cloathing at Annapolis.....
        Archives of Maryland, Vol. 21, p. 63.

        George Spalding, Pvt. enlisted in the 3rd. Reg. Md. Line, discharged 2/19/1779.
        Archives of Maryland Vol. 18, p. 164.

        James Thomas, Pvt. enlisted in the 3rd. Reg. Md. Line, a Drummer on 6/4/1778. Made Pvt. 6/11/1779 and discharged 11/1/80. He may have re-enlisted in 1780.
        Archives of Maryland, Vol. 18, p. 170, 298, 319, 329, 345.

May 2, 1778
        Zepha Williams, Pvt. enlisted in the 3rd. Reg. Md. Line and was killed 5/16/1780.
        Archives of Maryland Vol. 18, p. 176.

May 6, 1778
        John Thomas, St. Mary's County to Gov. Thomas Johnson
        Encloses return for purchases, part made with cash and part with certificates; 1200 is needed to pay off; Capt (George?) Walter can receive the money; 2316 lbs. bacon stored at Chaptico; 923 lbs. bacon are at "Lewellins", Wicomico River and 2851 lbs at Leonardtown.
        Calendar of Maryland State Papers No. 4, Part 1, p. 99 (Items 566 & 567).

        Arthur and Enoch McLane enlisted in the 7th Reg. Md. Line and served throughout the war and were Sergts. when discharged in 1783.
        Archives of Maryland Vol. 18, p. 233, 388, 546, 547.

May 7, 1778
        Council ordered the Commissary of Stores deliver to George Piercy of the Conqueror Galley as much white flannel as will make a Waist & Breeches. On May 16, 1778 he was delivered one hhd. Whiskey for the Conqueror and June 19, likewise a half hhd. of Whiskey. On January 22, 1779 he was paid 20 Ł.10s. per Acct.
        Archives of Maryland Vol. 21, p. 69, 86, 140, 282.

May 8, 1778
        Thomas Bond, Pvt. enlisted in Count Pulaski's Legion, as did James Carter, Pvt. on May 11, 1778 and Notley Tippett and Joseph Smith in July 1779, the latter two then being in Charles Town, S. C.
        Archives of Maryland Vol. 18, p. 593.

May 10, 1778
        Ignatius Craycroft, St. Mary's Co. to Gov. Thomas Johnson
        Bearer of letter Capt. (Wm.?) Waters brings 9 raw hides, salted meat goes to Llewellin's warehouse; (Baker?) Johnson promised salt pans by June 1.
        Calendar of Maryland State Papers No. 4, Part 2, p. 249 (Item 1581).

May 11, 1778
        George Plater of St. Mary's County, Delegate in Congress at his duties in Philadelphia.
        Archives of Maryland, Vol. 21, p. 75.

May 12, 1778
        Athanasius Thompson, Pvt. enlisted in the 3rd. Reg. Md. Line, made Corpl. 8/14/1778, Sergt. 1/1/1780 and Q. M. Sergt. 3/1/1780.
        Archives of Maryland Vol. 18, p. 298, 329.

May 13, 1778
     John Baptist Willingham, Pvt. enlisted in the 3rd. Reg. Md. Line, discharged February 1779.
     Archives of Maryland Vol. 18, p. 177, 329.

May 18, 1778
     Council ordered Treasurer pay to Capt. Nicholas Mauger $1680.00 to enable him to pay the $60.00 Bounty to each of the following substitutes enlisted to serve for three years or during the War from St. Mary's County, viz

Pat Kelly	William McGee	Charles McGee
John Rock	John Holmes	Austin Howard
Bennet Cheshire	Thomas Green Alvey	Justinian Pullock
John Blundell	Elias Henry	(Bullock?)
Richard Hall	Traverse Alvey	John Baptist Bailey
Joseph Shanks	Zephaniah Williams	James Thomas
Henry Harley	George Collins	William Holt
Edward Harley	John Farden	Jeremiah Scrabler
Thomas Curtis	John Sprague	Athans. Thompson
John Trueman	William Rock	

     Council to T. Richardson
     We have sent a Sloop of Mr. Eastman's which will carry 280 or perhaps 300 Barrels round to Mr. (E.) Magruder's...to load her with Fish....We received a Letter by the last Post from Mr. Blaine pressing us to forward the Provisions from the State to Charles Town, if Vessels can be got in Potomack and the River is clear...
     Archives of Maryland, Vol. 21, p. 90, 92.

     Charles and William McGee, Pvts. enlisted in the 3rd. Reg. Md. Line and served until the end of the war.
     Archives of Maryland Vol. 18, p. 141, 298, 329, 354, 435, 489, 490, 545.

     Edward White, Pvt. enlisted in the 2nd. Reg. Md. Line, Made Corpl. July 1780 and was discharged 11/1/1780.
     Archives of Maryland Vol. 18, p. 175.

     Edward and Henry Harley, Pvts. enlisted in Smallwood's Reg. Edward was discharged 11/1/1780. Henry missing 8/16/1780, but is shown as re-enlisted and served to 4/25/1781.
     Archives of Maryland Vol. 18, p. 121, 298, 384, 538.

     Elias Henry, Pvt. enlisted in Smallwood's Reg. Made Sergt. 10/1/1780. Discharged 11/1/1780. Note Elias Henry and the two Harleys above also are shown on the muster roll of the 3rd. Reg. Capt.-Lieut. George Armstrong's Company about these dates.
     Archives of Maryland Vol. 18, p. 121, 299.

     John Holmes, William Holt, Zephaniah Hoskins, Austin Howard, Phineas Hurst, Peregrine Howard, and William Howard, Privates, all appear in Smallwood's Regiment in 1778-1779. John Holmes, Austin Howard and Peregrine Howard also appear in the 3rd. Reg. Capt. Armstrong's Co. about these dates. Holmes was reported missing 8/16/1780 but was discharged 4/30/1781. Holt was discharged 10/14/1778. Hoskins was discharged 4/14/1779. Austin Howard was discharged 11/1/1780 and there are indications that he was in the service in 1782. Peregrine Howard was discharged 11/1/1780. William Howard was made a Corporal in Smallwood's Regiment and served until 11/1/1780. Phineas Hurst was promoted to Sergt. 1/18/1779 but the muster role is noted "deserted" (A.W.O.L.) 1/1/1780. He may have been killed or captured.
     Leonard Howard, Pvt. enlisted in the 2nd. Reg. Md. Line and was discharged 4/3/1779.
     Archives of Maryland Vol. 18, p. 121, 217, 298, 329, 330, 354, 357, 430, 436, 463, 490, 496, 617.

May 19, 1778

John McCalley, Pvt. enlisted in the 3rd. Reg. Md. Line and was discharged 4/4/1779.

Archives of Maryland Vol. 18, p. 142.

May 20, 1778

William Coode, Pvt. enlisted in the 2nd. Reg. Md. Line and was discharged 4/3/1779.

Archives of Maryland Vol. 18, p. 94.

May 21, 1778

Council to H. Hollingsworth

....We have ordered a Sloop which will carry 300 Barrels from hence to Potowmack for Shad without Convoy. From our latest Accounts the Men of War were as low as Hampton Roads, if there is a good Look out kept, we think small Craft may be prudently trusted to Potowmack....

Council to Genl. Smallwood

We enclose you two Letters received from Colo. Barnes respecting the Conduct of Lieut. Menger. We have not gone into an Examination of the Facts alledged by Colo. Barnes as we should not, on the Proof of them have undertaken to dismiss him from the Service, but Capt. Fenwick, who is referred to, in his State, confirmed what is said in the Letters. We are much inclined to forward the Business of the Officers and treat them as Gentlemen but are fully in Colo. Barne's Sentiment that Mr. Menger's Conduct deserves Reprehension.

Archives of Maryland, Vol. 21, p. 103, 104.

May 22, 1778

Council to Lieut. John Davidson

The Voluntary Offer of the Militia of Annapolis to go on the service requested by his Excellency General Washington necessary to be performed at and in the Neighbourhood of the Head of Elk is very acceptable. You are to proceed with the Company in the Vessel provided for that Purpose to the Head of Elk where you will join the other Militia engaged in the same service....under the Command of Charles Rumsey Esq. Lieut. of Cecil County....

Council to Maryland Delegates in Congress

....There is a perfect Coincidence of Gov. (Patrick) Henry's Sentiments and ours as to the Utility and Necessity of Manning our Gallies....if we could Man our Gallies they would cut off or greatly obstruct the Intercourse between the Enemys Ships and the Disaffected in this State and Virginia, prevent or punish the Depredations committed by the Tories on the Bay Craft and facilitate the Transportation of the Stores for the Army.....

Archives of Maryland, Vol. 21, p. 105, 106.

James Dyer, Pvt. enlisted in the 3rd. Reg. Md. Line.
Archives of Maryland Vol. 18, p. 103.

May 23, 1778

John Turner, Pvt. enlisted in the 3rd. Reg. Md. Line and re-enlisted in the 3rd. Reg. 1/15/1779. In the 3rd. Co. 3rd. Reg. 8/28/1781.

Archives of Maryland Vol. 18, p. 170, 329, 394, 419.

John Carpenter, Pvt. enlisted in the 3rd. Reg. Md. Line and was discharged 4/4/1779.

Archives of Maryland Vol. 18, p. 96.

May 25, 1778

Jesse Carter, Justinian Carter and Luke Carter, all Privates enlisted in the 3rd. Reg. Md. Line. Jesse is shown as deserted (A.W.O.L.) in June 1778 but appears in the Maryland Line February 25, 1782, having enlisted for 3 years. Luke

Carter served until 11/15/1783. Justinian Carter died 8/11/1778.
Archives of Maryland Vol. 18, p. 96, 329, 330, 417, 527.

Robert Swailes, Sergt. enlisted in the 3rd. Reg. Md. Line and was discharged February 1779.
Archives of Maryland Vol. 18, p. 165.

Robert Purtle, Pvt. enlisted in the 2nd. Reg. Md. Line. The muster roll is noted "time out (up?) discharged".
Archives of Maryland Vol. 18, p. 151.

Thomas Wise, Pvt. enlisted in the 2nd. Reg. Md. Line, and was discharged 4/3/1779.
Archives of Maryland Vol. 18, p. 175.

George Dent, Pvt. enlisted in the 2nd. Reg. Md. Line and was discharged 4/3/1779.
Archives of Maryland Vol. 18, p. 102, 329.
Note George Dent is buried in St. Andrews Episcopal Churchyard. He laid the corner-stone of the new St. Mary's County Court House in Leonardtown on August 16, 1831 at the age of 75.
Chronicles of St. Mary's Vol. 1, No. 1.

May 25, 27, 29, 1778
Council to Thomas Clagett, Piscattaway.
We are sending by your Brother the $4,000.00 as you desire. We have great Difficulties in procuring Craft for the Transportation of Provisions, the first we can Command...we shall send round to Potowmack with orders to take what you have on that River. What lies convenient to Patuxent had best be sent to convenient Landing there...we wish you in the mean time to hire a Vessel and send forward the Provisions inclusive of the Pork from Potomac, addressed to Colo. Henry Hollingsworth at the Head of Elk.....

Council to Capt. Stephen Ross
....If you should be disappointed in getting the Pork at Potomac Creek (in Virginia), in your Way down call on Mr. Bernard O'Neal on Wicomico, St. Mary's County and take in the Provisions he has or any other Public Stores....

Council ordered Treasurer pay to William Thomas $6000.00 to be delivered over to John Thomas Purchaser of Provisions in St. Mary's County to be accounted for.
Archives of Maryland, Vol. 21, p. 111, 112, 113, 114.

May 26, 1778
Notley Tippett, Pvt. enlisted in the 1st. Reg. Md. Line and later enlisted in Count Pulaski's Legion in July 1779, while on duty in South Carolina. He was discharged on 11/1/1780 and re-enlisted and served until the end of the war 11/15/1783.
Archives of Maryland Vol. 18, p. 168, 329, 432, 500, 557, 593.

May 28, 1778
Joseph Fields, Pvt. enlisted in the 3rd. Reg. Md. Line and was discharged May 1779.
Archives of Maryland Vol. 18, p. 110.

May 29, 1778
John Morris, Pvt. enlisted in the 3rd. Reg. Md. Line and was discharged 4/4/1779.
Archives of Maryland Vol. 18, p. 147.

Francis Fenwick, Pvt. enlisted in the 2nd. Reg. Md. Line and was discharged 4/3/1779.
    Archives of Maryland Vol. 18, p. 109.

James Wimsatt (Winset) Pvt. enlisted in the 2nd. Reg. Md. Line and was discharged 4/3/1779.
    Archives of Maryland Vol. 18, p. 175.

Barney Paine (Payne), Pvt. enlisted in the 2nd. Reg. Md. Line and was discharged 11/1/1780.
    Archives of Maryland Vol. 18, p. 151.

John Senior (Senner, Sanner?), Pvt. enlisted in the 2nd. Reg. Md. Line and died December 25, 1778.
    Archives of Maryland Vol. 18, p. 162, 329.

John and Sylvester Wheatley, Pvts. enlisted in the 2nd. Reg. Md. Line. John enlisted for 9 months and was discharged 4/3/1779. Sylvester enlisted for 3 years. He was reported missing 8/16/1780, probably a prisoner of war. He was discharged 7/1/1781.
    Archives of Maryland Vol. 18, p. 175, 329, 561.

May 30, 1778 *
    James Yates, Pvt. enlisted in the 2nd. Reg. Md. Line and was discharged 4/3/1779.
    Archives of Maryland Vol. 18, p. 180.

Joseph Reswick, Pvt. enlisted in the 2nd. Reg. Md. Line and was discharged 4/3/1779.
    Archives of Maryland Vol. 18, p. 156.

May 31, 1778
    Jeremiah Rhoades, Pvt. enlisted in the 3rd. Reg. Md. Line and re-enlisted 2/17/1779, and was discharged 2/17/1782.
    Archives of Maryland Vol. 18, p. 157, 298, 330, 359, 456, 552.

June 1, 1778
    Jonathan Woodburn, Pvt. enlisted in the 2nd. Reg. Md. Line and was discharged 4/3/1779.
    Archives of Maryland Vol. 18, p. 175.

Timothy Bowes, Clerk of the Commissioners of the Tax, St. Mary's County to the General Assembly writes that Richard Barnes has reported that the Act to assess and impose equal taxes on all property within this state and its supplements were revised in one general Act of the last session; the Commissioners request a Copy.
    Calendar of Maryland State Papers No. 4, Part 2, p. 253 (Item 1606).

June 6, 1778
    Circular to Counties, including St. Mary's, that the "Provisions purchased should be sent forward with all Expedition"....
    Archives of Maryland, Vol. 21, p. 124, 125.

June 8, 1778
    Council ordered Treasurer pay to William Molohon 34₤. 17s.6d. for expenses of bringing Recruits from St. Mary's to Annapolis....
    Also Treasurer pay to Richard Barnes 76₤.9s.6d. due him per Acct.
    Archives of Maryland, Vol. 21, p. 125, 127.

George Plater, St. Mary's County Delegate to Congress in York, Pa., with Charles Carroll of Carrollton.
    Calendar of Maryland State Papers No. 4, Part 1, p. 102 (Item 566).

June 10, 1778

Return of Substitutes, Drafts and Vagrants from St. Mary's County, June 10, 1778.

When Entered 1778	Name	Time of Serving	When Entered 1778	Name	Time of Serving
Apl. 20	Patrick Kelly	3 yrs	May 28	Notley Goldsmith	9 mo
30	Wm. Spalding, son of Jas.	9 mo	25	Stephen French	do
20	Wm. McGee	3 yrs	25	John Stone	do
28	Charles McGee	War	25	Robert Swales	do
24	John Duncaster	9 mo	29	Barnard Pane (Paine)	do
27	Edmd. Barton Cissel (Cecil)	9 mo	29	Stephen Greenwell	do
			29	John Wheatley	do
			29	Joseph Stone	do
26	John Rock	3 yrs	29	Thomas Jarboe	do
30	John Holmes	3 yrs	29	Robert Greenwell	do
30	Austin Howard	3 yrs	29	John Senior	do
26	Benj. Chesher, run off	War	29	James Wimseld	do
May 4	Bennet Cox, vagrant, deserted	9 mo	30	Edw. Barton Godart	do
			25	Geo. Dent	do
13	John Bapt. Willingham	9 mo	26	Notley Tippett	do
Apl. 21	Thos. Green Alvey	3 yrs	29	Peter Richie	do
24	Justinian Bullock	3 yrs	30	Norman Bouroughs	do
30	John Blundull	3 yrs	June 1	Jonathan Woodburn	do
May 4	Elias Henry	3 yrs	May 29	Edmund Hill	do
Apl. 24	John Bapt. Bailey	3 yrs	25	Thomas Branson	do
21	Richard Hall	3 yrs	28	Joseph Crook	do
28	Travers Alvey	3 yrs	28	Benj. Dailey	do
May 2	Joseph Shanks	War	13	James Graves	do
2	Zaphaniah Williams	War	Apl. 27	Rudolph French	do
1	James Thomas	3 yrs	23	John Fields	do
Apl. 25	Henry Harley	3 yrs	26	Leod. McAtee (Vagrants	do
26	George Collings (Collins)	3 yrs	26	John McAtee (or deserters	do
23	Wm. Holt	3 yrs	May 1	George Spalding	do
May 5	Edwd. Harley	3 yrs	Apl. 26	Wm. Rock	3 yrs
Apl. 27	John Farden	3 yrs	May 14	Justinian Carter	do
29	Jeremiah Scraher	3 yrs	16	Henry Causey	do
22	Thos. Curtis	War	Apl. 20	John Morris	do
28	John Sprague	3 yrs	May 14	Henry Gouldsburry	9 mo
May 13	Althas. Thomson	3 yrs	2	Silvester Wheatley	3 yrs
Apl. 30	John Truman	War	19	Luke Carter	War
May 26	Jeremiah Morgan	9 mo	Apl. 4	Thos. Biggs	9 mo
23	John Turner	do	May 16	Henry Philips	3 yrs
23	John Blair	do	14	Ignatius Downs	do
23	John Carpenter	do	19	John McCalley	9 mo
25	Edward Smith	do	31	Garbiner Lemmon	do
25	Leonard Branson	do	31	Geo. Shirley	do
25	Abednigo Jackson	do			
27	Edward McKarteney	do			
May 31	Jeremiah Rhoades	9 mo	May 30	Danl. Friend, a ship carpenter, a draft	9 mo
31	James Coachman	do			
30	Jesse Chiveral	do	25	Jesse Carter	do
23	David Johns	do	June 1	Jacob McKey	do
29	John Norris	do	1	John Medcalf	do
28	James Foster	do	1	John Barton Drury	do
23	Bennett McLeland	do	May 31	Thos. Mattingley	
22	Nathan Adams	do	31	Philip Mattingley	
22	Jeremiah King	do	31	Stanley Battin	
22	James Dyer	do		Joseph Johnston	do

May 25	Henry King	9 mo	May 31	Joseph Smith	9 mo
25	Thomas Wise	do		John Jones	do
25	Richard Smart	do		James Barnes	do
28	Smith Mahoney	do		Jonathan Riney	do
25	Robert Turtle (Purtle)	do	do	Rudolph Barnhouse	do
28	Thomas More	do		Joseph Moore	do
30	James Yates	do	10	Phineas Hurst	do
30	Zepheniah Hoskins	do	10	Michael Fields	3 yrs
30	Joseph Fields	do		James McBride	do
23	Leonard Howard	do	10	William Spalding, a draft	
30	Ignatius Clark	do		Benj. Morgan, a draft	
30	Charles Clarke	do		Benj. Thomson, deserter	
30	Joseph Reswick	do		from the Continental Army	

Archives of Maryland, Vol. 18, p. 329, 330.

June 10, 1778

William Spalding, Pvt. enlisted in the 1st. Reg. Md. Line and died 11/26/1778.
Archives of Maryland Vol. 18, p. 161.

Richard Ellis Gatton, Pvt. enlisted in the 1st. Reg. Md. Line and marked present on the muster roll 11/1/1780. Sylvester Gatton, Pvt. enlisted 10/4/1778 in the same Regiment. Richard enlisted for 3 years, was made a Corporal and was discharged 4/26/1781. Sylvester re-enlisted 7/3/1782 for 3 years and appears in the 2nd. Co. Northern Detachment of the Md. Line in 1783. He is also shown as an exchanged prisoner from Charles Town, S.C. in 1781, 1st. Reg. Md. Line.
Archives of Maryland Vol. 18, p. 112, 331, 359, 418, 465, 501, 536, 617.

Council ordered Treasurer pay to Samuel Abell 3 Ł.8s. per Acct.
Archives of Maryland Vol. 21, p. 132.

June 12, 1778

Council order Treasurer pay to John Allen Thomas 126 Ł.18s.6d. and 20 Ł.8s.3d. for the use of Richard Bond and 40 Ł.9s.9d. for the use of Capt. James Roach & his Company and 3 Ł.8s. for the use of Samuel Abell as per Accounts. Also pay to John Allen Thomas 60 Ł.12s.4d. per Acct.
Archives of Maryland, Vol. 21, p. 132.

June 13, 1778

Council of Maryland to Capt. Bennett Matthews
You are to proceed in the Independence Galley to Chaptico Warehouse on Wicomico River and receive of Capt. John Thomas, who lives within a mile of it, the Provisions that he has purchased, and call on your Way down at the other Landings on Patowmack, where he may have lodged any, and receive that also. If the Galley will as we expect take more than Capt. Thomas has of which you and he can judge, take so much of the Continental Provisions at Llewellins Warehouse in the care of Mr. O'Neal, as will about make up your Load. You are to proceed to the Head of Elk with the Provisions as soon as you well can, just calling in the Mouth of this River in your Way.
Archives of Maryland, Vol. 21, p. 134.

June 17, 18, 1778

Council ordered Treasurer pay to Athanasius Ford 19 Ł.6s.3d. per Acct. Also pay to Michal Fields $60.00 due him as Bounty, he having been enlisted in St. Mary's County.
Gabriel Williams a Substitute from St. Mary's County for nine Months is discharged, he having procured James McBride to serve in the Continental Army for a term of three years and having paid him the Sum of $80.00 in which the State Bounty is included.
Archives of Maryland, Vol. 21, p. 138, 139.

June 22, 24, 1778
	Council ordered that Joseph Moore, a substitute from St. Mary's County appearing to this Board to be altogether incapable of Service is hereby discharged.
	Lieut. Benj. Morgan of St. Mary's County mentioned as having been appointed by Gen'l. Smallwood as a Brevet Captain in the last campaign.
	Archives of Maryland, Vol. 21, p. 144, 149.

June 25, 1778
	Thomas Branson, Pvt. enlisted in the 3rd. Reg. Md. Line and was discharged 10/30/1778.
	Archives of Maryland Vol. 18, p. 86.

June 26, 1778
	George Plater from York, Pa. to Gov. Thomas Johnson
	Letter from Gen'l. Benedict Arnold was read in Congress on June 26; on June 18, Philadelphia was evacuated by the British; enemy cavalry was at Mt. Holly (N.J.); American Army was at Princeton (N.J.); 400 deserters from British forces have reached Phila. British fleet at Reedy's Island.
	Archives of Maryland, Vol. 21, p. 151.

June 30, 1778
	Council ordered Treasurer pay to Capt. Beriah Maybury 45 Ł.7s.9d. due to him and also 17 Ł.14s.3d. for the use of Capt. George Cooke per accts.
	Archives of Maryland, Vol. 21, p. 152.

	John Allen Thomas, St. Mary's County to Gov. Thomas Johnson
	Asks help for Justinian Pullock (Bullock), formerly a soldier in Thomas Company who was taken prisoner in the Winter of 1776; he escaped in the Spring and has tried twice to march but his legs are so swollen and painful that Dr. (Gustavus Richard?) Brown thinks he can do nothing to earn a living, nor has he any other means of support.
	Calendar of Maryland State Papers No. 4, Part 2, p. 257 (Item 1632).

	Council ordered Treasurer pay to....Capt. George Cook 17 Ł.14s.3d. per Acct. passed by the Principal Clerk to the Aud. Genl.
	Archives of Maryland Vol. 21, p. 152.

June - 1778
	Edward McCartney, Pvt. was discharged from the 3rd. Reg. Md. Line.
	Archives of Maryland Vol. 18, p. 142.

July 7, 1778
	Henry Hollingsworth, Head of Elk to Gov. Thos. Johnson
	Skirmishes reported on June 27-29; Gen't. Smallwood's Brigade was badly treated - on June 29 an action of 4 hours duration took place in New Jersey; 1300 British were killed and 900 Americans.
	Calendar of Maryland State Papers No. 4, Part 1, p. 105, 106 (Items 607, 608).

July 15, 1778
	John Metcalf (Medcalf) Pvt. who enlisted in the 2nd. Reg. Md. Line on June 1, 1778, died.
	Archives of Maryland Vol. 18, p. 139.

July 16, 1778
	Joseph Ford to Col. James Brice, Annapolis.
	Has been appointed by Col. (Ephraim) Blaine Commissary of Purchase for the Middle District as an Assistant for St. Mary's and Calvert Counties; wants to know by Uriah Forrest the prices allowed for beef and pork; postscript adds he has been offered Ł. 75 for the Lydia's long boat.
	Calendar of Maryland, State Papers No. 4, Part 3, p. 41 (Item 266).

July 17, 1778
      Council ordered Treasurer pay to John Thomas, Purchaser of Provisions in St. Mary's County 729 Ł.9s.4d. per Acct.
      Archives of Maryland, Vol. 21, p. 160.

August 4, 13, 1778
      Council ordered Treasurer pay to Zephaniah Turner 8 Ł.3s.2d. for the use of Capt. John Mackall, Balance of Acct.
      Also pay to John Davidson 1215 Ł.17s.10d. for the use of Norton and Beall on Account.
      Archives of Maryland, Vol. 21, p. 175, 184.

August 12, 1778
      George Armstrong, Capt.-Lieut. in command of the 3rd. Reg. Md. Line, and still in command at Kimbell's Farm on January 19, 1780.
      Archives of Maryland, Vol. 18, p. 298 and 299.

August 14, 1778
      Jeremiah King, Corpl. enlisted in the 3rd. Reg. Md. Line was discharged 4/14/1779.
      Archives of Maryland Vol. 18, p. 130.

August 18, 1778
      George Plater advises Gov. Thomas Johnson British fleet appeared off Rhode Island.
      Archives of Maryland, Vol. 21, p. 188.

August 24, 1778
      George Shirley, Pvt. who enlisted in the 3rd. Reg. Md. Line on 5/31/1778 died.
      Archives of Maryland Vol. 18, p. 164.

October 16, 1778
      Council ordered Treasurer pay to Philip Fenwick 6 Ł.18s.6d. for use of Enoch Fenwick and 5 Ł.19s.11d. for use of William Rapier and his Company.
      Archives of Maryland, Vol. 21, p. 217.

October 17, 1778
      Council ordered Treasurer pay to Philip Fenwick 12 Ł.16s. for the use of Alexander Watts and his Compy. per Acct. passed by the Auditor General.
      Archives of Maryland Vol. 21, p. 217.

October 23, 1778
      Council ordered Treasurer pay to Nicholas Sewall 15 Ł. per Acct....
      Archives of Maryland Vol. 21, p. 221.

October - 1778
      Henry King, Sergt. 3rd. Reg. Md. Line transferred to the Comy. Dept.
      Archives of Maryland Vol. 18, p. 130.

November 10, 1778
      Garbiner Lemmon, Pvt. enlisted in 3rd. Reg. Md. Line recorded as sick 1/19/1780.
      Archives of Maryland Vol. 18, p. 299.

November 20, 1778
      Council ordered Treasurer pay to John Allen Thomas 71 Ł. and the further sum of 17 Ł.18s.6d. for the use of Gerard Bond & his Company per Accounts.

ELLENBOROUGH
c. 1750

Home of Dr. Henry Reeder

DEEP FALLS
1745

RIVER VIEW
c. 1720

Home of Maj. Wm. Thomas

Home of Capt. Igantius Fenwick

Pictures courtesy of Charles E. Fenwick, Sr.

CHRIST CHURCH, CAPTICO
1736

ST. FRANCIS XAVIER, NEWTOWN
1766

ST. GEORGE'S, POPLAR HILL
1750

ST. ANDREWS, NEAR LEONARDTOWN
1766

Pictures courtesy of Charles E. Fenwick, Sr. and Robert E. T. Pogue

Commissions issued to the following as Justices of St. Mary's County:

Jeremiah Jordon	John Reeder, Jr.	Henry Greenfield Sothoron
Richard Barnes	Henry Reeder	Vernon Hebb
Ignatius Taylor	Henry Tubman	Bennet Biscoe
Hanson Briscoe	John Shanks	John Ireland
Ignatius Fenwick	Nicholas L. Sewall	Robert Watts
Robert Armstrong	John H. Reade	Thomas Bond
	William Kilgore	

Judges of the Orphans Court in St. Mary's Co.

Richard Barnes	Henry Reeder	John H. Reade
Thomas Bond	William Kilgore	

Dr. Wiesenthal to Gov. Thomas Johnson
In his lengthy report he mentions that he went down to St. Mary's County and amputated Col. Forrest's thigh.
Archives of Maryland, Vol. 21, p. 241, 242, 243.

November 21, 1778
Council ordered Treasurer pay to John Allen Thomas 3 Ł.11s.9d. for use of James Roach per acct.
Archives of Maryland Vol. 21, p. 248.

December 2, 1778
The humble Petition of Daniel Friend, Ship Carpenter to Gov. Johnson was drafted last June 1 from the Militia of St. Mary's County; at Annapolis was taken into service of the state as a ship carpenter; his wife and family are "greatly distressed"; his wages are inadequate to attend his plantation, now is a foreman and believes he deserves at least a salary equal to those under his supervision.
Calendar of Maryland State Papers No. 4, Part 3, p. 49 (Items 326-328).

December 15, 1778
Instructions of the General Assembly of Maryland to George Plater and other Maryland Delegates in Congress.
The injustice and inconvenience of permitting certain states to hold large territories is pointed out and the Delegates are instructed not to agree to the Confederation unless an article in conformity with the annexed declaration is added to it.
Calendar of Maryland State Papers No. 4, Part 1, p. 127 (Items 750, 751).

----1778?
The pork that was bought for the Militia of St. Mary's County is at Richard Bond's; if it is sent for, the arms at Leonardtown could be brought up at the same time.
Calendar of Maryland State Papers, No. 4, Part 2, p. 269 (Item 1711).

January 9, 1779
Robert Greenwell, Sergt. 3rd. Reg. Md. Line was discharged.
Archives of Maryland Vol. 18, p. 114.

January 11, 1779
Commission of Letter of Marque & Reprisal issued to Ignatius Fenwick, Commander of the Brigatine Sally, 90 Tons burthen, mounting 10 Carriage Guns, 4 Swivels and 15 small Arms....
Archives of Maryland, Vol. 21, p. 277.

January 15, 1779
John Blair, Pvt. enlisted in the 3rd. Reg. Md. Line and was discharged 11/1/1780.
Archives of Maryland Vol. 18, p. 90.

John B. Cecil (Cissell), Pvt. enlisted in the 3rd. Reg. Md. Line for 3 years.
Archives of Maryland Vol. 18, p. 97, 298.

February 3, 5, 1779
Council ordered Treasurer pay to Lieut. George Armstrong of the 3rd. Md. Regiment 150 Ł. due him by Resolve of the General Assembly. Also pay him 48 Ł. per acct. passed by the Aud. Gen'l.
Archives of Maryland Vol. 21, p. 290, 291. 294.

February 24, 1779
Joseph Shanks, Pvt. died. He had enlisted in the 3rd. Reg. Md. Line on 5/2/1778 for the duration of the war.
Archives of Maryland Vol. 18, p. 164, 329.

February - 1779
Joseph Crooke, Pvt. 2nd. Reg. Md. Line is reported on the muster roll as "not heard of". He enlisted on May 28, 1778 and probably was killed or a prisoner of war.
Archives of Maryland Vol. 18, p. 93.

March 3, 1779
Council ordered the Commissary of Stores deliver to George Spalding the amt. of 9 Ł.8s.9d. in Cloathing, being the balance due him p. Act of Assembly to procure Troops for the A. Army.
Archives of Maryland Vol. 21, p. 312.

March 30, 1779
Council of Maryland issues commission to John Eden as Agent to purchase provisions in St. Mary's County.
Archives of Maryland Vol. 21, p. 332.

April 3, 1779
John and Joseph Stone, Pvts. who had enlisted 5/25/1778 in the 2nd. Reg. Md. Line were discharged.
Archives of Maryland Vol. 18, p. 162.

Charles and Ignatius Clark, Pvts. who had enlisted 5/30/1778 in the 2nd. Reg. Md. Line were discharged.
Archives of Maryland Vol. 18, p. 93.

Abednigo Jackson, Pvt. who had enlisted 5/25/1778 in the 2nd. Reg. Md. Line was discharged.
Archives of Maryland Vol. 18, p. 126.

Robert B. Drury, Pvt. of the 2nd. Reg. Md. Line, discharged from service.
Archives of Maryland Vol. 18, p. 102.

April 4, 1779
Richard Smart, Pvt. who had enlisted in the 3rd. Reg. Md. Line 5/25/1778 was discharged.
Archives of Maryland Vol. 18, p. 164.

Deposition of Athanatius Jarboe - lost his vessel & supplies on Tangier Sound to pirates.
Calendar of Maryland State Papers No. 4, Part 3, p. 58 (Item 377).

April 14, 1779
Council ordered Treasurer pay to James Wimsatt (Winset) a 9 mo. Soldr. in the 2nd Reg., discharged, 5 Ł.5s.6d. the balance due him in lieu of Cloathing allowed by the Act of Assembly to procure troops for the American Army.

Also pay to James Yates (Yeates) a 9 mo. Soldr. in the 2nd. Reg. Dischd.
6 Ł. due him in lieu of a Blanket.
Archives of Maryland Vol. 21, p. 346.

Council ordered Commissary of Stores deliver Cloathing, and in some cases,
a blanket, to the following 9 months Soldiers, discharged, in the amt. indicated:

Zephaniah Hoskins, 3rd. Reg. Md. Line	14 Ł.5s.6d.
Notley Goldsmith, 3rd. Reg. Md. Line	21 Ł.5s.6d.
John Stone, 2nd. Reg.	7 Ł.15s.6d.
Thomas Biggs, 2nd. Reg.	5 Ł.9s.
Abednigo Jackson, 2nd. Reg.	20 Ł...6d.
John Norris, 3rd. Reg.	21 Ł.15s.6d.
James Yeates (Yates), 2nd. Reg.	10 Ł.18s.
Barton Goddert, 2nd. Reg.	17 Ł.10s.6d.
Steven French, 2nd. Reg.	2 Ł.1s.6d.
Joseph Drury, 2nd. Reg.	6 Ł.13s.
Barney Payne, 2nd. Reg.	13 Ł.10s.6d.
Thomas Beall, 2nd. Reg.	2 Ł.6s.6d.
Joseph Reswick, 2nd. Regt.	6 Ł.5s.6d.
Joseph Fields, 3rd. Regt.	20 Ł.5s.6d.
Philip Mattingly, 2nd. Reg.	19 Ł.18s.
Henry Garner, 2nd. Reg.	13 Ł.1s6d.
Rudolph Barnhouse, 3rd. Reg.	20 Ł.5s.6d.
Jacob McCoy, 2nd. Regt.	17 Ł.10s.6d.
Jonathan Riney, 2nd. Reg.	6 Ł.3s.
John Wheatley, 2nd. Reg.	12 Ł.10s.6d.
Thomas Wise, 2nd. Reg.	4 Ł.5s.6d.
Leonard Howard, 2nd. Reg.	7 Ł.14s.6d.
Ignatius Clarke, 2nd. Reg.	4 Ł.6d.
Robert Drury, 2nd. Reg.	4 Ł. 8s.
Francis Fenwick, 2nd. Reg.	20 Ł.5 s.6d.
Thomas Mattingly, 2nd. Reg.	16 Ł.5s.6d.
Joseph Stone, 2nd. Reg.	4 Ł.18s.
James Barnes, 2nd. Reg.	19 Ł.8s.
Jeremiah King, 3rd. Reg.	20 Ł.5s.6d.
Charles Clarke, 2nd. Reg.	1 Ł.1s.6d.

due them by an Act of the Assembly to procure Troops for the American Army.
Archives of Maryland Vol. 21, p. 345, 346.

April 16, 1779
Council ordered Treasurer pay to Lieut. George Armstrong of the 3rd. Md. Reg.
$2000.00, the Bounty of 1 Recruit, Peregrine Howard enlisted into the said Reg. and
also the further Sum of $16.00 allowed by the General Assembly for enlisting.
Archives of Maryland Vol. 21, p. 349.

April 17, 1779
Council ordered Commissary of Stores deliver Cloathing, and in one case a
blanket, to the following 9 month Soldiers, reinlisted, in the amt. indicated:

Jeremiah Rhodes, 3rd. Reg. Md. Line	7 Ł.3s.2d.
John Blair, 3rd. Reg. Md. Line	15 Ł.4s.4d.
John Beane, 3rd. Reg. Md. Line	6 Ł.4s.4d.
John Turner, 3rd. Reg. Md. Line	15 Ł.4s.4d.
William Griffin, 1st. Reg. Md. Line	16 Ł.19s11d.
Henry Goldsborough, 3rd. Reg. Md. Line	10 Ł.8s.9d.
Garbiner Lemmon, 3rd. Reg. Md. Line	11 Ł.18s.9d.
Edmond Barton Cecil, 3rd. Reg. Md. Line	7 Ł.14s.4d.
Richard Elliot, 1st. Reg. Md. Line	4 Ł.8s.9d.

Archives of Maryland Vol. 21, p. 351, 352.

April 20, 1779
    Council ordered Treasurer pay to Lieut. (George) Armstrong of the 3rd. Reg.
$200.00, the Bounty to James Jones enlisted by him & the further Sum of $16.00 for
enlisting Jones.
    Archives of Maryland Vol. 21, p. 354.

    Council ordered Treasurer pay to Lieut. John Bailey of the 3rd. Md. Reg.
$4000.00 to be expended in the Recruiting Service.
    Archives of Maryland, Vol. 21, p. 354.

April 21, 1779
    Council ordered the Commissary of Stores deliver to Lieut. George Armstrong of
the 3rd. Reg. 21 Pair Shoes to be charged to the 3rd. & 1st. Regs.
    Archives of Maryland Vol. 21, p. 356.

May 1, 1779
    Col. Richard Barnes to Gov. Thomas Johnson
    Enemy are in the Bay; can expect little of the Militia as arms and provisions
are lacking.
    Calendar of Maryland State Papers No. 4, Part 3, p. 60 (Item 392).

May 4, 1779
    Council ordered Treasurer pay to Stephen Greenwell, Pvt. a 9 mo. Soldier in
the 2nd. Reg. discharged the amount of 2 Ł.10s.6d. in Cloathing due him.
    Archives of Maryland Vol. 21, p. 378.

May 7, 1779
    Petition of William Wakely, Annapolis to Gov. Thomas Johnson
    Applies for position as a clerk; is a native of Ireland; has tutored the Children
of Henry Greenfield Sothoron for 2 years; served in Capt. Sothoron's Company in
Col. Jeremiah Jordan's Battalion against Lord Dunmore last summer; data in a letter
from Capt. Sothoron.
    Calendar of Maryland State Papers No. 4, Part 2, p. 156 (Item 1019).

May 9, 1779
    Ignatius Adams, Pvt. enlisted in the 1st. Reg. Md. Line and served to 11/1/1780.
    Archives of Maryland Vol. 18, p. 78.

May 11, 1779
    Letter from George Plater and other Maryland Delegates in the Continental
Congress to Gov. Thomas Johnson
    General Washington needs heavy cannon and hopes Maryland can supply
them; have sent $500,000 and have a warrant for $800,000 additional.
    Archives of Maryland Vol. 21, p. 74, 75.

May 12, 1779
    Council ordered the Commissary of Stores deliver to Robert Swailes a 9 Mo.
Soldr. in the 3rd. Reg. Discharged the amt. of 21 Ł.8s.9d. in Cloathing due him...
    Archives of Maryland Vol. 21, p. 388.

May 15, 1779
    Council ordered Treasurer pay to Lieut. John Bailey of the 3rd. Reg. $3000
on Acct. for the Recruiting Service p. G. Smallwood's Instns.
    Archives of Maryland Vol. 21, p. 393.

May 17, 1779
    Council of Maryland to Lieuts. of St. Mary's and Other Counties.
    Enemy in the Bay; we request you to give immediate notice to the Militia...
to prepare & hold themselves in Readiness to march on the first Order....captured and
burned Portsmouth & Suffolk, Va...
    Archives of Maryland, Vol. 21, p. 396, 397, 405.

May 22, 1779
        James Knott, Pvt. enlisted in the 1st. Reg. Md. Line is shown as a prisoner in January 1780. Exchanged and returned to service 1/1/1782 and served to the end of the war, discharged 11/15/1783.
        Archives of Maryland Vol. 18, p. 129, 543.

May 24, 1779
        Josiah Alvey, Pvt. enlisted in 1st. Reg. Md. Line and was discharged 5/24/1782.
        Archives of Maryland Vol. 18, p. 78, 523.

May 29, 1779
        Council ordered Treasurer pay to (Capt. ?) Lieut. John Bailey of the 3rd. Reg. $4000 to be expended in the Recruiting Service. Also pay him 24 Ł. ...(and) the Commissary of Stores deliver to him 10 yds. White Casmire...for Lieut. (George) Armstrong of the 3rd. Reg.
        Archives of Maryland Vol. 21, p. 430, 431.

May 31, 1779
        Council to Colo. Francis Ware
        ...We enclose you an order on Colo. Barnes for 100 lbs. of Powder...
        Archives of Maryland Vol. 21, p. 433.

June 1, 1779
        Council to Lt. Andrew Buchanan, Balto. County
        ...three large ships with 2 smaller vessels at the mouth of the Patuxent....

        George Plater & other Md. Delegates to Gov. Thos. Johnson
        ...A vessel...brings an Account of the British being defeated near Charles Town (S.C.)...
        Archives of Maryland Vol. 21, p. 436, 439.

June 3, 1779
        Council of Maryland to Gen'l. M. Gist
        ...Ships thought to be British in the Bay prove to be French ships...militia can be discharged.
        Archives of Maryland Vol. 21, p. 440.

June 4, 1779
        Council ordered Commissary of Stores deliver to George Dent a 9 Mo. Soldier in the 2nd. Reg. Discharged 3 Ł.5s.6d. in Cloathing and also to Johathan Woodburn a 9 Mo. Soldier in the 2nd. Reg. Discharged 8 Ł.10s.6d. in Cloathing due them p. Act of Assembly to procure Troops for the Amn. Army.
        Archives of Maryland Vol. 21, p. 442.

June 7, 1779
        Council ordered Treasurer pay to Lt. Colo. Uriah Forrest of the 1st. Regiment $3000.00 to be expended in the recruiting Service & Accounted for.
        Archives of Maryland, Vol. 21, p. 445.

June 10, 1779
        John Alvey, Pvt. enlisted in the 1st. Reg., Md. Line Marked present on the muster roll 11/1/1780.
        Archives of Maryland Vol. 18, p. 78.

June 11, 1779
        Council ordered the Commissary of Stores deliver to William Combs a 9 mo. Soldier in the 1st. Reg. Discharged the amount of 23 Ł.3s.6d. in Cloathing....
        Archives of Maryland Vol. 21, p. 450.

June 12, 1779
    Lt. Wm. Bruce, Port Tobacco to Gov. Thomas Johnson
    He and Lt. Saml. McPherson are about to go to St. Mary's County to recruit;
only $1000.00 is left...requests more funds. (Also recruiting in Charles County).
    Calendar of Maryland State Papers No. 4, Part 2, p. 270 (Items 1724 & 1728).

June 30, 1779
    Council to Colo. Forrest
    Inquiry as to propriety of appointing Robert Swailes to recruit men in St. Mary's
County - brought a letter from Colo. Plater but not sufficient recommendation.
    Archives of Maryland Vol. 21, p. 464.

July 7, 1779
    Robert Slye, Pvt. enlisted in the 4th. Reg. Md. Line. Muster roll noted
"Deserted" (A.W.O.L.) 1/17/1780.
    Archives of Maryland Vol. 18, p. 167.

July 9, 1779
    Council ordered Treasurer pay $2000...to Lieut. John Bailey of the 3rd. Reg...
for Recruiting.
    Archives of Maryland Vol. 21, p. 468.

    Richard Fenwick, Pvt. enlisted in the 4th. Reg. Md. Line and was discharged
11/1/1780. Was promoted to Corpl. 4/1/1780. Sergt. 7th. Co. 3rd. Reg. Md. Line
8/28/1781 and Corp.. 1st. Co. 4th. Battn. Md. Line 1/1/1782-1/1/1783. In service to
7/10/1784.
    Archives of Maryland Vol. 18, p. 111, 396, 456, 535.

July 13, 1779
    Council to Col. Uriah Forrest
    We have drawn the money for Lt. (John) Bailey...we wish to be furnished with
a Return of the Recruits and to which Regiments they belong...
    Archives of Maryland Vol. 21, p. 471.

    Council ordered Commy. of Stores deliver Serge Denim sufft. for 2 pr. Breeches
to be delivered to Colo. Forrest, 1 pr. to Lt. (John) Bailey...
    Archives of Maryland Vol. 21, p. 470.

    Council to Colo. Uriah Forrest
    We   have drawn the Money for Capt. (John) Bailey & Mr. Shelmerdine as you
desire....having Shirts and clothing delivered....
    Archives of Maryland Vol. 21, p. 471.

August 3, 1779
    Council ordered Treasurer pay to Lieut. John Bailey of the 3rd. Reg. $2000 to
be expended in the Recruiting Service....
    Archives of Maryland Vol. 21, p. 487.

August 18, 1779
    Council to Colo. Uriah Forrest
    The Assembly have been pleased to appoint you Auditor General with a Salary
of Ł. 3000 pr. year...The State of the Public Business makes it desirable an Auditor
should be soon qualified to act.
    Archives of Maryland Vol. 21, p. 498.

August 19, 1779
    Commission issued to Jeremiah Jordan of St. Mary's County to receive
Subscriptions under the Act entitled an Act to continue the Act of Assembly for enlarging

the Powers of the Governor and Council &c passed July Session 1779 and the Resolution of Congress of the 29th Day of June last.
Archives of Maryland Vol. 21, p. 499.

August 24, 1779
Col. Uriah Forrest takes oath as Auditor General.
Archives of Maryland Vol. 21, p. 502.

August 25, 1779
Council ordered Treasurer pay to Colo. Uriah Forrest $2000.00....
Archives of Maryland Vol. 21, p. 502.

September 7, 1779
Col. Uriah Forrest to Gov. Thos. Johnson
Cannot get to Annapolis before tomorrow afternoon; reports that Capt. Williams marched his detachment of 50 men before Sadler had collected 50 men; Sadler has prevailed upon no more than 14 Matrosses to take the Continental bounty; "he has every trouble"
Calendar of Maryland State Papers No. 4, Part 3, p. 77 (Item 484).

September 9, 1779
Council to Lt. Saml. Saddler.
Colo. Forrest mentions...that it may be useful to leave Saml. Chester of the Mattrosses behind, that he desired he might stay in the Fort....good recruiter...
Archives of Maryland Vol. 21, p. 517.

Council ordered Treasurer pay to.....Lt. John Bailey of the 3rd. Regt. $2000.00 for Recruiting....
Archives of Maryland Vol. 21, p. 517.

September 28, 1779
Council ordered Treasurer pay to....Captain Lieut. George Armstrong 750 Ł...
Archives of Maryland Vol. 21, p. 540.

October 12, 1779
Thomas Woolford and 12 others of the 2nd. Md. Reg. Buttermilk Falls (N.Y.) to Gov. Thomas Johnson. Memorandum to give ....$2000 for each signer, as voted by the General Assembly Signed.....Capt. John Davidson....
Calendar of Maryland State Papers No. 3, p. 50 (Item 246).

Capt. Joseph Ford Commissioned Ass't. Commisary of Purchases for St. Mary's and Calvert Counties.
Archives of Maryland Vol. 21, p. 554.

November 2, 1779
Joseph Ford, Leonard Town to Gov. Thomas Johnson wrote sometime ago concerning the Lydia's long boat; tried to send to Annapolis but could not get it done; in fairly good repair; Col. Barnes will purchase her or can advertise her for public sale.
Archives of Maryland Vol. 43, p. 360.

Commission issued to Zacha. Forrest, elected Sheriff of St. Mary's County.
Archives of Maryland Vol. 43, p. 7.

November 18, 1779
Lieut. John Bailey resigned from the 3rd. Md. Reg.
Archives of Maryland Vol. 18, p. 85.

November 18, 1779

Commissions issued to (the following by the Council of Maryland)
Lt. Col. John Thomas
Maj. John Hanson Briscoe

Capt. Charles Jordan
1st. Lt. Samuel Maddox
2nd. Lt. Meveral Locke
Ensign Raphael Neale

Capt. John Shanks in room of Gerard Bond
1st. Lt. John Blackiston
2nd. Lt. William Bayard
Ensign Samuel Tennison

Capt. Francis Millard in room of John Thomas
1st. Lt. William Thomas
2nd. Lt. Clement Power
Ensign James Thomas

Capt. John Hooper Broome in room of Thomas Attaway Reeder
1st. Lt. John Cartwright
2nd. Lt. Zachariah Hammett
Ensign Basil Hall

Ensign Robert Briscoe to John Mills Company

Capt. Richard James Rapier in room of James Roach
1st. Lt. William Rapier
2nd. Lt. Joseph Woodward
Ensign John Greaves

Capt. Edward Mattingly in room of William Bond
1st. Lt. Jonathan Edwards
2nd. Lt. William Cartwright
Ensign James Burroughs
Upper Battalion of Militia of St. Mary's County

Commissions issued to

Jeremiah Jordan	Henry Reeder	Vernon Hebb
Ignatius Taylor	Bennett Biscoe	Hanson Briscoe
John Shanks	John Ireland	Ignatius Fenwick
Robert Watts	Robert Armstrong	John H. Reade
Thomas Bond	William Killgore	John Mackall
	John De Butts	

appointed Justices of the Peace for St. Mary's County.

Henry Reeder	John H. Reade	Thomas Bond
William Killgore	John De Butts	

appointed Judges of the Orphans Court for St. Mary's County.
Archives of Maryland Vol. 43, p. 18.

November 25, 1779
Council of Maryland ordered Treasurer pay to Colo. Uriah Forrest 855£ for Paper purchased of him for the use of the Public.
Archives of Maryland Vol. 43, p. 25.

December 4, 1779
Council ordered Commissary of Stores deliver to Colo. (Uriah) Forrest 2 pr. French hose and flannel sufft. for 3 under waistcoats, he paying the current price for them.
Archives of Maryland Vol. 43, p. 30.

December 11, 13, 1779
        Council ordered Treasurer pay to Colo. Uriah Forrest $2000.00 for the use of
and to be delivered over to Barton Tabbs, Surgeon to the 7 Maryland Regiment due him
by an Act of Assembly...
        Also pay Colo. Uriah Forrest 775 Ł.14s.4d. for the use of Robert Buchanan...
        Archives of Maryland Vo. 43, p. 35.

December 18, 1779
        Council ordered that the Commissary of Stores deliver to Serjt. William
Bowles of the 2d. Regt. 1 Coat and also to Serjt. Thomas Guibert of the same Regimt.
1 Coat and 2 pr. Shoes to be charged to the same Regiment.
        Archives of Maryland Vol. 43, p. 38.

December 26, 1779
        Philip Key & Uriah Forrest to Gov. Thomas Sim Lee
        Sir. The Schooner, Union, Our Property, will carry about 450 barrels of flour.
She is now ready to take in her Load and will sail with the first Vessels that goes from
Baltimore, is a new Vessel & Promises to be a Prime Sailer. We expect half the
Proceeds in the West Indies and will take in freight free your Goods Provided they are
not of so Bulky a kind as to more than half fill the schooner & thereby Prevent our
Importing an equal quantity. If your Excellency shou'd Accept this offer Please signify
it as soon as Convenient as the Tobacco with which we mean to Load in case you
should not take her is an expence to us until on Board.
        Archives of Maryland Vol. 43, p. 389.

December 27, 1779
        Lt. Col. Uriah Forrest to the Command of the 7th Regiment on promotion of
Lt. Col. Peter Adams.
        Calendar of Maryland State Papers No. 4, Part 3, p. 87 (Item 539).

December 29, 1779
        Proclamations to County Commissioners and Sheriffs
        General Washington's forces in dire need of food and supplies - urgent
necessity of your most vigorous Exertions.
        Archives of Maryland, Vol. 43, p. 43, 44.

December - 1779
        Thomas Green Alvey, Corpl. and Traverse Alvey, Pvt. enlisted in Capt. Lieut.
Armstrong's Company, 3rd. Reg. Md. Line for the duration of the war.
        Archives of Maryland Vol. 18, p. 298.

January 3, 1780
        Council to Recruiting Officers in St. Mary's and other Counties....must...
pursue the Directions contained in the "Act for recruiting the Quota of Troops of this
State in the American Army", herewith sent....purchase Provisions sufficient for
subsistence of the Recruits....can draw $3000.00....use every Precaution to avoid
enlisting British or foreign Deserters....
        Archives of Maryland Vol. 43, p. 47, 48.

January 11, 1780
        Council ordered that the Collector of the Tax for St. Mary's County pay to
Lieut. Nicholas Mauger, James Thomas & John Armstrong Recruiting Officers for said
County $3000.00 each to be expended in the recruiting Service & Accounted for.
        Archives of Maryland Vol. 43, p. 54.

January 16, 1780
        Henry Phillips, Pvt. re-enlisted in the 2nd. Reg. Md. Line and was discharged
5/1/1781.
        Archives of Maryland Vol. 18, p. 151, 329, 360, 421, 472, 550.

January 19, 1780
George Armstrong, Capt.-Lieut. 3rd. Reg. Md. Line.
Archives of Maryland Vol. 18, p. 298, 299.

Council ordered for more effectual preventing forestalling & engrossing that the Counties of Maryland be laid out in eight districts - Charles and St. Mary's County to comprise the 5th District.
Archives of Maryland Vol. 43, p. 63.

January 25, 1780
Council ordered Treasurer pay to Uriah Forrest 3675 Ł. due him as Aud. Gen'l. to the 31 Decr. inclusive.
Archives of Maryland Vol. 43, p. 68.

January 26, 1780
Theophilus Tabbs, brother of Surgeon Tabbs of the 7th. Md. Reg. appointed Ensign in the 1st. Md. Brigade.
Archives of Maryland, Vol. 43, p. 69, 71.

January 29, 1780
Corn being supplied from "Islands in Potowmack".
Archives of Maryland Vol. 43, p. 73.

February 1, 1780
Cuthbert Abell, Sergt. in the 7th Reg. Md. Line served to 11/1/1780. He was a Sergt. in the 1st. Reg. Md. Line, Capt. Beatty's Co. in August 1781.
Archives of Maryland Vol. 18, p. 184, 389.

February 4, 1780
Ignatius Taylor to Gov. Thomas Sim Lee
Has taken into his possession 11 barrels of flour and 715 bushels of Indian Corn, 60 bushels of which is on board a vessel; wants instructions about storing.
Archives of Maryland Vol. 43, p. 415.

February 5, 1780
Council ordered Capt. Geo. Keeports deliver to Colo. Uriah Forrest Baise sufficient for 30 Blankets.
Archives of Maryland Vol. 43, p. 79.

February 6, 1780
Gabriel Williams was a Sergt. in the 7th. Reg. Md. Line and was assigned to the recruiting service from January - July 1780. Sergt. in the 1st. Co. 3rd. Reg. 8/28/1781 and discharged from the 2nd. Co. 2nd. Battn. 2/16/1783.
Archives of Maryland Vol. 18, p. 258, 389, 396, 442, 508, 560.

February - 1780
Council ordered the Commissary of Stores deliver to John Ford a Recruit, one suit of Cloaths, the Bounty allowed by...the Assembly.
Archives of Maryland Vol. 43, p. 96.

Febuuary 12, 1780
Council ordered Collector of Taxes for St. Mary's Co. pay to Lieut. Nicholas Mauger of the 3rd. Reg. $3000.00 to be expended in the Recruiting Service...Clothe sufficient for 10 suits of Cloaths and Overalls, 10 Shirts, 10 Pair of Stockings and 10 Pairs of Shoes...
Archives of Maryland Vol. 43, p. 85.

February 13, 1780
Baron deKalb, Commanding Maryland Division to the Governor and Council
of Maryland
...The other officer for whom I am to intreat your favours is Lieut. Col. (Uriah)
Forrest: This Gentleman is no longer able to continue his Services in his regiment
(had lost a leg in action) and his holding a Commission in it precludes the appointment
of another field officer, and throws all the hardships of the duty upon the Major....
the holding of Commissions by persons unable to discharge the functions...is prejudicial to the service...
Archives of Maryland Vol. 43, p. 427.

March 2, 1780
Council ordered Treasurer pay to Colo. Uriah Forrest, Aud. General 1041 £.13s.4d.
for one Month Salary ending the 29 February.
Archives of Maryland Vol. 43, p. 100.

March 11, 1780
Council to the Commrs. for Charles and St. Mary's Counties.
We request you to supply to the Recruiting Officers and others returned on
Furlough in your County, Provisions and Forage on their producing Gen'l. Smallwood's
Requisition for the same. Also forward all the Flour you have in Readiness and to
hasten the manufacture of the Wheat....
Archives of Maryland Vol. 43, p. 107.

March 18, 1780
Council ordered Collector of the Tax for St. Mary's County pay to Lieut.
Nicholas Mauger of the 3rd. Reg. $3000.00 to be expended in the Recruiting Service...
Archives of Maryland Vol. 43, p. 115.

March 26, 1780
Joseph Ford of St. Mary's Co. to Gov. Thomas Sim Lee
Purchased 40 barrels of corn from Charles Hayden but Wm. Kilgore one of the
Commissioners....seized 30 barrels of it from Hayden and paid a higher price; many
people complain of having two commissions on the necessaries for the Army; asks
for directions by the return of Athan Ford; in a postcript asks what to do with the
Lydia's long boat.
Calendar of Maryland State Papers No. 4, Part 3, p. 92 (Item 513).

April 1, 1780
Council ordered Treasurer pay to Colo. Uriah Forrest, Aud. Gen'l. 1041 L.13s.4d.
due him for 1 mo. Salary to this Inst.
Archives of Maryland Vol. 43, p. 126.

Edward Smith, Pvt. who enlisted in the 4th. Reg. Md. Line on 4/1/1777 was
discharged.
Archives of Maryland Vol. 18, p. 165.

April 2, 1780
John Blair, Pvt. enlisted in the 7th. Reg. Md. Line was discharged 11/1/1780.
Archives of Maryland Vol. 18, p. 190.

April 15, 1780
I. Taylor, St. Mary's County to Gov. Lee
As a Commissioner bought 844 1/2 bushels of Indian Corn; It lay a long time
on board a Vessel in the ice in January and 34 bushels rotted; stored remainder with
Col. Vernon Hebb and in the transfer came up 21 1/2 bushels short; the remainder 789
bushels has been shipped to the Head of Elk.
Archives of Maryland Vol. 43, p. 472.

April 18, 21, 1780

Council ordered that the Commissary of Stores deliver to Cuthbert Abell, Gabriel Williams, Cuthbert Stone and Arthur McLane, Recruits for the 7th Reg. a Suit of Cloaths... Also the Collector of the Tax for St. Mary's County pay to Serjt. Enoch McLane of the 7th Reg. $3000.00 to be expended in the Recruiting Service. Also Treasurer pay to Colo. Uriah Forrest $1100.00....for recruiting....Collector of Tax for St. Mary's County pay to Serjt. Enoch McLane of the 7th Reg. $3000...for recruiting ...and Commissary deliver Serjt. McLane & Aaron Spalding of 2nd. Reg. one Shirt each.

Archives of Maryland Vol. 43, p. 144, 147.

May 2, 1780

Council ordered Treasurer pay to Colo. Uriah Forrest 1041 Ł.13s.4d. due him for 1 month salary.

Council to Colo. U. Forrest

Capt. Middleton who commands the State Boat, Dolphin is now under Orders to proceed down the Bay to observe the Motions of the Enemy; he is in want of Hands and we must request of you to furnish 8 Men and such Officer as you may think proper to appoint, equipped and supplied with necessary Arms & Provisions....

Archives of Maryland Vol. 43, p. 160, 161.

May 9, 10th, 1780

Council ordered that John Shaw, Armourer Deliver to Colo. Forrest's Order Water Casks for a Transport taking Troops (1/2 of the Md. Division) to Virginia to be charged to the Continent, also 20 lb. of Musket Powder...

Also deliver to Colo. Uriah Forrest 40 lb. Cannon Powder & 3 lb. of the best glaized Powder for the Transports...

Archives of Maryland Vol. 43, p. 167, 168, 170.

May 15, 29, 1780

...Col. Forrest requests mattresses, blankets, etc. for 14 Md. Continental soldiers who are sick...visits ill Mother in St. Mary's Co...

Calendar of Maryland State Papers No. 4, Part 3, p. 97 (Items 607 & 612).

May 24, 1780

Leonard Turner, Pvt. enlisted in 3rd. Reg. Md. Line 5/24/1780 and was discharged 11/1/1780.

Archives of Maryland Vol. 18, p. 171.

May 24, 1780

Council ordered the Commissary of Stores deliver to....Capt. John Davidson of the 2nd. Regimt...33 Shirts, 33 pair Shoes, 31 Knapsacks and 14 Blankets to be by him delivered over to Capt. Joseph Marbury of the 3rd. Regimt. for the following Recruits for the said Regimet....Henry Johnson, Thomas Drury (Drugh), John Goddard, Chas. Mattingly, John Ferrel, Charles Williams... Nathaniel Knott, James Bailey, Leonard Turner, Charles Goldsborough (Goldsberry), John Drury, Nicholas Cecil (Sissel), James Armstrong....each 1 Shirt and 1 pair of Shoes, the Bounties allowed them by the Act of Assembly, the Blankets and Knapsacks to be charged to the Continent....

Archives of Maryland Vol. 43, 180, 181.

June 20, 1780

Capt. George Cook loaned the State $1000.00.
Archives of Maryland Vol. 43, p. 520.

Joseph Ford, St. Mary's County to Gov. Thomas Sim Lee

As requested by the Governor and Council has applied to many of the inhabitants thought likely to have money to lend; could obtain none.
Calendar of Maryland State Papers No. 4, Part 3, p. 98 (Item 618).

June 22, 1780
>Commissions issued to:
>Capt. Zacha. Forrest in room of John Smith
>1st. Lt. Zepha. Forrest
>2nd. Lt. John Smith
>Ensign Francis Brooke
>
>Capt. Barton Abell in room of Ignats. Abell
>
>Capt. Bennett Combs in room of John Greenwell
>1st. Lt. Jas. Williams
>2nd. Lt. Robt. Ford
>Ensign Jno. Heard
>>of the Lower Batt. of Militia in St. Mary's County.
>Archives of Maryland Vol. 43, p. 201.

June 23, 1780
>Council ordered Treasurer pay to Uriah Forrest 1562 Ł.10s. for 172 (?) Months
Salary as Aud. Gen'l. to the 15th Inst.
>Archives of Maryland Vol. 43, p. 202.

July 1, 1780
>Jno. Taylor of Williamsburg (Va.) to Gov. Thos. Sim Lee
>About 25 sail of the enemy are in the (Chesapeake) Bay; forced their boats to
return into the James River, the enemy at Hampton Roads; they have taken about 20
prizes lately in the bay.
>Archives of Maryland Vol. 45, p. 2,3.

July 5, 1780
>Council ordered the Commissary of Stores deliver to Ignatius Adams of the
1st. Reg. 1 shirt, 1 pr. Overalls & 1 pr. shoes.
>Archives of Maryland Vol. 43, p. 212.

July 8, 12, 18, 1780
>Joseph Ford appointed Commissary for Purchases in St. Mary's County
>Pay Colo. Uriah Forrest 750 Ł. on account
>Pay Col. Uriah Forrest 1040 Ł.13s.4d. for one month as Aud. Gen'l.
>Archives of Maryland Vol. 43, p. 215, 219, 222.

July 11, 1780
>Wm. Fitzhugh, Rousby Hall, Patuxent to Gov. Thos. Sim Lee
>Recommends Doctr. John Reeder Egan as a surgeon for the Militia; a fleet of
more than 20 ships, Brigs &c went down the Bay & meeting some of the Enemy near
Smith's Point on the Potomack were forced back and have gone up the Patuxent.
>Archives of Maryland Vol. 45, p. 10.

July 16, 1780
>Thomas Guibert was mustered as a Sergt. between April & June and was
discharged from the 2nd. Reg. Md. Line on 7/16/1780.

July 23, 1780
>Richard Barnes, Leonardtown to Gov. Lee
>Our recruiting business in this County goes on much worse than I expected;
have little expectation of being able to make up our complement; greatest part of
those enlisted are free Negroes & Mulattoes, all of which amounts to 15;
>Archives of Maryland Vol. 45, p. 24.

July 26, 1780
>Affadavits of Benjamin Prior and Notley Tippett that they, in the company of

Joseph Smith, enlisted in Count Pulaski's Legion, sometime in the month of July 1779, being then in Charles Town, S. C. Said Smith is now before Richard Barnes, Lt. of St. Mary's County taken up as a deserter.

Sworn before me, Jeremiah Jordan
St. Mary's County, July 26th, 1780

Archives of Maryland Vol. 38, p. 593.

July 28 , 1780

Council of Maryland to the Maryland Delegates in Congress
...Our Coast...much infested with the Privateers and Crusers of the Enemy, our Trade & Navigation obstructed & many of our Vessels captured.... 20 of our vessels now blocked up in the Patuxent...want Frigates at the Capes...

Archives of Maryland Vol. 43, p. 238.

Richard Barnes, Leonardtown to Gov. Lee

On the 26th of this month we had a meeting of the Field Officers of the County together with the Commissioners of the Tax in order to assess Paupers and issue Warrants for the Collection of the 15 p.Ct. due from those that did not by that time find their proportion of men at which time we had only inlisted 31. From the shortness of the time allowed the People to procure their proportion of men and knowing that hardly any money would induce the number the County was to have supplyed to Inlist during the war and having just received a letter from F. Stone informing me that the Field Officers of Charles County, had agreed to inlist their men for three years, which as they could not be got for the war he advised should be done. This added to the certainty that it would not be in the power of the People to procure the money in time to raise the men, and knowing that it would distress many to be obliged to sell their effects to raise the money, Induced me together with the unanimous advice of the Field Officers and Commissioners of the Tax for the County, to give a further time to Tuesday next, for the Classes to find their men, and at the same time to take them for three years. Which proceeding I trust will meet with the approbation of my Country, as it was done for the best. If men can be raised by bounty, money will be wanted, you will therefore consider the propriety of supplying me with some for that purpose. I do very sincerely wish that I was clear of this purplexed (sic) disagreeable business, which has been rendered exceedingly troublesome and has been attended with considerable disadvantage to our raising the men by that absurd scheme of making two Classes of property, which in my opinion did, as it now doth surpass all the schemes for absurdity that I ever met with.

Archives of Maryland Vol. 45, p. 32, 33.

August 1, 1780

Ignatius Adams, Pvt. enlisted in the 8th Co. Md. Line and served to 1/1/1781.
Archives of Maryland Vol. 18, p. 358.

Travers Alvey, Pvt. enlisted in Capt. James W. Gray's Company, Md. Line and served to 1/1/1781.
Archives of Maryland Vol. 18, p. 354.
John Alvey, Pvt. enlisted in the 7th. Co. 1st. Md. Reg. and served to 1/1/1781. He, with Thomas Green Alvey and Travers Alvey served in the Md. Line until 11/15/1783, after re-enlisting.
Josias Alvey served until 5/24/1782.
Archives of Maryland Vol. p. 357, 522, 523.

August 15, 1780

Uriah Forrest to Gov. Lee

The bearer John McCoy who served faithfully in the 3rd. Md. Reg. & has had the misfortune to lose his Leg, is upon furlough and endeavouring to get to his friends in St. Mary's, he has no money & represents he has recd. no pay for between two and three years....I would beg leave to recommend him as a Man who merits Indulgence & favor.
Archives of Maryland Vol. 45, p. 48.

August 16, 1780
    John Drury, Pvt. in the 3rd. Reg. Md. Line was reported missing in action.
He probably enlisted in the Spring of 1778.
    Archives of Maryland Vol. 18, p. 104.

August 20, 1780
    Jeremiah Jordan, St. Mary's County to Gov. Lee
    Agreeable to the Supplementary Act to the Act entitled an "Act for the
immediate Supply of Flour & other Provisions for the Army" I have sent to the head of
Elk 900 bushels of Corn & should have sent the remainder procured by me, but the
mouth of our River being so infested by the Enemy, I thought it too hazardous to
risque it, Since which being Stored in a very Close room there is about 200 Bushels
damaged, which if you think advisable I could get exchanged for new corn at the fall.
    Archives of Maryland Vol. 45, p. 55, 56.

August 25, 1780
    Uriah Forrest to Gov. Lee
    The bearer Mr. Jacob Gray who is a Sergt. in the 2nd. Md. Reg. has been
some time from the Army, owing to the loss of his arm; he has made repeated
applications to me for to request that your Excelly. would be pleased to order him a
shirt, overalls, shoes and some other articles but from my knowing the scarcity of
these things, I have hitherto denied him. The furnishing him with these few articles
cannot make any great detention in forwarding these Troops and will be rendering
his situation much more Comfortable.
    Archives of Maryland Vol. 45, p. 61.

August 26, 1780
    Council ordered Treasurer to pay to Key and Forrest 4,510 Ƚ. due them p. acct.
    Archives of Maryland Vol. 43, p. 265.

August 30, 1780
    Council of Maryland
    In Virtue of the "Act for the Regulation of the Staple of Tobacco" the following
Persons are hereby appointed Inspectors, viz
                        St. Mary's County
Chaptico, Thomas Nicholls   St. Inegoes , Capt. John Horn Abell
Wicomico, Gerard Bond   Leonard Town, Igns. Abell
St. Cuthbert's Creek, Capt. John Smith,   St. Mary's River, John Taylor
                Town Creek, Enoch Breedon
    Archives of Maryland Vol. 43, p. 270.

September 4, 1780
    Address from Sundry Inhabitants of St. Mary's County to His Excellency Thomas
Sim Lee, Governor of the State of Maryland and His Honourable Council
    May it please your Excellency & Honours, We the subscribers in behalf of
ourselves and other Inhabitants of this County take the Liberty of addressing your
Excellency and Honours on a subject (as we conceive) highly important and Interesting
to every true friend to this State.
    The Dangers we are exposed to daily from our Enemies who have lately robb'd
several of the Inhabitants between the Mouths of Potowmack and Patuxent Rivers of
their property, calls for immediate assistance, not only to protect us in our property
so openly exposed, but likewise that of all those who shall or may attempt to transport
their Effects to or from any part of Chesapeake Bay. We therefore hope and make no
doubt but your Excellency & Honours will take this matter under your consideration
and endeavor to redress our Grievances by ordering some Vessels properly equipped
to cruze as soon as possible in said Bay for the purpose above mentioned.
    We also beg leave to recommend to your Excellency and Honours one Thomas
Price, a resident in the County (who we are fully convinced from his Knowledge of
the Bay, of a Vessell, his Conduct, Activity and Spirit) would exert himself in

Annoying, taking or destroying the Enemy, who, we are informed intend seizing all our property they can; and if not timely prevented, will, in all probability, render us incapable of supporting our Families, For an Account of the Depredation which have been committed by the Enemy we refer you to Mr. Henry Sewall who will deliver you this.

We are with all due respect Your Excellency & Honours most Obedient & very Humble Servts.

Nicholas Sewall	W. Bellwood	Robert Watts
N. Lewis Sewall	Robt. Jarboe	Thomas Dillen
Geo. Biscoe	William Holton	

N.B. Application having been made to the Lieutenant of this County for a Temporary relief without Effect Occasioned this Address.

Archives of Maryland Vol. 45, p. 77, 78.

September 8, 9, 1780

Council of Maryland ordered John Fenwick Collr. of Tax for St. Mary's County pay to Jos. Ford Contractor for Horses in said County 5,000 Ł. to be accounted for.

Also Cuthbert Abell, Collr. of the Tax for St. Mary's County pay to the said Joseph Ford 5,000 Ł. to be accounted for.

That the Treasurer pay to Joseph Ford 150 Ł. on Account.

Archives of Maryland Vol. 43, p. 281, 282.

September 11, 1780

Council to Jeremiah Jordan Esq.

Sorry corn on hand damaged when so badly needed by the Army - gives instructions.

Archives of Maryland Vol. 43, p. 286.

September 16, 18, 19, 1780

Council ordered Treasurer pay to Athanasius Ford 3500 Ł. to be delivered over to Joseph Ford Contractor for horses in St. Mary's Co.

Also pay to Honble George Plater, Esq. 37 Ł.10s. of the new Emission of this State on Acct.

That John Bullen, Esq. deliver to Colo. Forrest's Order five good Horses.

Archives of Maryland Vol. 43, p. 293, 294, 295.

September 20, 1780

Council to Joseph Ford, Esqr.

Sir. We received yours of the 14th Inst. and send by your Brother Ł 500 in new Bills. We do not know on what you founded your Opinion that the Commissioners will not allow the Collector to receive Money for Taxes, or that they have any Power to direct what Money shall or shall not be received. The Law for sinking our Proportion of the Continental Bills of Credit, makes the new Bills a Tender for Taxes at 40 for 1. and the State Money, we apprehend, is to be received under the same Regulation. This will be, in our Opinion, agreeable to the Intention of the General Assembly & the Treasurer if there is any Doubt with him, will have our Directions to receive it at that Rate. No Certificates should be given obligatory on the State to discharge them in Continental Bills of Credit. We enclose three Certificates amounting to 3500 Ł., having given an Order in your Favor for that Sum to Mr. Athanasius Ford.

Archives of Maryland Vol. 43, p. 297, 298.

Richard Barnes, Leonardtown to Gov. Lee

We have in this County for a considerable time past been alarmed by Vessels of the Enemy composed of some Boats and small Sloops. Maj. Igns. Taylor's House on Wicomico they the other day plundered of all they could take away with them, the ballance they wantonly destroyed. They have likewise plundered Mr. Robt. Armstrong's House at Point Lookout & have taken many negroes together with stock from different parts of the County. In short they are a pack of the most abandoned Fellows that ever hath molested us. They are now in Potomack and its more than probable will do considerable dammage before they leave us. Their force from the best information I can collect is but trifeling and in my opinion reflects disgrace on this State to let them pass unmolested. I have been informed they have done considerable damage to many Gentlemen on the Virginia side of Potomack. We are in this County the most exposed to them of any Coty. in the State without its being in our power to protect ourselves for the want of arms, not more than 50 of these Guns, the property of the State, sent here will make a tolerable shift. I have so frequently given my opinion of them that I should not now mention them, if the People of the County did not urge me to it by their complaints. If those that were here unfit for service were properly sold to the People of the County they, I am Satisfied would do their endeavours to get them repaired, which would be making them contribute to the defence of the State. Most of the People that had guns on the commencement of the war has sold them to trading Vessels, the impropriety of which they are now fully convinced of.

Archives of Maryland Vol. 45, p. 113.

September 21, 1780

Robert Armstrong, St. Mary's County to Gov. Lee

Sir. Your Publick letter of August last came safe to hand. Agreeable to your directions therein. I have done all in my Power to procure for the Publick either Money or Tobacco from the Inhabitants of this Neighbourhood, but find my Solicitation to be of no Effect; the people Generally complain that they will be compelled to sell part of their Property to pay their Taxes and of Course have nothing to Lend. The damage done me the 23rd of August and the 16th Instant by the Enemy has wholy disabled me from rendering my Country any Service in that way. I have received of Capt. John Mackall one crop note and agreeable to the acct. for procuring a Loan have forwarded it to the Treasurer of the Western Shore.

Archives of Maryland Vol. 45, p. 115.

September 23, 1780

Wm. Webb Haddaway, Talbot Co. to Gov. Lee

Has returned from convoying a Schooner to Sharps Isle; returned to St. Jeromes where he took on fresh supply of new Hands; Enemy plundered several houses on Potomac a few days ago.

Archives of Maryland Vol. 45, p. 118.

September 24, 1780

Edmund Plowden to Gov. Thomas Sim Lee

Sir. The sum of Tobacco I have received on loan for use of the State since your last amounts to 22,781 pounds, a list of which I have inclosed to the Treasurer by this conveyance. I was called upon some time past by the purchasing Commissary of this County with an order from you for all the money and Tobo. in my hands, however I had not any at that time and if I am not otherways directed I shall continue to send all I receive to the Treasury, where I apprehend it is most wanting. The extract you sent me of the subscription made by the gentlemen of the Assembly from this County I believe is paid into the hands of some of the other Commissioners. It does not appear to me there will be any considerable quantity of Tobo. obtained. I shall use my best endeavours to get all I can.

Archives of Maryland Vol. 45, p. 119, 120.

September 28, 1780

Council to Commissaries of Purchase St. Mary's & other Counties

...We are informed that the Distress of the Army for want of Meat is so pressing that it is absolutely necessary to procure and send forward to the Head of Elk immediately 500 head of neat Cattle...have sent new Bills...consider one new Dollar equal to 40 Continental....earnestly entreat you to exert yourself on this trying Emergency....

Archives of Maryland Vol. 43, p. 307.

September 29, 1780
      Council to Colo. Richd. Barnes
      We received yours of the 20th Inst. and request you to have all public Arms in St. Mary's which are unfit for Service, sold to the best Advantage to the People in your County. We shall have Occasion to send the State Boats down and shall, by that Opportunity, send you some Arms from the State Armory.
      Archives of Maryland Vol. 43, p. 308.

September 30, 1780
      Council ordered Treasurer pay to Colo. U. Forrest Aud. Gen'l. 2604 Ł.3s.4d. due him for 2 1/2 Months Salary to 1st Inst.
      Also pay the said U. Forrest 500 Ł. of the new Emission to be delivered over to Capt. Joseph Ford, Commissary for St. Mary's County on Account.
      Archives of Maryland Vol. 43, p. 309.

October 5, 1780
      Council ordered Treasurer pay to Thomas Guibert late a Soldier in the 2d. Maryland Regimt. six and a quarter Dollars of the new Emission in lieu of $250.00 due him as Bounty p. acct. passed by the Depy. Aud.
      Archives of Maryland Vol. 43, p. 314.

October 6, 1780
      Charles Jordan appointed Inspector of Wicommoco Warehouse in the room of Gerard Bond, resigned.
      Archives of Maryland Vol. 43, p. 315.

      Joseph Ford, Leonard Town to Gov. Thomas S. Lee
      Your Excellencies letters of the 20th & 28th Septemr. by Mr. Ford and Collo. Forrest I received Each accompanies with 500 Pounds of the New Bills and have to say in Answer that the number of Steers from St. Mary's will I fear fall short of what I expected Owing to Mr. Jenifers Giving a greater Price in Charles County. I have Purchased from fourty to fifty good Steers from four to seven Grasses five and a half Dollars of the New Bills (except some few which I gave certificates and old circulating currency for and them I think I shall get settled with this new Money) with a promise of a Higher Price if any Commissary gives it in the Lower Counties by authority, the People in this County I am well assured would have been contented with the 5 1/2 Dollars If a greater price had not been given.
      I shall send off next fryday or Saturday from fourty to fifty and thirty more will, I think, be as many as I shall be able to have Ready to forward Shortly after, and this I shall be deceived in probably if the other purchasers continue to give a greater Price. There is to be had here Three or four Hundred good whethers and from an Experience the meat comes much Lower than Beef and keeps in Pickle Better, I speak from a Trial I had last fall.
      I must begg leave to mention to yr. Excellency that there is but one Cooper in this County and he has no particular place of Residence, who I have kept for Better than four weeks expecting to know whether the Staves I have on hand is to be made up, he has promised to wait Ten days before he sets off for Baltimore, his price is much Reasonabler than I Believe a professed cooper is to be got for in the State, one Hundred and fifty Pounds p. month and will make Two Barrels a day. I have not purchased any Cattle to Slaughter here. If any is (to be had?) the best time is (passing?) in my opinion, before they can be bought, collected & Slaughtered it will be late in the fall. I have not been well since I left Annapolis or It think I should have had my first Drove of Steers at the Head of Elk Before this. Your Excellency may depend my Utmost endeavors will be used to make up a good Proportion of the Supplies wanted, the Bacon and Wheat that I've purchased is still with me, there has been no possiblity of geting it away with any Safety. Could not one (of) the State Boats come for it and about four Hundred Bushels corn that Coll. Jordan has in his Care, they would be able to keep the Barges off.
      Archives of Maryland Vol. 45, p. 136.

October 13, 1780

   Council of Maryland ordered the Collector of the Tax for St. Mary's County pay to Joseph Ford, Contr. for Horses in said County 3125 Pounds and also the further Sum of 4691 Ł.10s. on Account.
   Archives of Maryland Vol. 43, p. 326.

October 16, 1780

   Joseph Ford, Leonard Town to Gov. Lee
   I have sent Under care of **Mr. Robert Greenwell** Fourty Four Steers Agreeable to the Return Coll. Barnes will Deliver your Excellency. I have not money sufficient to carry them to the Head of Elk, have therefore directed Mr. Greenwell to call on your Excellency for a Supply. I've furnished him with $700 which was all the Continental currency I had. I have not Received the money for the Orders I had on the Collectors by 300 Pounds or I could have forwarded them without Troubling your Excellency. I have given an order on the commissaries Between this and the Head of Elk to furnish them with Provisions and forage but as your Excellencies would be much better I should be Glad of it.
   Archives of Maryland Vol. 45, p. 148.

October 18, 1780

   Council ordered Treasurer pay to Richard Fenwick a Recruit for the 4th Regimt. four Pounds four shillings and four pence half penny of the new Emission in lieu of $450.00 the State and Continental Bounties.
   Archives of Maryland Vol. 43, p. 332.

October 20, 1780

   A Return of Wheat Mutton and Bacon purchased by Joseph Ford for the use of the Continental Army, St. Mary's Co.
   From July 25 to Oct. 5, bought provisions from George Abell, Robert Abell, James Alvey, Bennett Aprice (Bennett A. Price?), Barnet W. Barber, Cornelius Barber, Thomas Bond, William Bowles, Nicholas Brown, Stephen Cawood, Robert Clarke, Joseph Daviss, Owen Daviss, Joseph Dunbar, James Fenwick, John Fenwick, Philip Fenwick, William Fenwick, Athanias Ford, Robert Ford, William Fowler, Joseph Gates, Basil Hayden, Bassell Hayden, Clement Hayden, George Howard, John Horrell, John Johnson, Philip Key, Charles Llewellen, Francis Mattingly, Henry Medley, Joseph Medley, James Mills, Clem Morriss, Francis Plowden, Phillip Read, William Reswick, Clement Sewall, Joseph Shamwell, Wm. Shaw, Anthony Simms, Basil Smith, Richard Sothoron, Henry Spalding, Thomas Spalding, Joseph Stephens, Joseph Stone, William Thomas, Zachariah Thomas, John Thompson, Raphael Thomas, Jesse Wharton, James Wimsatt and Misael Wood. Ford swore before Henry Reeder that the return was a true one.
   Calendar of Maryland State Papers No. 4, Part 3, p. 113 (Items 714-716).

   A Return of Forage purchased by Joseph Ford for the Continental Army, St. Mary's County.
   Purchased 25 bushels of oats from John Greenwell on Aug. 4 and 7 1/2 barrels of corn from Stephen Tarlton on Aug. 10. Ford made oath before Henry Reeder that the return was true.
   Calendar of Maryland State Papers No. 4, Part 3, p. 114 (Item 717).

   Joseph Ford, Leonardtown to Gov. Lee
   Sir. I Herewith send your Excellency Returns of all Purchases made by Mr. Sims my appointment as Commissary. The Sickly situation of my family and self for some time past and the Unexpected Trouble with the Steers, Bucking them to the Rod (sic), Put it out of my Power to comply with your Excellencies Command by the 17th Inst. Out of the fourty Eight then Returned, four was strayed before I parted with them & I have heard of one more since, they were So ungovernable at first that I had some doubts whether I should get any of them away. I expect with the Strays to make

up about Thirty Steers in Ten days. There will be but little Pork to be had here this fall. Would it be adviseable to contract for a Quantity of Barrel Staves and Heads. I have shipt off about half the Bacon I purchased. Craft is so Difficult to be got that I cannot say when I shall be able to get to the Ballance. The People who I owe Tobacco too for Horns are now constantly Teasing me for it. I should be Glad to discharge their Debts. A good Crop of Indian Corn made with us.

A Return of Beef on the Hoof Purchased by Joseph Ford, Commissary of Purchases for St. Mary's County from the 5th till 14th Octr. 1780.

Date Oct.	No Vou.	Vouchers Name	No. Steers	Supposed Weight	Rate New Dollars	Rate Old Money	Old Money	New Money
5	1	John Smith	2	1000	5 1/2			20·12·6
6	2	Basil Smith	1	400				8·5·0
8	3	John Tarlton	1	320			250·0·0	
	4	Hanson Briscoe	2	800	6			18·0·0
9	5	James Mills	2	650	5 1/2			13·8·4 1/2
10	6	John Eden	2	800	ditto			16·10·0
13	7	Luke Mattingly	2	800		82·10·	660·0·0	
14	8	Col. Richd. Barnes	36	13850	5 1/2			285·13·1 1/2
			48	18620		82·10·	910·0·0·	362·48·9·

Errors Excepted October 20th 1780 Joseph Ford Comry of Purchases.

Then Came Joseph Ford Before me one of the Magistrates for St. Mary's County and made oath on the Holy Evangelist that the Above Return is Just and true as it stands Stated.   Sworn before Henry Reeder

Archives of Maryland Vol. 45, p. 155, 156.

October 21, 1780

Council ordered Treasurer pay to Robert Greenwell forty Dollars of the new Emission to be delivered over to Capt. Joseph Ford, Commissary of St. Mary's County on Account.

Archives of Maryland Vol. 43, p. 336.

October 23, 1780

Joseph Ford, Leonard Town to Gov. Lee

Sir. I Received a letter Signed by Mr. (Thomas) Johnson Your Excellencies Clerk wherein he mentions Two Orders on the Collectors of this County which I never Received. I suppose they were mislaid. I made a mistake in adding My Returns of Wheat, Bacon &c of Ł. 1000·0·0 which I hope may be Rectified.

Archives of Maryland Vol. 45,, p. 157.

October 27, 1780

Council ordered Treasure pay to John Brewer 4 Ł...3d. of the new Emission in lieu of 160Ł.10s. due him....

Archives of Maryland Vol. 43, p. 341.

October 28, 1780

Council ordered Commissary of Stores deliver to Capt. Charles Jordan of the 1st Regimt....Cloth and Trimmings for a Suit of Cloaths and Linen for 2 Shirts....

Archives of Maryland Vol. 43, p. 342.

October 29, 1780

Col. Uriah Forrest to Gov. Thomas Sim Lee

Not less than 300 men who served their full terms and were discharged from the Army have been unable to obtain the pay and clothing for which they have proper certificates; this has left them dissatisfied and has influenced their associates; asks that the General Assembly be told.

Calendar of Maryland State Papers No. 4, Part 3, p. 115 (Item 724)

Archives of Maryland Vol. 45, p. 165, 166.

October 31, 1780

        Council ordered that Clement Briscoe one of the Collectors of the Tax for St. Mary's County pay to Joseph Ford Commissary for said County 1975 ₺. on Acct.

        Also Richard Clarke one of the Collectors for said County pay to Joseph Ford 200 ₺. to be by him Accounted for.

        Archives of Maryland Vol. 43, p. 344, 345.

November 1, 2, 1780

        Council ordered Treasurer pay to John Davidson 240 ₺. due him p. Acct. passed by the Aud. Genl.

        Also pay William Bowles $20.00 of the new Emission to be delivered over to Joseph Ford on Account.

        Archives of Maryland Vol. 43, p. 345, 347..

November 3, 1780

        Council ordered Treasurer pay to John Brewer 10 ₺. of the new Emission in lieu of 400 ₺. due him....

        Archives of Maryland Vol. 43, p. 348.

November 6, 1780

        Council to Colo. Moses Rawlings

        ....We have requested Colo. Forrest to send up (to Fort Frederick) such of the Soldiers of the Extra Regiment rejected by the Board of War, as are able to march at this Time.

        Archives of Maryland Vol. 43, p. 351.

November 8, 1780

        Return of Tobacco stored in various warehouses, exclusive of transfers

        Shows weights of 477 hogsheads (1770-1780) 445, 524 pounds. The warehouses included those at Cedar Point, Coles at Patuxent, Leonardtown, Llewellen's at Wicomico, St. Inigoes, St. Mary's River and Taylor's Landing.

        Calendar of Maryland State Papers No. 4, Part 3, p. 116 (Item 732).

November 9, 1780

        Joseph Wilkinson, Mouth of the Potomac to Gov. Thomas Sim Lee

        Ordered the Militia on duty before receiving the Governor's letter of Nov. 8. The enemy came into Patuxent River on Nove. 5, three arm'd Schooners, one with 8 and 6 & one 4 Guns supposed to be 3 & 4 Pounders, Swivels & small arms & proceeded up river to Point Patience; burned John Parran's house & furniture, took several negroes & what stock they could collect & two Vessels loaded with 8 hhds of Tobacco; then proceeded down River opposite Col. (Peregrine?) Fitzhugh's, sent a flag, demanded Provisions & if received would do no damage; were refused & they immediately Cannonaded & burnt the Colonel's house.

        Archives of Maryland Vol. 45, p. 173.

November 18, 1780

        Council ordered Treasurer pay to Hon. George Plater 3000₺. on account. Also pay him 103 ₺. 0s.11d. of the new Emission on acct.

        Archives of Maryland Vol. 45, p. 216.

November 20, 1780

        Council ordered Treasurer pay to Wm. Bowles $20.00 of the new Emission to be delivered over to Joseph Ford on Account.

        Archives of Maryland Vol. 43, p. 347.

November 21, 1780

        Council ordered Treasurer pay to Vernon Hebb 5 ₺.12s.3d. of the new Emission in lieu of 224 ₺.10s. due him per Account passed by the Aud. Genl.

        Archives of Maryland Vol. 45, p. 219.

80

November 24, 1780
    Council ordered Treasurer pay to John Brewer 4 Ł. of the new Emission in lieu of 160 Ł. due him...
    Archives of Maryland Vol. 45, p. 223.

November 25, 1780
    The Justices of the Peace and Orphans Court for St. Mary's County....are reappointed and Continued under their former Commissions.
    Archives of Maryland Vol. 45, p. 224.

December 2, 1780
    Council ordered Treasurer pay to Colo. Uriah Forrest 3125 Ł. for three months salary to the first Instant.
    Archives of Maryland Vol. 45, p. 233.

December 10, 1780
    A Return of Beef on the Hoof Purchased by Joseph Ford, St. Mary's County.
    Ford, the Commissary of Purchases for St. Mary's County, from Oct. 14 to Nov. 6 purchased a total of 26 head of cattle from Robert Armstrong, John Baptist Barker, Col. Richard Barnes, Timothy Bowes, John Hanson Briscoe, Eliazer Daviss, Enoch Fenwick, Samuel Jennifer, Solomon Jones, Francis Plowden, Joseph Stone and Jesse Wharton.
    A Return of Wheat Purchased by Joseph Ford, St. Mary's County.
    From Oct. 20 to Dec. 10, purchased wheat from Edward Barber, William Hamarsley, William Proctor, Basil Smith and Zachariah Swan.
    Calendar of Maryland State Papers No. 3, p. 119 (Items 755, 756).

December 13, 1780
    Council ordered Treasurer pay to Joseph Ford $160.00 of the new Emission and 500 Ł. Continental on Account.
    Archives of Maryland Vol. 45, p. 242.

December 20, 1780
    John McKay to Gov. Lee
    His leg has gotten very bad; doesn't want to go back to the hospital; appeals for help in paying the Doctor.
    Archives of Maryland Vol. 45, p. 206.

December 27, 1780
    Council Circular to Commissaries of St. Mary's And Other Counties
    ...have the most pressing Demands for Provisions; use every exertion in purchasing Pork and Beef and have it salted; are not to exceed three pounds Gold p. hundred for Pork; buy Beef on best terms you can.
    Archives of Maryland Vol. 45, p. 255.

December 29, 1780
    ....Andrew McCurty and _____ Clark, Pilot of St. Mary's County and David Hunter, Pilot...of Calvert County have been seen with the Enemy ....we hereby authorize, require and Command the Lieutenants of the said Counties to arrest (them)..
    Archives of Maryland Vol. 45, p. 256.

----- 1780
    Signals by which vessels from the Potomac may be known. In the night, a light hoisted at the flag staff and in the day a Union flag at the foretop.
    Archives of Maryland Vol. 45, p. 211.

January 1, 1781
    John Davidson Commissioned Major of the 5th Reg. Md. Line.
    Archives of Maryland Vol. 18, p. 364, 380, 481.

George Armstrong Commissioned Capt. of the 1st. Reg. Md. Line on 2/11/1780.
Archives of Maryland Vol. 18, p. 362.

January 3, 1781
    Joseph Ford, Leonard Town to Gov. Lee
    Letter of 27th of last month received this morning; quantity of Pork to be
purchased in St. Mary's will be small, 5000 weight; may be disappointed in getting
this quantity; cost 150 to 200 ₤.; some Beef to be had but price asked is too high, 25
to 30 shillings a pound; 4000-5000 weight may be had at these prices; has purchased
460 bushels of Corn at $20.00; continental money or Tobacco of new Inspection is
wanted in payment; not less than 20,000 bushels of corn available in St. Mary's
County; will keep the cooper close at work; has 50 or 60 bushels of good allum
Salt, purchased for the public; enemies Barges so closely watch Patuxent and Potomac
Rivers, is too dangerous to send forward supplies; is entirely out of money; needs
₤. 10,000 Continental money & ₤. 250 of the new Bills with an order on the Sheriff
in case needed; George Leigh will deliver letter, is a good opportunity to send money.
    Archives of Maryland Vol. 47, p. 1, 2.

January 5, 1781
    Capt. (Ignatius) Fenwick loaned 16 Hheads Tob. to the State.
    Archives of Maryland Vol. 47, p. 3.

    Council of Maryland to Capt. Joseph Ford
    We send you by Mr. George Leigh ₤. 250 of the new Emission and shall
continue to supply you with a further Sum as you may have occasion. The public salt
in your Hands is to be applied in curing Pork and Beef you may purchase.... forward
the Cattle you procure on the Hoof...to Frederick Town for the use of the Convention
Troops and desire this may be done as fast as you can make up 15 or 20 Head....
desire to be informed at what Price you can dispose...of Tobacco laying in St. Mary's
and Charles Counties. It will not be proper to risk any the Supplies by Water until you
receive our further orders.
    Archives of Maryland Vol. 45, p. 264.

January 11, 1781
    Council Circular to the Lieutenants of the several Counties
    ...have information that a Party of the Enemy...about 2500 or 3000 strong,
headed by General (Benedict?) Arnold took possession of Richmond.....and sent a
strong Detachment to...Petersburgh....it is more than probable they will visit us...
immediately...put the State in proper Posture of Defence....order the Whole militia
of your County to put themselves in readiness to march at a minutes Warning...
    Archives of Maryland Vol. 45, p. 270.

January 12, 1781
    Council ordered John Fenwick, Collector of Taxes of St. Mary's County pay to
Joseph Ford, Purchaser of Horses for said County 2400 ₤. to be by him Accounted for.
    Archives of Maryland, Vol. 45, p. 271.

January 17, 1781
    Igns. Fenwick to Richard Barnes, Esq.
    You will receive herewith by Mr. Forrest one George Clarke of St. Georges
who is the person described by the Govr. also one Lee who lives with him & as I have
been informed has been on Bd. with Clarke. My brother Jo. I think would have been
able to satisfy the Govr. of there going on Bd but has been from home & could not be
now Summoned. Doctor Brihon they have been after at two or three different places
& could not be found. They shall be summoned to attend as soon as possible.
Andrew McCurty could not be found tho they were some time after him, he is an old
worthless fellow scarcely worth notice, but I believe Clark is a hardened daring
bold fellow of the worst character & I think a very dangerous one to go at large at this
time. I could wish he could be detained untill proper evidence could be sent up

as I think the matter may be proved upon him & Lee.
Archives of Maryland Vol. 47, p. 25, 26.

January 18, 1781
Council to Robert Armstrong, Esq.
The General Assembly have requested us to establish a Chain of Expresses from Point Lookout to this City (Annapolis) for the purpose of communicating Intelligence of the operations of and Movements of the Enemy to us with the greatest speed. Your convenient situation and Readiness to contribute your Assistance for the Defense of the State on all Occasions have induced us to apply to you to employ an Active, Diligent, and trusty Person to ride Day and Night from Point Lookout to Annapolis who is to be ready to set off at any Hour with such Dispatches as you may deliver....all expenses will be faithfully and punctually discharged.
Archives of Maryland Vol. 45, p. 278.

January 20, 1781
Council ordered Treasurer pay to Francis Fenwick 40 Ł.14s. of the new Emission in lieu of 1628 Ł..5d. due him per Account passed by the Aud. Genl.
Archives of Maryland Vol. 45, p. 282.

January 22, 1781
Council to Capt. Gilbert Middleton
You will apply to Col. Forrest for and take into your charge George Clarke of St. Mary's County mentioned in the enclosed...and deliver him to the Sheriff of Baltimore County...
Archives of Maryland Vol. 45, p. 284.

January 24, 1781
Council ordered that the Commissary of Stores deliver to Colo. Uriah Forrest Cloth and Trimmings for a suit of Cloaths for the year 1780 and Cloath for a Coat and Trimgs. for a Suit of Cloath's and Linen for two shirts in part of the Articles for the year 1781.
Archives of Maryland Vol. 45, p. 286.

January 24, 1781
Joseph Ford, St. Mary's County to Gov. Lee
Received 250 Pounds of the New Bills; fears shall not make up number of steers worth sending to Frederick having bought only 4 and little prospect of getting more; New Tobacco sells for 50 Pounds with an Allowance of 4 p. Ct. for cask; shall not make up quantity of Pork had expected, having lost 1200 weight for want of Continental money; has purchased upwards of 1500 bushels of Corn at $20.00 & can purchase a larger quantity; was told Mr. Jenifer can buy cheaper in Charles County; has laid out money received by Mr. Leigh in Beef, Pork and Corn; received upwards of 2000 weight of Pork and has engaged for 1500 weight more; if corn is continued to be purchased should send a sum sufficient to pay for 3,000 bushels; is indebted 6000 weight of Tobacco and has advanced 7800 on account of the Horses purchased.
Archives of Maryland Vol. 47, p. 36.

January 25, 1781
Sam Smith (of Baltimore), Cedar Point, Major Taylors, to Gov. Lee
The Cato & Nautilus are both on shore between Cedar Point & St. Jerome's Creek near the house of Mr. Bellwood where they were driven by the Iris on the 22nd Inst.; The Nautilus is high up & will be saved; near 200 Bbles. of her flour saved already; the Cato is further out; The enemy after boarding began to plunder; went into Magazine which blew up carrying off 10 of theirs & six of our people; has blown Cato stores as far forward as the pumps and entirely away; water ebbs & flows in her; trying to save the flour but without much success; necessary to dispatch the 5 State Boats & some other Craft to secure what is saved; will be little risk as our Guns are planted properly for defence & nothing dare come near the wrecks;

Capt. Bull for want of ammunition has lost his Brig; she is burnt, however he saved 200 Bbls; the avarice, avidity & Lazyness of the inhabitants does not admit of a comparison; for Heavens sake dispatch the vessels; more than one half of the flour may be saved, water does not penetrate more than an inch into the flour; the frigates went down yesterday & are now quite out of sight; pay bearer Ł. 150 plus his expenses; needs at least 4000-5000 Ł.

   Archives of Maryland Vol. 47, p. 37, 38.

January 26, 1781
   Robert Armstrong, St. Mary's County to Gov. Lee
   Agrees to establish Chain of Expresses from Point Lookout to Annapolis per his letter of the 18th; enemy is "before Our Doors"; their force are two ships, one a small Frigate, the other a Sloop of War, one Brig and a schooner; (reports on the Cato and Nautilus); the ships are now at anchor off St. Georges Island; yesterday, about three o'clock landed 40 men at Point Lookout and deprived Joseph Milburn, a tenant of all bedding, clothing and provisions and plundered me of a part of what I had on the plantation; fired several balls from the schooner through the houses, landed at Mrs. Egerton's and took some stock; were preparing to land a considerable force but were prevented by the Militia who are poorly provided with arms and worse for ammunition; County at their mercy; many negroes from this neighborhood have gone to the enemy.
   Archives of Maryland Vol. 47, p. 38, 39.

January 27, 1781
   Council ordered Treasurer pay to John Mills 100 Pounds and 29 hhds. of Tobacco at St. Mary's Warehouse in 1780 to be delivered over to Joseph Ford Commissary of St. Mary's County on Acct.

   Council to Joseph Ford
   You will have enclosed the Notes of 29 Hogsheads of Tobacco of the year eighty, weight 27.626 Net Proceeds which we hope will be adequate to your Demands. You may continue to purchase Corn at least as far as the Amount of the Tobacco will extend. We have furnished the Bearer with 100 Pounds Continental Currency to defray his Expenses with which you are charged.
   Archives of Maryland Vol. 45, p. 290.

January 28, 1781
   Sam Smith, Mr. Sewalls, to Gov. Lee
   The schooner's situation & great probability of her preservation induced me to advise Maj. Taylor to offer every 8th barrel of (flour) which the Militia can save; the Schooner's crew do not hold it to their duty to preserve anything but their rigging & furniture; yesterday she was unloaded and this day have begun to pump & bail & think will soon clear her; much of her cargo is embezzled; the inhabitants have offered such prices to the sailors as induced them to sell the State's property; I followed a different plan for the Brig; discharged her unruly crew in part & hired Negroes with about 20 people; in one day saved 600 Bbls & have now 700 Bbls. landed & hope to secure 100 more; if vessels don't come down tomorrow, shall haul it from the beach and store in the yard of Mr. Bellwood; if a general search warrant could be procured it would answer the purpose of saving much & would deter them from future attempt to steal the provisions.
   Archives of Maryland Vol. 47, p. 40.

January 29, 1781
   Council to Capt. Robert Berry
   You are to proceed immediately with the Arms and Ammunition for which you have an Order on Mr. Shaw to St. Mary's River if it can be done with any Degree of Safety, if not to a Place the most convenient to that River and deliver them with the Letter enclosed into the Hands of an Officer not under the Rank of Captain and at the same time request him to give immediate Information to the Lieutenant of St. Mary's

County or the Officer next in Command of such Deposit. If you should have any information of the Enemies coming up or you should discover them yourself, you must with all the Expedition possible return to this Place and give Information immediately to the Governor and Council.

Archives of Maryland Vol. 45, p. 293.

January 30, 1781

Robert Armstrong, St. Mary's County to Gov. Lee

Since writing on the 26th, a 10 Gun Schooner of the Enemy came up Smith Creek, landed about 50 men under cover of their cannon, took possession of the schooner Kitty, Capt. Smith from Annapolis, loaded with Tobacco; the schooner was aground and partly unrigged and they burned her; they put 3 prisoners on shore, by whom we learn that there is a fleet of 60 sail, including Transports and Privateers, down the Bay and they they intend a plundering voyage to Baltimore and Annapolis and intend to destroy all Salt works enroute.

Archives of Maryland Vol. 47, p. 41.

February 1, 2, 1781

Council ordered Treasurer pay to Colo. Uriah Forrest 9.958 ₤.6s.8d. and also 308 ₤.9s. of the new Emission.

Also pay to Colo. Forrest 10 Pounds of the new Emission to be delivered over to John McKay, a soldier in the 5th Regimt. to enable him to get his Leg cured.

Archives of Maryland Vol. 45, p. 296.

February 3, 1781

Council ordered Treasurer deliver to Colo. Uriah Forrest 150 hhds. of Tobacco on Account.

The Commissaries of....St. Mary's (County)....have orders to send forward immediately all the Provisions they may have for the use of the Convention Troops and Guard.

Archives of Maryland Vol. 45, p. 299, 300.

February 5, 1781

Benjn. Wickes, Cedar Point, to Gov. Lee

This will inform you that Mr. Shepard in a Sloop, in company with a Schooner ....arrived here on the 2nd, since which time I have put on board the sloop 435 barrels of flour and think it prudent to send her off without the schooner as there is a fair wind and an apparent good chance to get safe up, the schooner shall be loaded tomorrow if possible, there will be about 100 barrels left of the Cato's Cargo after the schooner is loaded.

Archives of Maryland Vol. 47, p. 53.

February 7, 1781

Council to Ignatius Taylor, Esqr.

We received your letter of the 22d. Ult. and are much obliged to you for your assistance and Activity in preserving the Cargoe of the Nautilius, Col. (Sam) Smith informes us that he hired Negroes to save the Cato's Cargoe and that the whole of that Cargoe except what was purloined by some of the Inhabitants is lodged in Mr. (Wm.) Bellwood's yard. This Board have determined to have the Flour transported to Baltimore Town to be baked or repacked and have appointed you to take care of the Interest of the State and have the whole of the Flour as well the Cato's as the Nautilius Cargoe put on Board the Craft we have sent down and will make you ample Compensation for your Trouble and Care in Superintending and managing this Business. We are willing to make the Militia the usual and customary Allowance for Salvage (which is one tenth Part of the Property saved) and will pay one tenth Part to you or your order to be distributed among those who assisted you. We request you would use your Endeavours to find out Persons who have embezzled our Flour and transmit a List of their Names to us as soon as possible that we have them prosecuted. If the Craft sent will not carry the whole of the Flour, be pleased to procure a Vessel

immediately. Since writing the above, Capt. Shepherd has arrived with 435 Barrels Part of the Cato's Cargoe and we are informed that the rest of that Cargoe except about 100 Barrels is put on Board the Schooner and now request you to ship the remaining 100 Barrels with the Nautilius' Cargoe on such Craft as can be obtained.
    Archives of Maryland Vol. 45, p. 303,304.

February 8, 1781
    Sam Smith, Baltimore to Gov. Lee
    "By Constant Attention: he has saved 800 barrels of flour on the Cato; one third of the Brig was blown away; needs Ł.3000 more to pay for salvage work; plunder has been extensive.
    Archives of Maryland Vol. 47, p. 60.

February 9, 1781
    Col. Uriah Forrest resigned as Auditor General.
    Archives of Maryland Vol. 45, p. 307.

February 10, 1781
    Thomas Drury, Pvt. of the 3rd. Reg. Md. Line discharged from service. Probably enlisted in the Spring of 1778.
    Archives of Maryland Vol. 18, p. 277.

February 12, 1781
    Col. Uriah Forrest, Phila., to Gov. Thomas Sim Lee
    Has been unable to sell the Maryland tobacco, so cannot procure the goods required (blankets, paper, cloth, trimmings, linen, etc.); injury may arise from Maryland's not being represented in the Congress (if so the Confederation could be signed) on questions of duty on imported goods and on appointment of civil officers; British fleet damaged by a storm.
        Note; Maryland very wisely refused to join the Confederation until
            Virginia gave up her extravagant claim to the western lands.
    Archives of Maryland Vol. 47, p. 66, 67.

February 16, 1781
    Council ordered Treasurer pay to Robert Miles 4 Ł.4s.4d. half penny of the new Emission in lieu of 168 Ł. 15s. due him p. Acct.
    Archives of Maryland Vol. 45, p. 312.

    Richard Barnes, Leod. Town to Gov. Lee
    We have for sometime past been ravaged in this Coty. by the Enemy. They, on Friday last landed and plundered several familys on Smith's Creek, together with a quarter of mine there, from which unless a proper force by Water can be procured to drive them away (as there are many of their Vessels, as I am informed constantly about our Shores) I am well satisfied they will do much damage in this County. If any of the Militia are called on to do duty we shall be at a loss for Bread. Would it not therefore be prudent to reserve a part of the flower (sic) that was saved from the vessels that were drove on shore for that purpose.
    Archives of Maryland Vol. 47, p. 72.

February 17, 1781
    Joseph Ford, Leonard Town to Gov. Lee
    Four Certificates that I gave for Draught Horses have been brought to me within this few days the People requesting I would take them in and Pay them the money Urging that they had offered them to the Treasurer and he would not pay them. They Amount to 6550 Pounds. I should be glad if convenient that that sum of money may be sent by the Bearer Mr. Athanasius Ford to discharge that Debt. We have a Mill now that Makes good flour, shall I have the wheat manufactured that I have of the Publick, what will be the terms I may agree with the Miller on?

Col. Uriah Forrest, Phila. to Gen'l. James Wilkinson

Send notes for tobacco belonging to Maryland; dispose of on most advantageous terms & at least Ł. 60p. Cent., after sending Gov. Lee Ł. 30,000 in Continental money, purchase soldier's clothing and paper for printing bills of Credit, laws and proceedings of the General Assembly.

Archives of Maryland Vol. 47, p. 73.

February 18, 1781

Richard Barnes, Leod. Town to Gov. Thos. Sim Lee

Enemy recently have taken many vessels loaded with Tobacco and kept the inhabitants on the Potomac in constant alarm; is sending a map of the County in order judgment can be made of propriety of furnishing us with cannon; thinks 5 pieces would contribute very much to the security of the County and prevent enemy Barges and small vessels from doing damage and make them cautious in attempting to take vessels-they now pass up & down our Rivers with impunity; enemy have constantly landed on St. Georges Island; much in want of Cartouch Boxes to the guns sent, about 60 would be useful; the Acct. of Arms &c sent by Capn. Berry don't agree with the acct. of them:

50 Stand of Arms, one half of which has Bayonets
A Cask of powder abt. 80 lb. wt.
2 large Cartridges of powder about 10 wt.
8 doz. ditto not filled
49 Cartridge Boxes with Hoops
100 6 lb. Ball
A six pound Cannon, the Carriage in bad order
2 Rammers & Spunges
1 Ladle of Worm
Archives of Maryland Vol. 47, p. 75, 76.

February 19, 1781

Lt. Col. Uriah Forrest resigned his Commission in the lst. Reg. Md. Line.
Archives of Maryland Vol. 18, p. 378.

February 20, 1781

Council ordered Treasurer pay to Athanasius Ford 150 Ł. of the new Emission in lieu of sixty pounds specie for a Horse sold (to) Colo. Lee's Corps...

Council to Mr. Joseph Ford

Your request of a Supply of Cash is not in our Power to comply with. We think it very proper that the Wheat should be manufactured, as we are unacquainted with the Terms of Grinding, leave you to make what Contract you may think just and customary.

Archives of Maryland Vol. 45, p. 318 , 319.

February 23, 1781

Council to Col. Barnes

We are of the opinion with you that a part of the Flour saved from the Vessels that were forced on shore by the Enemy should be reserved for the Militia if there is any Prospect of their being called on soon into Service of which you are certainly the best Judge and...leave it wholly up to you and have requested Maj. Taylor to deliver to your Order such Quantities as you may think necessary for that Purpose.

Archives of Maryland Vol. 45, p. 324.

Unsigned letter or report (bottom torn off) date Annapolis 6/25/1790.

Uriah Forrest (Lt. Col.) lost his leg in the action of German Town and resigned the 23rd. of Feb. 1781 as will appear by the votes and proceedings of Congress. The State of Maryland advanced him a sum of money equal to seven years half pay of a Lt. (Col.)....

Archives of Maryland Vol. 18, p. 628, See also p. 109, 362, 378, 520.

February 26, 1781
          Council ordered Treasurer pay to Francis Brooke 15 Ł.16s.6d.... due him per
Acct.
          Archives of Maryland Vol. 45, p. 325.

          Sam. Huntington, President, Phila., to Gov. Lee.
          Your Excellency will receive enclosed the Extract of a resolve of the 23rd
Instant requesting the State of Maryland to advance to Lt. Col. (Uriah) Forrest, an
Account of the United States a Sum equal to seven years half pay of a Lieut. Colonel,
in lieu of the half pay he might otherwise have been entitled to during his natural Life.
Upon resignation of this Officer, Congress have thought proper, in Consideration of
his past Services & particular Misfortune of the Loss of a Limb in the public Service,
to grant him the Benefit & Emoluments contained in the enclosed resolution.
          Archives of Maryland Vol. 47, p. 86.

March 1, 1781
          Council to Ignatius Taylor
          Being informed that you cannot get Vessels to transport Flour in your care to
this place or to Baltimore, we therefore desire you will deliver it to Mr. John Dorsey
or his Order who has engaged to procure Vessels and to transport it to Baltimore.
          Archives of Maryland Vol. 45, p. 332.

          Council ordered Treasurer pay to John Brewer 68 Ł.6s.10 1/2d. ... due him
per Account.
          Archives of Maryland Vol. 45, p. 332.

March 2, 1781
          Council ordered Treasurer pay to Robert Miles 11 Ł.5s. of the new Emission
in lieu of 450 Ł. due him per Account.
          Joseph Ford appointed auctioner of St. Mary's County under the "Act to Reg-
ulate Auctions".
          Archives of Maryland Vol. 45, p. 334.

March 5, 1781
          Ordered that the Commissary deliver to Colo. Uriah Forrest 32 pounds of sugar
due him to the month of Febry. inclusive.
          Archives of Maryland Vol. 45, p. 337.

March 10, 1781
          Council order Commissary of Stores deliver to Gabriel Williams of the 7th Reg-
iment and Serjt. (Richard) Fenwick of the 4th Regimt. each a suit of Cloaths...for the
year 1781.
          Archives of Maryland Vol. 45, p. 347.

March 14, 1781
          James McHenry Esq. to Gov. Thomas Sim Lee
          Capt. (A) McLane reports one frigate and a brig off St. Jerome's; two more
vessels have come to this morning within 5 or 6 miles of the Nesbit, which probably
gave rise to Marquis' intelligence.
          Note: McHenry was Aide de camp to Marquis de Lafayette. On March 3, 1781
                    the Council of Maryland had ordered all necessary vessels be impressed
                    to convey Major General Lafayette, his troops and guns to Virginia.
                    Among the vessels impressed were two of William Fenwick, of St. Mary's
                    County and later Kentucky, a sloop of 50 tons and a pilot boat, the
                    Fair Maid. He, with his vessels, was employed on the Chesapeake
                    until after the surrender of Cornwallis at Yorktown (see pension claim
                    5444, U.S. National Archives).
          Archives of Maryland Vol. 45, p. 337; Vol. 47, p. 127.

March 25, 1781

Richard Barnes, Leod. Town to Gov. Thomas Sim Lee

From the information I have rec'd. of the Select Militia we have about 70 engaged for that service which I now inform you of in order that we may be supplied with that quantity of Arms which are necessary for us to make any tolerable defence for the protection of the Calry. And unless something is done for the securety of the Inhabitants, bad consequences may arise, as I have been well informed that many of the Inhabitants of the Coty. on the water had much rather lay at the mercy of the Enemy than have the Militia called to protect them owing, as I suppose, to their knowledge of the defenceless situation they are in. If we could be supplyed with about 70 stand of Arms more than what we have, I should be glad of your opinion whether it would not be advisable, whilst the Enemy are in the Bay to keep about 60 more men constantly patroling from one part of the Coty. to the other in order to prevent disatisafction and the negroes going to the Enemy as from the late conduct of the Negroes when those Ships were in St. Mary's. I am well satisfied the greatest part of them that are in the Coty. would join them. I am well informed upwards of 25 offered themselves to those Ships the night they were in St. Mary's. Your answer to the above will oblige Your Most obt. servt.

Archives of Maryland Vol. 47, p. 148.

March 27, 1781

Joseph Wilkinson, Calvert County to Gov. Lee

In consequence of five of the enemys Vessels laying off the Clifts, I have ordered the Militia on Guard and directed them to secure all Craft on the Bay & River. The enemy has been several times in the mouth (of) Patuxent, they landed last Wednesday night in St. Mary's and plundered several Gentlemen of the whole of their furniture, wearing apparel, corn, meat &c....

Archives of Maryland Vol. 47, p. 151.

March 28, 1781

Council ordered Treasurer pay to Colo. Uriah Forrest 412 £.10s. of the new Emission due him per Acct.

Archives of Maryland Vol. 45, p. 364.

March 30, 1781

Council ordered Treasurer pay to....and Colo. Uriah Forrest Commissioner for the preservation of Confiscated British property 40 £. of the new Emission on Account.

Archives of Maryland Vol. 45, p. 367.

Note: For an interesting study of the Confiscation of British Property in Maryland, and in particular St. Mary's County, see Chronicles of St. Mary's Volume 5, No. 7 by Mrs. LaVerne Fenwick.

April 1, 1781

Stephen West, Upper Marlbro to Gov. Lee

....Letter from Col. Lyles dated 2 Hours ago at Piscataway, "We have certain Intelligence that the Enemy are under full sail up the Potowmack River....their force are are 3 ships, 1 Brig or Snow & severall sloops and schooners....

Archives of Maryland Vol. 47, p. 157.

April 2, 1781

Council ordered Treasurer pay to Robert Miles 5 £.12s.6d. due him per Account.

Archives of Maryland Vol. 45, p. 371.

April 3, 1781

Richard Barnes Leod. Town to Gov. Lee

Encloses letter from Cols. Jordon, Hebb & Thomas recommending 100 Militia with their horses be raised immediately for the defence of the County; has ordered the Upper Batln. of Militia to hold themselves in readiness until answer received; if something is not immediately done for the protection of the County, ruin must be the

consequence to many inhabitants; the enemy have plundered many since last letter
and are now on St. George's Island; party consists of 4 Sloops and 4 or 5 Barges;
there have been several brushes with them by the Militia in which one man was
wounded; would like Capt. Ford supply provisions and the Sheriff be directed to supply
Ford with money for that purpose; doesn't think Tobacco in payment of taxes should
be carried to Warehouses at this time.

      Cols. Jeremiah Jordan and Vernon Hebb & Lt. Col. Jno. Thomas to Col.
      Richard Barnes
      ...Armed Force now in St. Mary's River and landed on St. George's Island;
need at least 200 good Muskets with Bayonets & Cartouch Boxes; also 8 Cannon;
100 men mounted on horses will immediately turn out for service if they can be armed.
      Archives of Maryland Vol. 47, p. 159, 160.

April 4, 1781
      Council to Col. Barnes
      Yours of 25 Ult. received; understand necessity for arms but can't convey,
the Navigation being impeded by the Enemy Vessels off the harbor (Annapolis) and
all carriages impressed for transportation of stores and men of La Fayette; will
furnish 70 stand of arms on your sending for them; think use of mounted troops would
be effective but think 30 sufficient.
      Archives of Maryland Vol. 45, p. 376.

April 5, 1781
      Council to Richard Barnes, Esq.
      Received yours of 3rd Instant; think 30 mounted troops sufficient; the extra
number of Cartridge Boxes with such a Quantity of Powder as you think necessary
shall be sent with the Arms; order on Capt. Ford enclosed to supply provisions for the
Militia.

      Council to Capt. Ford
      You will furnish the Militia of St. Mary's County with such provisions as
Col. Barnes may order.
      Archives of Maryland Vol. 4, p. 377, 378.

      Zacha Forrest, St. Mary's County to Gov. Lee
      Negro man was condemned at last Court to be hanged; have no Gaol in the
County and must keep the Criminal at his own house; hopes he will send warrant for
the execution or a reprieve as he has no way of securing him properly; the fellow is
very likely and not more than 19 years of age.
      Archives of Maryland Vol. 47, p. 164.

      Council ordered Treasurer pay to...John Greenwell 5 ₤.5s., Wm. Pratt
16 ₤.10s.10d., Joseph Wimsatt (Winset) 11 ₤.6s.8d. and John McKay (McCay)
10 ₤.5s.6d...due them...
      Archives of Maryland Vol. 48, p. 120.

April 7, 1781
      Richard Barnes, Leod. Town to Gov. Thos. Sim Lee
      Mr. J. A. Thomas comes to you at my particular request to get such necessarys
as can be possibly spared. I am in hope that more than 70 stand of Arms you mention
may be spared as Arms are not wanted in the interior parts of the Country and the whole
of this Coty. is exposed. I am satisfied the Men would turn out freely if we could
Arm them...There are many other things necessary which Mr. Thomas will inform you..
request the Arms be delivered (to him)...I refer you to him for all Intelligence that we
have. I have no money and therefore request that the Expences may be paid by you.
      Archives of Maryland Vol. 47, p. 168.

April 8, 1781

Daniel Jenifer, Port Tobacco to Gov. Thomas Sim Lee

Two armed schooners with a cutter and some Barges came above Cedar Point; plundered Young's ferry, pillaged Walter Hanson & carried off his son, Samuel; plundered Rev. Ignatius Matthews (Port Tobacco); Militia prevented them from landing at Gerard Blackistone Causin's; plundered the "Elegent Seat" of George Dent; removed most of the tobacco from the Cedar Point Warehouse.

Archives of Maryland Vol. 47, p. 172, 173.

Council to Marquis de Lafayette

Col. Beall reported that six of the Enemy's Ships have burnt Col. Barnes' house on St. Mary's River and plundered him of all of his property; are proceeding up Potomac River to Alexandria; submit to his consideration the propriety of detaining the Detachment under your Command in this State and marching such a part as you may deem necessary to our assistance in Baltimore and in this City (Annapolis).

Council to Gen'l. Buchanan

....This Morning two Ships, a Brig and a Schooner appeared off this Harbour. ..recommend removal of all valuable property and provision into the County....

Archives of Maryland Vol. 45, p. 383.

April 9, 1781

Council to Col. Joshua Beall

....We wish you to be more explicit (in) report...so we may be better enabled to judge what conduct to pursue...cannot spare the number of arms you request as it has been necessary to embody part of the Militia of this County and pressing demands are made by the Lieutenant of St. Mary's Connty....

Archives of Maryland Vol. 45, p. 386.

April 10, 1781

S. West to Gov. Lee

....the intelligence from Col. (Joshua) Beall was exaggerated...they had not burned Col. Barnes's...on Saturday when it was so foggy 1 or 2 barges came all the way up the Patuxent...Every hours experience shows the necessity of having some armed vessels in...the Patuxent & Potomac.

Joseph Wilkinson, Lower Marlbro to Gov. Lee

....at the mouth of (Patuxent River)...they met the two Ships and Brig that have been up the Bay....I am informed that a barge came yesterday evening to Cedar Point and last night a House was seen on fire near the place supposed to be Mr. Nicholas Sewall's....

Archives of Maryland Vol. 47, p. 177, 178.

Council ordered that Capt. Philemon Warfield deliver to John Allen Thomas Esq. 100 Stand of arms with Accoutrements complete and two quarter Casks of Musket powder to be delivered over to Colo. Richard Barnes, Lieutenant of St. Mary's County and also 25 Muskets with Accoutrements, complete, two quarter Casks of Musket powder 500 Gun flints and two quire of Cartridge paper for the Lieut of Charles County for the use of the Militia of said Counties.

Council to Col. Richard Barnes

We have given John Allen Thomas, Esq...100 Stand of Arms with Accoutrements complete, all the small Cartridge Boxes, two quarter Casks of Musket Powder, 500 gun flints and 5 Quires of Cartridge Paper which is everything that can possibly be spared....You will remove all the Horses, Stock and provisions...where you think there is any probability of their falling into the Hands of the Enemy and if the Inhabitants of St. George Island should refuse to remove and you should think their continuance there prejudicial to the State, you will also have them removed to the main. We hereby empower you to take such Vessels with their Hands, Carriage Horses and other

Draft Cattle, Geers and Drivers as you may judge necessary and proper for the service of the State to perform, Carriage mount the Militia to go on Expresses....
Archives of Maryland Vol. 45, p. 387, 390.

April 12, 1781
Council ordered Treasurer pay to John Allen Thomas, Esq. 24 Ł. due him per Account.
Archives of Maryland Vol. 45, p. 392.

April 14, 1781
Agreeable to an Act to embody a number of select Militia and for immediately putting this State in a Proper posture of Defence, the Council proceeded to establish the relative Rank of the Lieutenants appointed by the General Assembly by placing each of their names in a Balot Box and drawing them out one by one, their names were drawn in the following order: George Dashiel, Christopher Birkhead, Richard Barnes....
Archives of Maryland Vol. 45, p. 398.

April 15, 1781
Richd. Barnes, Leod. Town to Gov. Lee
I have sent the Bearer, Mr. John Mills for the ballance of the Arms which Mr. Thomas says he had an order for. If a few Gun Locks could be spared, they would be very useful. At any rate, should be obliged to you to send me some bullet Molds that will make an Oz and Oz and quarter Ball as it is not in my power to get them made here and the greatest part of the Lead we have is in Bars and Ball of a very improper size. I shall have those people that are on St. Georges Island removed to the main. You will be kind enough to pay Mr. John Mills the whole expence of sending for the Arms &c, as I have no money....It will not be in my power to do what is proper unless I am supplyed with money....Enemy Vessels .... are up Potomack. Several ships & Brigs have just appeared off St. Georges...added to those that went up the Potomack will make their force to us very formidable.
Archives of Maryland Vol. 47, p. 190.

April 17, 1781
Joseph Ford, Leonard Town to Gov. Lee
What flesh provisions procured were sent...to George Town, except two Steers...delivered to the Militia...by Col. Barnes orders we have had constantly on duty for two weeks about 200 men. I have furnished them so far with provisions but ...with some difficulty as I had no money....indebted between 4000 and 5000 Pounds Continental money...If it can be conveniently spared will be glad to have about 250 Pounds of the new money...may with safety be sent by the Bearer, Mr. John Mills. ..has had much trouble with a horse received from Reverend Mr. Stephens a non juror and finally sold at low price...the Lard, Tallow & hides of the Public in my care, I should be glad to know what to do with. I enclose Docr. Reeder's certificate that St. Mary's Warehouse is Burnt.

Zacha Forrest, St. Mary's County to Gov. Lee
The bearer, Mr. Mills brings with him a deserter from the Continental Army, not having a Gaol in our County....one other has escaped...begging your excellency will order....some Officer to take....Please send some order respecting negro man under sentence of death, he is young and healthy and would make a fine Soldier.

Thomas Stone, Port Tobacco to Gov. Lee
Yesterday a 16 Gun, Brig appeared off Swan Point and sent a Boat with 6 hands to destroy a vessel on the Stocks. Near that place 8 Militia under Col. Harris attacked them and took the Boat & Crew, the Prisoners are ordered to Annapolis. This morning the enemys vessels which were above sailed down Potomac and were below Cedar Point at 11 O'clock....
Archives of Maryland Vol. 47, p. 195, 196, 197, 198.

April 18, 1781

Thomas Stone, Port Tobacco to Thomas Johnson, Jr.

On Apr. 12 British landed maruders at Portobacco and stole church furnishings; on the 13th, landed at Capt. George Dent's and burned the houses; Cedar Point was robbed of tobacco on the 14th; there were 5 or 6 barges and 300 men; 2 or 3 cannon are needed; British vessels rounded Cedar Point on the 17th and are anchored at Swan Point.

Calendar of Maryland State Papers No. 4, Part 1, p. 191 (Item 1108).

April 21, 1781

Council ordered Treasurer pay to John Mills $100.00 to be delivered over to Richard Barnes, Esq. on account.

Council to Capt. Joseph Ford

We have yours of the 17 Instant. You will have the Tallow and Lard sold for the best Prices you can obtain in ready money; this with the Order enclosed you on the Collector of St. Mary's County we think will be Sufficient to answer your present necessities. The Hides you will have tanned for the State.

Archives of Maryland Vol. 45, p. 408, 409.

April 24, 1781

Richard Barnes, Leod. Town to Gov. Thomas Sim Lee

I find that it is impossible for the County to be protected against our present Enemy by the Militia....In consequence....have taken advice of Cols. Jordan, Fenwick and Thomas....that 120 men should immediately be raised, part of which to be Horse (30) .... and to have them stationed till the Enemy return down the Bay at the Mouth of the Patuxent...On return of the Enemy down Potomack one George Howard from this Neighbourhood went to them and carryed 5 negroes that was known of, 4 of which were the Revd. Mr. (James) Walton's. Mr. James Adderton who was taken by the Enemy when they landed at St. Inigoes, informed me that when he was on board one of their Ships in St. Mary's, one of the Ship's Crew who he was acquainted with asked him if he knew Geo. Howard and told him....that he had brought 9 negroes with him... Howard was a Native and had taken the oathes to Government...observe your Senti- ments relative to the militia being furnished with spirituous liquor...intention was only to give it to those men that were on guard, in bad weather and when they were fatigued in marching....in general our People are very poor and there are times when it will be proper for them to be supplyed with it....I am informed that the officers in the upper Battn. got the quarter Master to supply the Militia that were on Wicomico with some Brandy while the Enemy were up Potomack, without my knowing anything of it which in future I shall prevent...I have inclosed Mr. Mills Acct. of the expense of sending to Annapolis by him for Arms.....

Archives of Maryland Vol. 47, p. 203, 204.

April 26, 1781

Joseph Ford, Leonard Town, St. Mary's County to Gov. Lee

Your Excellencies favor of the 21st Inst. enclosing an Order on the Collector of the Tax for 200 Ł. I Received. I shewed it to him and he informed me he had not Received one Shilling of the Tax in money more than he had Remitted, nor did he expect Shortly to Receive any. If 200 Ł. could be conveniently spared, I should be glad and sent by the Bearer Mr. Robert Greenwell.

Archives of Maryland Vol. 47, p. 214.

April 27, 1781

J. Taylor to Colo. Richard Barnes, with 7 Prisoners under Guard of Serjeant Daffin & others

The Capts. Folgier and Cole belonging to Baltemore who are just arrived from the West Indies, on their Passage up the Bay met with a New York Privateer Schooner & a Sloop, her prize, a little below Cedar Point, which they Captured.... 7 of the Prisoners were put on board the above mentioned Sloop, having no guard over them, they made their escape....were this day taken up by Mr. Belwood, Jarboe

& others who I have ordered to Carry them to you....The Chaps had with them a Pretty deal of very good wearing Apparel such as Shirts, Breeches, Waistcoats &c, Summer Ware and which they say partly belonged to the Marques La Fayette, which I imagine is truth, they (the Privateer) took Middleton's Boat in which the Marques's baggage was shiped...
Archives of Maryland Vol. 47, p. 214.

April 30, 1781
Ricd. Barnes, Leond. Town to Gov. Lee
As many of the Militia as we can arm are now on duty in the different parts of the Coty. and as this will be the case the greatest part of the summer or as long as the Enemy are in the Bay, I am fully satisfied that if some plan is not fel on to keep a select number of men constantly together for the year, they will not answer the intended purpose of defending the Coty. and will in a great measure prevent them making a support for their Familys. For the constant changing and the trouble of getting men to relieve those that have been on duty, the whole affair must be conducted in a very confused and purplexed manner, without the mens being qualified in their duty and their not having that confidence in each Other that men have by continuing a time together.. And will have a very bad tendency, I am apprehensive, in harrassing the People more than their feelings can well bear. Great difficultys we shall in all probability have...but the time now approaches that makes it highly necessary for us to conduct our affairs with the greatest propriety. I have directed Capn. Ford to endeavour to purchase some Brandy for the use of the Militia on duty as it can't well be expected that men can do duty without it. I am informed that two Ships came into Potomack yesterday with several sloops & Barges. Those that Capn. Thomas will inform you of are now up Potomack, some where above this. I should be glad to have your sentiment on the above.
Archives of Maryland Vol. 47, p.223.

May 2, 1781
Council of Maryland to Richard Barnes, Esq.
We have received your letter of the 24th and 28th Ult. We think it proper to order such a Part of the Militia as you may deem necessary for your Protection to hold themselves in Readiness to march upon every Emergency. Howard's Property we have no Authority, but think Grand Jury of the Genl. or your County Court ought to be informed of his conduct and a regular Prosecution carried on against him. Every Militia man whose Situation in Life will not enable him to furnish himself with every part of a Ration ought to have it provided for them while on Duty, but those who can ought to furnish themselves and make Returns of their Accounts to this Board for Payment. The Account of Mr. Mills we have settled...The 7 Prisoners mentioned in yours of the 28th have arrived and are safely lodged in this City.

Council ordered Treasurer pay to John Mills 53 £.6s.3d. and also 73 £.13s. due him per Account.

Council to Mr. Joseph Ford
The Order given you on the Collector of St. Mary's County we hope will shortly be discharged by him; and it is the only Mode we can adopt to supply you.
Archives of Maryland Vol. 45, p. 422, 423.

May 3, 1781
St. Mary's County, Came Benja. Williams before me one of the Magistrates of this County and made Oath on the Holy Evangels of Almighty God, That he this deponent took this Paper out of the Pocket of the Person who called himself Arthur Gage & who stands on the other side as a Subscriber thereto.
Sworn to before J. Taylor.
Archives of Maryland Vol. 47, p. 230.

May 4, 1781

    Ricd. Barnes, Leod. Town to Gov. Lee

    I herewith send you under Guard 3 Prisoners, part of the same Crew that I sent to you, takin in a Canoe at Point Lookout, together with John Taylor, who was takin up in consequence of a paper signed Arthur Gage &c. which was found in the pocket of one of the Prisoners sent to you, who acknowledged to me that he was at the House of John Taylor and got Provision from him....on hearing that Docr. Robertson and Austin Milburn were at Taylors at the time the Prisoner was there, I have procured the inclosed deposition of Austin Milburn. Taylor is a man of infamous character, with a good deal of property, and has for a considerable time had a difference with Mr. J. Adderton....He has two sons that go by water and I believe not well attached to our cause....Captn. John H. Abell informs me that on his ordering James Theobalds & Dan'l. Dris to join the Company that we are raising they left the parts and that a Canoe of Theobalds Father (who lives at Point Lookout) was seen with two Men in it Standing to the Eastern Shore....he (Theobalds) took with him one of the Public Arms with a Bayonet & Cartouch box....(Complains of quality of Officers and recommends a list of new officers)...can send the Commissions by the Bearer....Mr. John Wood.

    Deposition of Austin Milburn, St. Mary Co. before Henry Reeder

    ....the Prisoner that acknowledged the Paper signed Arthur Gauge was 2nd Lt. Mr. Doyal & Mr. Mullin and was in the following words "Mr. James Adderton have a great deal of property of Negroes & Plate, he lives in St. Inegoes Creek near the Warehous, whom is a great foe to Mr. John Taylor living in St. Marys County near the same place which have Behaved as a good friend to the Union flagg In distress made their Escape from the Prisonment of & the captured Jack of the Lanthorn...deponant further sayeth that he with Doctr. Robinson went to John Taylors Blue stone and found the aforesaid Arthur Gauge, Mr. Doyal & Mr. Mullin there.....asked them where they were from and they answered him from Annapolis last on which Mr. John Taylor told him they were Acquaintances of his son Billeys and that they wanted to cross over to Virginia to get to Rappahanock to get out to Sea....(copy of the paper taken from Arthur Gage follows attested by Benja. Williams, a County Magistrate.)

    Archives of Maryland Vol. 47, p. 228, 229, 230.

May 5, 1781

    Philip Key to the Council

    As the State have a quantity of Tobacco on Chaptico, Leonard Town & Llewellins Ware Houses, I will undertake conveying it to Philadelphia as soon as Possible. If the Governor & Council will place the sale of it under Mr. Wm. Molohon who shall not make any engagement for it without their approbation. Mr. Molohon to have a right to deduct from the sales of the Tobacco the charges incident to the transportation and the usual Commission.

May 6, 1781

    Richd. Barnes, Leod. Town to Gov. Lee

    I received yours of the 2d May and must confess that I am at a loss to know by it, whether the plan we have adopted of calling out on duty 100 of our Militia, to be kept constantly together, whilst the British are in force in the Bay, meet with your approbation or not...could wish (directions) were given in such a manner as I might not mistake them...shall keep men together...until I am directed to the contrary... would like them to be furnished with some Spiratuous liquor to be given generally.... the draft directed by the Assembly in my opinion improper....could wish you would suspend it in this County, due to our peculiar situation.

    Archives of Maryland Vol. 47, p. 231.

May 7, 1781

    Commissions issued to

    Capt. William Sommerville in room of Alex. H. Watts

1st. Lt. John Mills
2nd. Lt. Robert Greenwell
Ensign Henry Abell   of Capt. Barton Abells Compy.

1st. Lt. James Attwood   of Capt. John Mackalls Compy.

1st. Lt. Richard King
2nd. Lt. Polard Hopewell
Ensign Edwd. Swan   of Capt. Sam'l. Jenifer's Compy.

Capt. John Chesley in room of Hugh Hopewell

1st. Lt. George Hopewell
2nd. Lt. Robt. Daffon
Ensign Wm. Bellwood

1st. Lt. John Shadrack
2nd. Lt. George Cole   of Barton Smoot Compy.
        Lower Bat. Militia St. Mary's County

        Council to Colo. Richard Barnes
        The 3 British Prisoners with Taylor were yesterday delivered by John Wood and were immediately ordered into Confinement. We have not yet determined what to do with Taylor, as soon as we do, you shall have Information. His Excellency being out of Town prevents our sending the Commissions you request, on his return you may depend upon having them immediately sent.
        Archives of Maryland Vol. 45, p. 426, 427.

May 9, 1781
        Council ordered Treasurer pay to Zachariah Forrest 157 Ł.4s. for the use of Capt. John Horn Abell and his Company due them per Acct. passed by the Aud. Genl.
        Archives of Maryland Vol. 45, p. 428.

May 10, 1781
        Council ordered Treasurer pay to Isaac Simmons 43 Ł...3d. due him.
        Archives of Maryland Vol. 45, p. 429.

May 12, 1781
        Joseph Ford to Gov. Lee
        The Confusion the enemy has Kept us In for this month past and my Books being removed some distance from home has prevented my making a Return of Purchases in April...but as I have obtained nothing more than will serve the Militia on duty here for a little time, I do imagine it is not so material. Country make Salt is rising Very fast here, I have a sufficiency for this Post but Perhaps some others are not supplied, in that case it may probably be right to procure some. It sells currently for Ł. 5 new money.

        John Taylor, Prison, Annapolis, to his Excellency the Governor and the honble Council of the State of Maryland.
        ....Your petitioner being near Sixty years of age and a native of this Country was apprehended (notwithstanding the natural tie of a man's attachment to his Country) and taken on Suspicion of his being friendly and assisting to the Enemy....charges... will be found groundless and Migatory....prays to cause him to be removed from his present place of Confinement...not adopted for the Confinement of even the basest Criminal...to another place of security....until the matters alleged against him be fully heard....
        Archives of Maryland Vol. 47, p. 239, 240.

May 14, 1781
        Negro Joe the property of John Eden of St. Mary's County captured in the

Jack Oth Lanthorn by Capt. Folger in the Antilope and now confined in the Gaol of this
City is delivered to said John Eden upon his agreeing to restore him on the order of the
Governor and Council or to pay the Customary Salvage whenever called on by the
Governor and Council.
        Archives of Maryland Vol. 45, p. 435.

May 17, 1781

        George Plater, J. A. Thomas, St. Mary's County to Gov. Thomas Sim Lee
        From the particular situation of our County, we are induced to request that your
Excellency would suspend the Draft of the Militia of that County for fitting up the
Quota of Troops until the 3rd. day of June next.
        Archives of Maryland Vol. 47, p. 245.

        Council to Lieutenant of St. Mary's County
        The peculiar Circumstances of the Militia of St. Mary's County as represented
to us by Messrs. Plater and Thomas have induced us to suspend the Draft until the
3rd. Day of June.
        Archives of Maryland Vol. 45, p. 438.

June 1, 1781

        Council Circular to the Lieutenants of Several Counties
        From the Intelligence we have received of the rapid Movements of the Enemy
in Virginia, we have reason to apprehend an Invasion of this State, it will be necessary
that every Precaution be taken preparative for our Defence. We therefore request you
to order the Militia in your County to hold themselves in perfect Readiness to march
at a moments warning to such Place as may be thought necessary, and to have all the
Arms in your County proper for Defence, immediately repaired and put in the best Condition. Cartridges made and everything ready to take the Field.
        Archives of Maryland Vol. 45, p. 453.

June 5, 1781

        Council ordered Treasurer deliver to Philip Key Esq. 533 hhds. of Tobacco
on Chaptico, Llewellins and Leonard Town Warehouses in St. Mary's County to be by
him transported to Philadelphia and to be accounted for.
        Joseph Ford appointed Purchaser of Clothing in St. Mary's County.

        Council to Collector of St. Mary's County
        We request you to make an immediate Return of all the Tobacco belonging to
the Public in Llewellins and Leonard Town Warehouses, which is so much exposed that
we think proper it should be removed but it cannot be done until the Notes are returned.

        Council to Philip Key, Esqr.
        Yours of this Day we received. We agree to your Proposals and have drawn an
Order in your Favor for 233 Hogsheads of Tobacco on Chaptico, Llewellins and Leonard
Town Warehouses which we would have immediately transported by the way of back
Creek and the Head of Elk to Philadelphia subject to our further Orders.
        Archives of Maryland Vol. 45, p. 461, 462, 463.

June 7, 1781

        Joseph Ford, St. Mary's County to Gov. Lee
        Enclosed Your Excellency will Receive my Return of Purchases in April and May
with an Account of what Stores I have on hand....We are again Visited by 3 of the
enemies ships, Two are in St. Mary's River, the other a little above in Potomack....
the Steers that are on hand perhaps had better be kept and the Militia fed with Bacon
and Mutton....I sent an Application to the General Assembly for a Relief from the
Tobacco burnt in St. Mary's Warehouse....hope..Board....give an order on the
Collector of Tax for the Balance due....and the Amount due on the enclosed Returns,
the whole 26, 985 Pounds of Tob. Mr. Mills...brings the Account as Settled by the
Auditor General My Account of charges and coopers wages will amount to about

5000 Pounds of Tobacco More. I should be Glad if that could be included....
Archives of Maryland Vol. 47, p. 273, 274.

June 8, 1781
Francis Ware, Port Tobacco to Gov. Lee
May it please your Excellency. I have this moment Received information by Express from the Sciper of our Lookout boat That there were Several Sail of Vessels this forenoon Standing up the River Potomack, one of which a Large Ship as high as Blackistone's Island....
Archives of Maryland Vol. 47, p. 276.

June 9, 1781
Council to Commissary of St. Mary's County
We request you will procure some Whiskey or Brandy for the Militia of St. Mary's County to be delivered out to them in small Quantities when called into actual Service and only at Such Times as the Lieutenant of the County may think absolutely necessary.

Council Circular to Commissaries of St. Marys, Prince George and Charles County.
Summary. Orders Commissaries to buy or seize if necessary, Stock in exposed places to prevent falling into hands of the enemy and send by a safe route to Georgetown.
Archives of Maryland Vol. 45, p. 467, 469.

June 11, 1781
Council ordered Collector of Tax for St. Mary's County pay to Joseph Ford Comy. for said County 15,000 pounds of Tobacco on Acct.

Council to Richard Barnes, Esq.
We request you will direct the Tobacco in the several warehouses within your County, exposed to the Enemy to be removed to such Places of Security as you may think....give us the earliest Intelligence of any interesting Movements of the Enemy.

Council to Joseph Ford, Esqr.
....received yours of the 7th...proper to supply the Militia with fresh Provisions and to preserve the salt Provisions....enclose Order..for 15,000 Pounds of Tobacco...Assembly have not taken any Order respecting Tobacco in your Hands burnt in St. Mary's warehouses, when they do, Your Account may be finally settled...
Archives of Maryland Vol. 45, p. 470, 471.

June 12, 1781
Daniel of St. Thomas Jenifer and Daniel Carroll to Gov. Lee
....If the Tob. that Mr. Key is to transport lies on the Potomack we cannot hope for any relief from it as we shall be under the necessity of decamping before he can get it to this place...
Archives of Maryland Vol. 47, p. 284.

Council to General Assembly
Concerns Negroes found in the capture of the British Ship "Jack O' Lanthorn", one the property of John Eden.
Archives of Maryland Vol. 45, p. 473, 634.

June 15, 1781
George Collins, Pvt. discharged from 3rd. Reg. Md. Line after serving 3 years.
Archives of Maryland Vol. 18, p. 96, 298, 329.

June 16, 1781
Council ordered that John Taylor be confined to the District of Montgomery County and not to depart the limits without leave and post bond of 1000 pounds Specie.

Col. Richard Barnes was advised of action.
Archives of Maryland Vol. 45, p. 476, 478.

Richard Barnes, Leod. Town to Gov. Lee
On my return to this County I found a small Ship under a Flag near Blackistone's Island (since which she has proceeded up Patowmack) and a six and thirty gun Frigate with two schooners laying at the mouth of St. Mary's River where they have been for several days and have ever since continued without ever attempting to land but on St. Georges Island which they have regularly done every day. On the 13th a Brig with two Schooners appeared off the mouth of Clements Bay and landed two barges loaded with men at Mr. Herbert Blackestons   House which they burned and carryed Blackeston with them, where he has continued. The Brig and Schooner having gone to the mouth of Nomany (Nomini) where they were seen to land from this side Potomack. The object these Vessels have in view further than plundering &c I am apprehensive is to git information of our situation before the arrival of the force bound to Potomack which we were informed of before I left Annapolis. I have just rec'd. directions from the Council for the removal of the Tob. in the Ware houses, all of which I shall endeavour to have removed except that in Chaptico Warehouse which is nearly as secure as any place we can move it to.
Archives of Maryland Vol. 47, p. 295, 296.

June 17, 1781
Henry Goldsborough, Pvt. 3rd. Reg. Md. Line died.
Archives of Maryland Vol. 18, p. 114, 298, 536.

June 18, 1781
Richard Barnes, Leod. Town to Gov. Lee
All the Vessels of the Enemy left Potomack on Saturday last. They landed at Mrs. Egertons house below Smiths Creek and plundered and destroyed all her Household furniture. Since I last wrote to you I have been informed the Crew of the Frigate that layed at the mouth of St. Mary's River were imployed the whole time they were there in getting Masts &c. for Ships off St. Georges Island where there is good Pine for the purpose. Some of the Inhabitants above St. Mary's River I have been informed furnished the Enemy with Provision whilst they were there. I shall do my endeavors to find them out, the Law that passed for the punishing such chaps, I shall be glad you would supply me with, as some examples may be necessary. If ammunition should be wanted I should be glad to be informed. If you have any to spare as we shall soon be in want of some owing to our not having Cartough Boxes and the pilfering of the Militia.

Capt. Joseph Ford to Col. Forrest
I have taken the Liberty of enclosing you a Letter for his Excellency, Tho. Sim Lee Esquire Respecting the Goods Mr. Campbell has Liable to a seizure by Law. It is my opinion that such goods as he has may be laid in upon better terms in Annapolis and Baltimore & for that Reason I have though best to lay the matter before the Council and that we may get there determination more Speedily. I shall be obliged to you to wait on them and forward there answer by the Return of Charles Lansdale. Mr. Campbell has suspended the Sale of them till I have their directions. If the Assembly have taken order in my matter be so obliging as to inform me of their decree.
Archives of Maryland Vol. 47, p. 299, 300.

Francis Revelly succeeded as Capt. of the 1st. Reg. Md. Line upon the death of Capt. George Armstrong.
Archives of Maryland Vol. 18, p. 477.

June 19, 1781
Council to Colo. Samuel Smith
....The Tobacco delivered (to) Mr. (Philip) Key is for particular Purposes and will be solely under his directions in Consequence of his Engagement to advance the

Money for transporting and superintending that Business without a Reward.
Archives of Maryland Vol. 45, p. 480.

Joseph Ford, Leonard Town, to Gov. Lee
I am Honour'd with Letters from your Honorable Board of the 5.9. & 11th Instant, that of the 11th enclosing an Order on the Collector for 15,000 pounds of Tobacco. I have been collecting Cattle Agreeable to Orders and Must say for that part of the people that I have been with that they parted with them with willingness. I shall be able in Ten days to forward my number and must observe that there is at Least one Thousand as much exposed. I do immagine that it will not be wrong to send those steers Returned on Hand forward with them, many people here would willingly discharge there Class money in Bacon but it is determined here that it was not the intention of the Assembly.

Mr. Archibald Campbell, Merchant in this Town has Two or Three pieces of Oznabgs. and a few pieces of Low priced dutch Linnens for sale. I applied to him for them, he says they belong to Mr. David Steward, Baltimore and that Steward has already furnished large supplies for public use. I should have taken them Agreeable to Law but was of opinion that such goods were to be had in Baltimore on better terms as these were brought from there. He has promised me not to sell them till I get directions Respecting them which I Hoped your Excellency and the Honble. Council will take under consideration and inform me what I shall do in the Matter. The Enemies Ships has left Potomack except the one thought to be a flagg, without doing any damage Except the Burning one Mr. Blackstone's House.
Archives of Maryland Vol. 47, p. 303.

June 22, 1781
Council to Maryland Delegates in Congress
We were honored by yours of the 12th Instant, be assured that your very disagreeable Situation for want of remittances from this State has given us real Concern and that it would give us considerable Relief to remove them immediately. We have delivered Philip Key, Esqr. 230 Hogsheads of Tobacco to be immediately transported to Philadelphia, 80 Hogsheads of which are now a Float from the sales thereof you are to be supplied with Money. Mr. Key drew an Order on Mr. Mollohan for 60 Pounds Specie to be delivered to you which we imagine you have received. You may rely, Gentlemen that if our Abilities were equal to our Inclinations, you would not be left in such embarrassing Circumstances.

Council to Capt. Joseph Ford
Yours of the 19th we have received and as we are not acquainted with the Circumstances of the Goods, must refer you to the Law for your Guide. We are pleased to hear that the Inhabitants of your County part with their Cattle with Chearfulness. We do not think it proper at this time to enlarge the order. In case of Invasion the Lieutenant of the County has full Powers to remove all the Stock exposed to the Enemy.
Archives of Maryland Vol. 45, p. 483, 484.

June 26, 1781
Daniel of St. Thomas Jenifer, Dan'l. Carroll and Richard Potts Phila., to Gov. Lee
....Believe difficulties of being supported will be relieved by safe arrival of tobacco under Philip Key and that William Mullahon will honor Key's order....

David Stewart, Baltimore to Col. Uriah Forrest, Annapolis
Capt. Joseph Ford has seized property belonging to George Salmon, William Taylor and self; Col. Saml. Smith has completed all purchases locally; order of Council is needed to compel Ford to return property; packet should be sent to Mr. (Archibald) Campbell.
Archives of Maryland Vol. 47, p. 316.

June 29, 1781
Council to Philip Key, Esq.
Mr. James Skinner, Inspector of Hunting Creek Warehouse informs us that

there was a Vessel loading State Tobacco at that Warehouse and could not get a full
load and has offered 14 Hogsheads to be put on Board this Vessel. We have wrote him,
if it is public Tobacco to deliver it to you or your Order, and if the Craft is under your
Direction and you approve of the Tobacco, you will forward it in the Manner you have
engaged to forward the Tobacco heretofore delivered.
Archives of Maryland Vol. 45, p. 490.

June 30, 1781
Members of the House of Delegates
We promise to become Subscribers of the Sums affixed after our names...for
an Emission...of Bills of Credit not exceeding 200,000 Pounds....to defray the
expences of the present Campaign for St. Mary's County Philip Key 500 Pounds, Edmd.
Plowden 500 Pounds.
Archives of Maryland Vol. 47, p. 326.

John Barnes loaned the State 500 £.
Archives of Maryland Vol. 47, p. 327.

James Foster, Pvt. who enlisted in the 3rd. Reg. Md. Line on 5/28/1778, re-
enlisted in the 3rd. Reg. on 11/1/1780 and died 6/30/1781.
Archives of Maryland Vol. 18, p. 110, 298, 534, 619.

July 2, 1781
Philip Key, Chaptico, to the Council
I have received your...favor 29th. to which I shall pay the utmost attention.
My stay at Annapolis retarded the forwarding your Tobacco very much...have this
day finished shiping on board craft 55 Hhds. 25 from Potomack & 30 from Patuxent that
I have carted over, the whole will be forwarded this month as I have got the business
now under my own direction. If you have more Tobacco at Chaptico that you wish to
forward it can be carted to Patuxent with more ease than from any other House on
Patomack....Tobacco...is of the best Quality....Tobacco now sent will net the
State 23 s. clear of charges or at least 22s.6d.
Information of John Anderson, a Deserter from one of the British Barges taken
2nd. July 1781. Sworn to in Council before Thos. S. Lee
....that Edwd. Fenwick of St. Mary's County was sevl. Times on St. George's
Island while the Barges were there, he came for a Negro and bot Goods of the Barges-
that Josiah Langley of same County brot. some meal for the Barges and went up Potow-
mack as a Pilot of the Barges & returned in her and left her at St. Geos. Island.
Langley was to carry the Barge to Leonardtown but was fired on by the Militia on the
Shore.
Archives of Maryland Vol. 47, p. 333, 334.

July 9, 1781
Genl. Geor. Washington Hdqtrs. near Dobb's Ferry to George Plater, Esqr.
Pres of the Senate, Wm. Bruff, Speaker House of Delegates, Maryland
....as the troops of Maryland compose part of the Southern Army now under
immediate command of Maj. Gen'l. Greene. I think there wd be an impropriety ....
(for) General Smallwood to remain in Maryland...(should make) application to General
Greene....
Archives of Maryland Vol. 47, p. 340; Manual of State of Maryland 1973-1974
p.825.

July 13, 1781
Council ordered Commissary of Stores deliver to...John Turner of the 3rd. Reg.
1 suit of Cloaths, 2 shirts, 1 pair overalls, 1 pair Shoes and 1 hat...in part of Cloathing due him.
Archives of Maryland Vol. 45, p. 500.

July 14, 1781

    R. Bond, St. Mary's County to Council(?)

    Received yours of the 12th Inst. and have pleasure to advise you the number of Horses required from this County are ready to be delivered to your order.

    Archives of Maryland Vol. 47, p. 349

July 17, 1781

    Council ordered Treasurer pay to Capt. John Barton Abell 28 £.12s.1/2d. Specie for use of himself and his Compy of Militia.

    Also pay to Lt. William Rapour (Rapier) 23 £.16s.4d. Specie due himself and the Militia under his Command.

    Council ordered Treasurer pay to Isaac Simmons 11 £.10s.7d. per Account.

    Archives of Maryland Vol. 45, p. 506, 507.

July 18, 1781

    Wm. Fitzhugh, Calvert County to Gov. Lee

    ....It appears Clearly that (James?) Anderson is both a Pirate & a spie; believes John Mackall, a Magistrate of St. Mary's County deserves censure because his administering the oath of allegiance to Anderson influenced Col. Richard Barnes to grant him a pass...(followed by several depositions of persons who identified Anderson).

    Archives of Maryland Vol. 47, p. 343, 355, 356, 357, 358.

July 19, 1781

    Council to Commissioners for the Preservation of British Property

    Mr. Shaw informs us you have a Quantity of Pewter taken as confiscated British Property. We shall be obliged to you to reserve it to make Buttons for the Soldiers Cloathing.

    Archives of Maryland Vol. 45, p. 510.

July 23, 1781

    Council order Treasurer pay to Capt. Joseph Ford, Commissary for St. Mary's County 20 £. of money appropriated for the present Campaign.

    Pay to Capt. Joseph Ford 76 £.11s.5d. Specie of same; also pay him 4178 pounds of Tobacco due him per Acct.

    Archives of Maryland Vol. 45, p. 515, 516.

    Richard Barnes Leod. Town to Gov. Lee

    By the last law raising Troops for 3 years, I passed two, one of which I sent up to you. The other was a considerable time before he could git his pay from the Class. ...could not oblige him before he had recd. his cloathes...(Has gone) in a Brig to Alexandria of Inga. Craycroft....where he may be secured if you think proper...His name is Henry Brian (Bryan) passed as a Substitute for 3 years the 3rd. Apl. 1781.

    Archives of Maryland Vol. 47, p. 364.

July 27, 1781

    Council Circular, Commissaries of St. Mary's & Other Counties

    As there will not be an immediate Occasion for a further supply of Cattle at George Town, we request you not to send any more thence but wait our further Orders, and in the mean Time have the Cattle put in good Pastures.

    Archives of Maryland Vol. 45, p. 524.

    A Return of Draughts and Substitutes sent from St. Mary's Co. under the Act of May Session to join the Troops at Annapolis.

Substitutes

James Adams	28 July '81	Edward Harley	1 Aug. '81
John Jennings	31 July '81	Igns. Griffin	2 Aug. '81
Joseph Kerby	31 July '81	Walter Buckler	5 Aug. '81

Substitutes

Igns. Adams	23 July '81	Bernard Paine	31 July '81
Wm. Kirkpatrick	26 July '81	Moses Adams	31 July '81
Thos. Curtis	26 July '81	Peter Jarboe	31 July '81
Joseph Wimsett	27 July '81	Edwd. Hazel	1 Aug. '81
Igns. Paine	28 July '81	Joseph Brown	2 Aug. '81
John Maddox	28 July '81	William Pike	2 Aug. '81
Joseph Reswick	28 July '81	John Norris	2 Aug. '81
John Dent Suit	28 July '81	John Greenwell	2 Aug. '81
Baptist Gough	29 July '81	Thos. Wise	5 Aug. '81
Elisha Burrowes	30 July '81	Cuthb. Jones	Aug. '81
(Burroughs ?)		Charles Gough	31 July '81

Draughts – All draughted 27 July '81

Joseph Newton	Charles Attwood	Nicholas Goldsbury
Henry Briscoe	Jeremiah Hazel	Igns. Brion (Bryan ?)
Edward Monark	Solomon Dixon	William Adams
Jeremiah Herbert	Henry Norris	Bennet Anderson
Struton Edwards	Robert Jarboe	Igns. Mattingly
Igns. Howard	John King	William Pratt
Arnold Norris	Charles Tawney	
Zacha. Newton	Charles Cole	

Archives of Maryland Vol. 18, p. 384.

July 30, 1781

Council Circular to Richard Barnes Esqr. and Col. Jeremiah Jordan

We have considered the Papers and Depositions....against Solomon Tyler and it not appearing to us there is any good and sufficient Cause to justify the Detention of his Property, we request...such Property be delivered to Rachel Tyler, his wife.

Archives of Maryland Vol. 45, p. 528.

Richard Barnes, Leod. Town to Gov. Lee

I have directed the Militia to be raised here for reinforcing the Continental Army to be at this place on Thursday next.... There are many men drafted that have large Familys without any one to assist them to work and have rent to pay which will be the ruin of themselves....what must be done with such....

Archives of Maryland Vol. 47, p. 373, 374.

August 3, 1781

Council to Richard Barnes, Esqr.

....received your Letter of the 30th July and agree...that sooner the draughted Men are sent here the better...wrote on the 23rd July ordering them to this Place, the regiments are filling fast by the 9 months men enlisting for the war. When the Person draughted is indigent and has a wife and child or two or more children who depend on his Labour or...is sick...infirm, we have requested the Lieut. to give a discharge and therefore wish you to inquire into all such Complaints and if they are well founded to discharge the Draughts.

Archives of Maryland Vol. 45, p. 538.

August 4, 1781

Col. Uriah Forrest, Leonard Town to Gov. Lee

"Humanity" causes him to intercede on behalf of Joshua Hebb one of the drafts of this County...has 5 small children who have "Hooping" Cough & expects every hour that his Wife will furnish him with a sixth; his labor their only subsistance; only two others merit Interposition: Clerk Spalding and Luke Mattingly both of whom are very Poor, Rent Land and have a number of children who must inevitably starve the men are not permitted to return; they bring recommendations from Col. Richard Barnes. (Note on papers says the drafts marched "today".)

Archives of Maryland Vol. 47, p. 387.

Council Circular to Collectors of Horses for Western Shore
....40 Enemy vessels reported coming up the Bay; need a number of Teams to remove Public Stores and Papers...forward immediately to this Post....

Council Circular to Lieuts. of St. Mary's and Calvert Counties
We request you to Station Persons on whom you can depend upon such Points as command the most extensive view of the Bay to give Information of the Approach of the Enemy....communicate to this Board by Express immediately.
Archives of Maryland Vol. 45, p. 542.

August 6, 1781
Joseph Ford to Gov. Lee
....enclose account of Expences in collecting and driving 95 Steers to George Town...(funds) being nearly exhausted hopes will give an order for payment...to Mr. (John) Mills who had charge of the drove and drovers....
Archives of Maryland Vol. 47, p. 392.

August 7, 1781
Council to Richard Barnes, Esqr.
We are informed by Mr. Richard Lee of Virginia that two Deserters of the Virginia Continental Line are in St. Mary's County on the east side of St. Mary's River, their names Reuben McKenny, and John McKenny. John is married to a woman of St. George's Island. Tarply Nash is another Deserter. Mr. Lee describes them as atrocious, piratical Villians who have armed themselves and attempted to plunder and raise a Crew of Deperadoes to ravage both sides of the river Patowmack. We request you to take effectual measures to apprehend those Men and send them under a Guard to Mr. Lee.
Archives of Maryland Vol. 45, p. 548.

August 9, 1781
Richd. Barnes, Leod. Town to Gov. Lee
Mr. James Thomas an Officer in the Militia of the Coly. that has behaved himself in that station very well was taken by the Enemy's Barges going to the head of the Bay and carryed to the Enemy at Portsmouth. His Father, Mr. Wm. Thomas is very desirous of supplying him with some money, which he is much in want of and has applyed to me to request your kind assistance to give him such liberty as will enable him to do it. Gentlemans Father and Family have conducted themselves as Friends to our cause.
Archives of Maryland Vol. 47, p. 402.

August 14, 1781
Council ordered Treasurer pay to John Mills 59 Ł.7s. ...appropriated for this campaign per Account.

Council to Capt. Joseph Ford
We have received yours of the 6th Instant by Mr. Mills and have ordered Payment for the account of Expences incurred in driving and collecting Cattle. We have also delivered to him Ł. 50 of the new Emission to defray Expences of your Department arisen due since the 19th of June last.
Archives of Maryland Vol. 45, p. 558, 559.

August 15, 1781
Council to The Commanding Officer of the British Navy or Land Forces at or near Portsmouth.
....we have also to inform you that about the 1st July past one of the British Barges captured in the Mouth of Patuxent a small Bay Schooner laden with Tobacco, on board of which was a young Gentlemen, Mr. James Thomas, Owner of the Vessel and Tobacco. His Parents who are People of Credit have heard that he is very ill in Jail at Portsmouth, and since he was a Prisoner, badly wounded, and that he suffers

for the Conveniences of Life. Under these Circumstances common Humanity induces us to comply with the request of the Parents and Relations of Mr. Thomas, in giving the Bearer hereof Lieut. Col. John Thomas of the St. Mary's Militia permission to go with a Flag to endeavour to obtain the Release of his Brother, either on Parole or on Exchange, at the same Time to carry him some Money and Necessaries for his Support and Recovery. He will be attended by Doctr. Mudd and four Hands to navigate the Boat. There are in Maryland several Persons who have been taken by the Inhabitants plundering on the Shores. If you think proper to release Mr. Thomas, we will immediately release in his Stead any British Citizen who is a Prisoner here in like Circumstances....

Archives of Maryland Vol. 45, p. 562.

August 15, 1781

William Watts commissioned as Surgeon's Mate in the 2nd. Reg. Md. Line. In the 3rd. Reg. Jan. 1, 1783 and served until the end of the war, November 15, 1783.

Archives of Maryland Vol. 18, p. 476, 480, 522.

August 17, 1781

Richd. Barnes, Leod. Town to Gov. Lee

This will be delivered to you by Nicholas Goldsbury (Goldsborough) and Cutht. Jones of the drafted Militia to serve till the tenth of Decr. 1781. The Ballance of the men I have not been able to collect and I am apprehensive it will not be in my power to do, as most of them have left the Coty.

Archives of Maryland Vol. 47, p. 426.

August 23, 1781

Joseph Ford to Gov. Lee

...received letter...of the 14th. Inst. Informing me that Mr. Mills was furnished 50 ₤....he informs me he never Received it...Mr. Campbell will Receive and forward it to me....(wants) Instructions what is to be done with the Corn and Wheat...purchased in...last eight months past, it is much exposed to loss by Rats... there is not a Mill...in the County fitting to Manufacture it into flour. Mr. Ford's will do with some repairs...but...not till late in the fall.

Archives of Maryland Vol. 47, p. 441, 442.

August 25, 1781

Council to Capt. Joseph Ford.

Yours of the 23d Augt. is received; from the Multiplicity (of business) before the Board the money mentioned in ours of the 14th was omitted to be sent, we now send it; Mr. Calhoun, the Commissary for this Shore will give you Directions respecting the Wheat and Corn...

Archives of Maryland Vol. 45, p. 582.

August 28, 1781

John Mills to Honourable The Governor & Council

I being a draught of this county, obtained leave of Gen'l. Smallwood to return home to try to get a Substitute but have not yet met one. I shall return to Annapolis as soon as I get well of boils...which occasions me to overstay my Furlough...am ready to take the Horses with me if your Honours think proper to Give an Order to Mr. Bond ...I offered to bring the Horses when I brought The Drafts but (Richard) Bond would not deliver them at the Request of Captn. Ford, without your order...if...give me an order for the Horses I can bring them at very little Expence...(has recommendations from Col. Barnes and Capt. Joseph Ford)...Enemys Vessels left the River Patuxent on Sunday last with three crafts they Took some...was loaded with Tobacco.

Archives of Maryland Vol. 47, p. 452.

August 30, 1781

Richd. Barnes, Leod. Town to Gov. Lee

This will be delivered you by Mr. Wm. Belwood an Officer in the Militia who

with a party of Men have retaken a Vessel from the Enemy with two white men on board and a Negroe Boy of Mr. John Henry's that say he was takin a few days before by the Enemy. I have sent them to you by Mr. Belwood who is impowered to dispose of the Vessel for the benefit of the men that took her agreeable to Law for which purpose I shall be obliged to you to advise him the proper steps to be takin.
Archives of Maryland Vol. 47, p. 459.

Council to Colo. Richard Barnes
A Detachment from the main Army is expected at the Head of Elk, on the 8th of next month on their way to Virginia and it will be necessary to have there all the Vessels that can be procured ready to receive them. We have directed Impress Warrants to all the Counties where there is any Probability of obtaining Vessels and have enclosed one to St. Mary's which we shall be obliged to you to direct the Person in your County who you think the most proper for the Business.

Council Circular to the Commissaries of the several Counties
A Detachment from the Main Army with the French Troops to the number of 7000 will be at the Head of Elk in eight days....to act against Lord Cornwallis. Gen'l. Washington....(needs) immediate and large supply of flesh Provisions....Purchase Beef Cattle...where most exposed...to the Enemy...seize them if necessary...also purchase Bacon, barrelled Pork and Beef, seize if necessary...number of cattle in St. Mary's (wanted) 200....
Archives of Maryland Vol. 45, p. 589, 590.

August – 1781
Petition of Michael Spalding of St. Mary's County To his Excellency Thomas Sim Lee Esqr. and the Honourable Gentlemen of the Council
Has only one Horse that is of any use for family service as going to the mill, Church, &c; was taken for use of the States; understands it was not intent of the Law to distress those who was unable to find a Horse which is his case; has gotten several Creditable Neighbours to attest to truth; signed by Zacha Forrest, John Smith 1st, John Smith, Jr.
I hereby certify that it is my knowledge many in this County can much better spare a Horse than Michael Spalding.
Jno. Reeder
Archives of Maryland Vol. 47, p. 463.

September 1, 1781
Richd. Barnes, Leod. Town to Gov. Lee
Has sent one of the Men you directed to Col. R. H. Lee; has given further directions to have the other two apprehended and to fire on them if necessary.
Archives of Maryland Vol. 47, p. 468.

September 3, 1781
John Taylor of St. Mary's County is permitted to move wife and belongings to Montgomery County.
Archives of Maryland Vol. 45, p. 598.

September 5, 1781
Council Circular to the Commissaries of the Several Counties
French Fleet of 28 Ships of the Line and 4 Frigates came into the Bay on Aug. 26th and landed 3000 Troops in Virginia; Relying on your Patriotism, Zeal and Activity, we trust you will do every Thing in your Power to procure the Cattle; not a moment to be lost; can call on the Lieut. of the County for help if necessary who will order out the Light Horse Militia to aid you money sent to St. Mary's County 500 Ł.
Archives of Maryland Vol. 45, p. 603, 605.

September 6, 1781
   Council ordered Treasurer pay to...William Kilgour 36 Ł.17s.8d. specie...
   Archives of Maryland Vol. 45, p. 604.

September 7, 1781
   Council ordered Treasurer pay to...Joseph Ford, Esqr. Commissary of St.
Mary's County 500 Ł....
   Archives of Maryland Vol. 45, p. 608.

September 8, 1781
   Capt. Wm. Belwood captured a sloop that had been taken by a British Galley,
the Revenge...
   Archives of Maryland Vol. 47, p. 481.

September 9, 1781
   Benjamin Ford, Pvt. enlisted in the 5th Reg. Md. Line for 3 years.
   Archives of Maryland Vol. 18, p. 402.

September 10, 1781
   Richd. Barnes, Leod. Town to Gov. Lee
   Appointed Robert Armstrong to be stationed at Point Lookout; saw two Ships and
a Brig above Smith Point; sent his Messenger, John Lee to report who is to be paid 10s.
hard money; if French Fleet in Bay may be unnecessary to keep man at Point Lookout;
appoint Hugh Hopewell to send all the Vessels that can be got to the head of Elk,

   Hugh Hopewell, St. Mary's Co. to Gov. Lee
   Agreeable to a Letter delivered to me by Col. Richard Barnes from you, I have
impressed 2 Sloops and a Schooner; the Sloops are about 35 Tons Burthen, the Schooner
12, the Sloops I expect is at the Head of Elk before this, the Schooner sets off today..
..needed repaires.
   Archives of Maryland Vol. 47, p. 483, 484.

September 17, 1781
   Permission given to Colo. Uriah Forrest to Load two Vessels with Flesh Pro-
visions &c for the French Fleet in Chesapeake Bay.
   Archives of Maryland Vol. 45, p. 614.

September 18, 1781
   Council ordered Treasurer pay to Colo. Uriah Forrest 800 Ł....of the money
appropriated for the present campaign to be delivered over to Joseph Ford, Commissary
of St. Mary's County on Acct.
   Archives of Maryland Vol. 45, p. 617.

September 21, 1781
   Council order Treasurer pay to Colo. Uriah Forrest 65 Ł.... in part of his Salary
as Commissioner and pay to John Shanks 1 Ł.1s.9d. due per Account.
   Archives of Maryland Vol. 45, p. 621.

September 24, 1781
   Richard Bond, St. Mary's County to the Governor and Council
Cant keep the State Horses any longer; if they are to remain in this County, Col. Barnes
will undertake the care of them.
   Archives of Maryland Vol. 47, p. 501.

September 27, 1781
   Deposition of John Mills
   ....made oath that he Entered himself in the Select Militia in St. Mary's
County before the Draught...and that he hath Considered himself bound as one of the
Select Militia...
   Archives of Maryland Vol. 47, p. 508.

September 28, 1781
        Council ordered John Mills discharged as not being liable to be Draughted.
        Archives of Maryland Vol. 45, p. 628.

September 29, 1781
        Council Circular to The Collectors of Horses
        Send all Horses collected immediately to this place (Annapolis) and give particular directions to have the Horses well taken Care of on the Road.
        Archives of Maryland Vol. 45, p. 629.

October 17, 1781
        John Chiverall (Chivel) received Ł. 21 as an exchanged prisoner from Charles Town, S. C.
        Archives of Maryland Vol. 18, p. 617.

October 18, 1781
        William Smallwood to Gov. Lee
        Doctor Murray has recommended the persons mentioned below as proper objects for Discharges...not fit for duty...
        St. Mary's County Nicholas Goldsborough
                       Solomon Dixon
                       Zachariah Newton
        Archives of Maryland Vol. 45, p. 646; Vol. 47, p. 526.

October 20, 1781
        Joseph Ford, St. Mary's County to Gov. Lee
        Sending returns by Edward Fenwick; has purchased 353 Head of Beef cattle; 153 sent to Georgetown; about 60 to be collected and branded; not possible to make up 500 without distressing the People; shall make up 400 without much seizure but if the whole it must be done by Violence; account follows:
        400 Beeve each including the 5th qr. 435 4d. is Ł. 2900
            expences collecting & driving to Georgetown   300
                                                 3200
        Cash Recd. by Post & Col. Forrest   13 00
                     Bal   L. 1900
        Archives of Maryland Vol. 47, p. 529.

October 22, 1781
        Council ordered Treasurer pay to Edward Fenwick 1300 Ł. ...to be delivered over to Joseph Ford Commissary of St. Mary's County to be by him expended in the purchase of Provisions for the Army on Account.

        Council to Joseph Ford, Esqr.
        We have yours of the 20th Instant and have sent you by Mr. Fenwick 1300 Ł. to pay for the Cattle which with 600 Ł. sent by Charles Lansdale, make the sum you request. You will not for the present collect more than 400 Beef Cattle in the whole which you will continue to forward to George Town. We have this Day received certain Information of the Capture of Lord Cornwallis and his whole Army.
        Archives of Maryland Vol. 45, p. 647, 649.

October 23, 1781
        Council ordered Treasurer pay to William Cartwright 6Ł.5s.6d. specie agreeable to the Act to adjust Debts....
        Archives of Maryland Vol. 45, p. 650.

October 25, 1781
        Council ordered Treasurer...deliver to John Chiverall (Chival) 2 Ł.10s.....
and...Commissary of Stores...one Blanket....
        Archives of Maryland Vol. 45, p. 652, 653.

108

October 29, 1781
Council ordered Treasurer pay to Patrick Carbery 4 £.5s.11d.... of the money approd. for the Defence of the State per Acct...
Archives of Maryland Vol. 45, p. 655.

October 30, 1781
The following Draughts and Substitutes to serve till the 10th of December next being represented unfit for service for which they were intended are hereby Discharged. St. Mary's County, Ignatius Griffin, Henry Norris and Joseph Reswick.
Archives of Maryland Vol. 45, p. 656.

October - 1781
Ignatius Fenwick, Henry Spalding, and Barnett W. Barber jurors in Annapolis at the General Court, with others complain that inhabitants of the town refuse to take any money except Gold or Silver and they have only "Red" money.
Archives of Maryland Vol. 45, p. 676.

November 5, 1781
Council Circular to the Commissaries of St. Mary's and other Counties
We request you to forward all the Cattle now in your Possession or that maybe collected to Frederick Town...
Archives of Maryland Vol. 45, p. 662.

November 10, 1781
Council ordered Treasurer pay to the Honble George Plater, Esqr. 77 £.15s.4d. ....to be delivered over to Joseph Ford Commissary of St. Mary's County on Acct.
Also pay to Colo. Forrest 4 £.4s.9d.....for the use of William Kilgore per Acct.
Archives of Maryland Vol. 45, p. 664.

November 18, 1781
Joseph Ford to Gov. Lee
His returns have been delayed because of problems Collecting the Cattle and Mrs. Ford being dangerously ill; will send last drove of Cattle to Frederick on Tuesday next about 150 in number; with those delivered at George Town makes the 400; has on hand 1200 Bushels of Wheat; trying to get a Craft to carry to Baltimore.
Archives of Maryland Vol. 47, p. 552.

November 24, 1781
Council ordered Treasurer pay to....John Egerton 1 £.11s.8d. and 15s. to John Dunbar due them per account passed...
Archives of Maryland Vol. 48, p. 2.

Council order Treasurer pay to William Bailey (Bayley) Esqr. 2 £.6s.8d. ....1 £.11s.8d. to be delivered over to John Egerton and 15s. to John Dunbar due them per Account.
Archives of Maryland Vol. 48, p. 2.

November 26, 1781
Hanson Briscoe, Chaptico, to Gov. Lee
Has been informed that the Wheat Collected in this County for Taxes would be Exchanged for "Flower" in Baltimore; offers to take the whole in this County at the Current Cash Price and give Flower in Exchange at the Baltimore Price; if such an order is acceptable will be much obliged to the Governor to make an application; if they choose rather to Transport to Baltimore or George Town has Vessels and would undertake at the Accustomed Freights.
Archives of Maryland Vol. 47, p. 557.

Council ordered Treasurer pay to John Allen Thomas, Esqr. 10 £.11s.4d.....

to be delivered over to John Llewellen per acct.
        Archives of Maryland Vol. 48, p. 4.

November 27, 1781
        Council ordered Treasurer pay to Nicholas Lewis Sewall 68 ₤.15s.8d. specie...
to adjust the Debts due from the State per Account of Philip Knight.
        Archives of Maryland Vol. 48, p. 5.

November 29, 1781
        Council ordered Treasurer pay to Edmund Plowden Esqr. 28 ₤.1s.11d...
Cuthbert Jones and Charles Taney from St. Mary's Substitutes to serve 'till
the 10th December next are hereby Discharged.
        Archives of Maryland Vol. 48, p. 6.

December 1, 1781
        Council to Jas. Calhoun
        Mr. Hanson Briscoe, St. Mary's County, has Vessels and will engage to trans-
port all the Wheat in that County, and perhpaps in the neighboring ones.
        Archives of Maryland Vol. 48, p. 9.

December 3, 1781
        The following Draughts and Substitues (St. Mary's County) to serve 'till the
10th of December are hereby Discharged:

Jeremiah Herbert	John King	Jeremiah Hazel
John Maddox	Arnold Norris	Henry Briscoe
Charles Cole	Stratton Edwards	Ignatius Bryan
Nathaniel Kahill	Bennet Anderson	

        Council to Richard Barnes, Esqr. Lieut. St. Mary's
        We are informed that a certain Jacob Hayward is now in St. Mary's County, at
or near the Dwelling of Mr. Briscoe, Naval Officer on Patuxent River. He is charged
with treasonable Practices against the State; we therefore hereby direct and empower
you to make diligent Search for and apprehend the said Jacob Hayward and send him to
this City under a sufficient Militia Guard.
        Archives of Maryland Vol. 48, p. 10, 11.

        The following Draughts and Substitutes to serve 'till the 10th of Decr. Instant
are hereby Discharged -
                        St. Mary's County

Thomas Wise	John Greenwell	Ignatius Paine
Barney Paine	Edward Hazel	John Norris
Elisha Burroughs	Peter Jarboe	Charles Gough
Baptist Gough	William Pike	Joseph Kelly
William Killpatrick	Joseph Wimsatt	

        Archives of Maryland Vol. 48, p. 11.

December 7, 1781
        Petition of Robert Gilchrist of Caroline County
        Wishes as "a native of Britain" to remove to Great Britain or the Island of
Jamaica.
        Recommended by Geo. Plater, J. A. Thomas and Uriah Forrest.
        Archives of Maryland Vol. 47, p. 565-566.

December 11, 1781
        Council ordered Treasurer pay to Capt. Joseph Ford 230 ₤.5s.4d.....due him..
..also pay him 17 ₤.16s.7d specie to adjust the Debts due from this State and,22061
pounds of Tobacco due him per Acct....
        Archives of Maryland Vol. 48, p. 18.

December 14, 1781

Council ordered Commissary of Stores deliver....John Shanks, soldier in the Maryland Line a suit of Cloaths, 2 shirts, 1 pair Stockings and one pair Shoes on Account.

Archives of Maryland Vol. 48, p. 22.

December 15, 1781

Council ordered Treasurer pay to Col. Uriah Forrest late a Comm. for the pre-servation and sale of Confiscated British property 302 Ł....

Archives of Maryland Vol. 48, p. 25.

December 20, 1781

Council to Majr. Ignatius Taylor

Your letter of the 20th Novr. we have received...endeavour to get the Vessel and have her with her sails, Rigging....secured....and appoint a person to ascertain the Damage...If the Vessel cannot be got off without incurring a greater Expence than she will sell for it is advisable to dispose of her as she lies for Tobacco or Specie. It will be proper for you to send the Military Stores to Annapolis with the Flour. When you furnish on Account of the Expence that may attend this Business, it shall be paid.

Archives of Maryland Vol. 48, p. 30.

December 21, 1781

Council ordered Treasurer deliver to Athanasius Thompson & Elias Henry late in the Maryland Line, each, one suit of Cloaths, one hat, one shirt, two pr. Stockings & one Blanket & one pair Shoes to Sergt. Henry, Part of the Clothing due them.

Archives of Maryland Vol. 48, p. 31.

----1781 (?)

St. Mary's County Property Destroyed by the British

Lists property destroyed by the enemy with valuations, the owners are:

Rebecca Adderton	Edward Fenwick	Benedict Moore
John Armstrong	George Gough	Ignatius Moore
Robert Armstrong	Bennett Henny	Nicholas Moore
Joseph Arters	Caleb Henny	Peter Morrise
Joseph Bennett	Barbary Herbert	Albert Rhodes
Belwood & Holton	Mary Herbert	James Ritchie
Ignatius Biscoe	Wm. Herbert	Geo. Robertson
Herbert Blakiston	George Hopewell	H. Lewis Sewall
George Brewer	Matthew Jones	Nicholas Sewall
William Carpenter	James Jordan	Bartholomew Smith
Charles Chilton	William Leigh	John Smith
✓ John H. Clarke	William Lilburn	Bennett Tarlton
Francis Drury	Thomas Loker	William Taylor
John Drury, Jr.	John Marshall	Sarah Watts
John Drury, Sr.	Austin Milburn	George Wiseman
Mary Egerton	Joseph Milburn	Ignatius Wooten
Philip Evans		

Calendar of Maryland State Papers No. 5, p. 142 (Item 1047).

Losses sustained by "inhabitants of this State"

Richard Watts makes a return from St. Mary's County of losses by Capt. George Cook and Jonathan Hudson.

Calendar of Maryland State Papers No. 5, p. 142 (Item 1048).

An Alphabetical List of discharged Soldiers of the two Battalions of Militia (by counties) raised to serve in the Continental Army in the year 1781.

St. Mary's County

John Adams	Baptist Gough	Edward Monarch
Moses Adams	Charles Gough	Zachariah Newton
Wm. Adams	John Greenwell	Arnold Norris
Bennett Anderson	Azariah Gatton	Henry Norris
Ignatius Adams	Edward Hazle	John Norris
Henry Briscoe	Jere Herbert	John Norris
Ignatius Bryan	Ignatius Howard	Ignatius Payne
Elisha Burris (Burroughs)	Peter Jarboe	Barney Payne
Joseph Brown	Robert Jarboe	William Pratt
Moses Black	Cuthbert Jones	Joseph Risswick
Wm. Card (Chard)	Nathaniel Kahill	John Sute
Charles Cole	Wm. Kirkpatrick	Charles Taney
Thomas Curtis	Ignatius Mattingley	Thomas Wise
Solomon Dixon	John Maddox	Joseph Wimsett
Stratton Edwards		

Archives of Maryland Vol. 18, p. 406-413.

Joshua Bennett was a soldier in the Continental Army in 1781.
Archives of Maryland Vol. 18, p. 406.

January 1, 1782

Ignatius Adams, Pvt. enlisted in 1st. Battn. 2nd. Co. Md. Line.
Archives of Maryland Vol. 18, p. 432.

John Blair, Pvt. enlisted in 1st. Battn. 5th. Co. Md. Line was invalided 6/10/1782.
Archives of Maryland Vol. 18, p. 438, 526, 632.

Josias Alvey, Pvt. enlisted in 2nd. Battn. 2nd. Co. Md. Line   was discharged 5/24/1782.
John Alvey, Pvt. enlisted in 2nd. Battn. 3rd. Co. Md. Line
Travis Alvey, Pvt. enlisted in 1st. Battn, 4th Co. Md. Line
Archives of Maryland Vol. 18, p. 444.

John Brewer, Pvt. enlisted in 2nd. Battn. 4th Co. Md. Line and died 7/7/1782.
Archives of Maryland Vol. 18, p. 446, 525.

John Shanks, Pvt. enlisted in the 4th Battn. 3rd. Co. Md. Line and was invalided 11/15/1783.
Archives of Maryland Vol. 18, p. 461, 506, 555.

Cuthbert Abell, Sergt. in 1st. Battn. 5th. Co. Md. Line, Capt. Lloyd Beall's Co., was discharged 2/1/1783.
Archives of Maryland Vol. 18, p. 507, 523.

January 9, 1782

Council to Joseph Ford, Esqr.
We have yours of the 5th Instant and have sent you by Mr. (Jeremiah) Tarlton Ł. 100 of the last Emission to enable you to procure the Salt you may want. The account you enclosed should be settled, in the first Instant by the Auditor.
Archives of Maryland Vo. 48, p. 41.

January 17, 1782

Commissions issued by the Council of Maryland to:

Jeremiah Jordon	Vernon Hebb	Ignatius Taylor
Hanson Briscoe	John Shanks	John Ireland
Ignatius Fenwick	Robert Watts	Robert Armstorng
Thomas Bond	William Killgore	John Mackall
John De Butts		

Justices of the Peace for St. Mary's County
Ignatius Taylor   Ignatius Fenwick   Thomas Bond
William Killgore   John De Butts
   Judges of the Orphans Court for said County.
   Archives of Maryland Vol. 48, p. 44, 45.

January 19, 1782
   Council ordered Treasurer pay to Colo. Uriah Forrest 3 Ł.18s.5d... for the use
of Capt. Samuel Jenifer and also 26 Ł.0s.10d. for said Jenifer & his Comy of Militia.
   Archives of Maryland Vol. 48, p. 49, 50.

   Council ordered Treasurer pay to....Edmund Plowden 347 Ł.19s.5d. per certificates and Account passed...
   Archives of Maryland Vol. 48, p. 49.

January 23, 1782
   Council ordered Treasurer pay to Edmund Plowden 28 Ł.7s....due him
   Archives of Maryland Vol. 48, p. 53.

January 28, 1782
   Council ordered John Crisall, Issuing Commissary receive of Capt. (Wm.)
Bellwood a Load of Flour and have it stored.
   Also ordered Treasurer pay to Capt. Bellwood, 24 L.5s. per Account passed.
   Archives of Maryland Vol. 48, p. 57, 60.

   Council ordered Treasurer pay to Colo. Uriah Forrest 41 Ł. 6s.7d. ... to be
delivered over to Capt. John Mackall for the use of his Company of Militia...
   Also pay to Colo. Uriah Forrest 138 Ł.5s.9d. of the Emission, 68 Ł.18s.
thereof to be by him retained and 69 Ł.7s.9d to be delivered over to James Wilkinson
Esqr. due them per Certs. settled by the A. Gl.
   Also pay to Colo. Uriah Forrest 115 Ł.17s.6d...due him for half pay and also
the further sum of 19 Ł.2s.3d. due him p. Acct....also pay him 11200 pounds of
Tobacco including four per Cent due him for two hhds of Clarret for the Hospital De-
partment.
   Archives of Maryland Vol. 48, p. 58.

January 29, 1782
   Council ordered Treasurer pay to Robert Jarboe .7 Ł.4s.2d. per account passed.
   Archives of Maryland Vol. 48, p. 60.

January 31, 1782
   Council order Treasurer pay to Majr. John Davidson 107 Ł.7s.5d...to adjust
the Debts &c. and 1 Ł.10s. specie for 1 Cord Wood purchd. for the soldiers.
   Archives of Maryland Vol. 48, p. 64.

February 1, 1782
   Council ordered Treasurer pay to...Colo. Uriah Forrest 81 Ł.9s.2 1/2d. specie.
Balance on last year's Salary per acct...
   Archives of Maryland Vol. 48, p. 65.

February 4, 1782
   Council ordered Treasurer pay to Major John Davidson 21 Ł.14s...due on acct..
   Archives of Maryland Vol. 48, p. 66.

February 19, 1782
   Council ordered Treasurer pay to...Joseph Ford 79 Ł.4s....and also 53 Ł.10s.
8d. due on a Certificate for a Horse...
   Archives of Maryland Vol. 48, p. 81.

113

February 23, 1782
    Council ordered Treasurer pay to....Joseph Ford 284 Ł.15s.5d...due him...
    Archives of Maryland Vol. 48, p. 85.

    Council ordered Treasurer pay 97 Ł.1s.8d. to Capt. John Mills for use of him-
self & Company of Militia, 53 Ł.1s.10d. to William Spink for himself & Compy.
1 Ł.5s.6d. to John Mackall and 15 Ł.5s. to Henry Medley per Acct...
    Archives of Maryland Vol. 48, p. 85.

February 26, 27, 1782
    Council to Major John Davidson
    Information having been given to this Board, by Gen'l. Smallwood that several
soldiers of this State in the Continental Service have deserted...and (believes) they
are secreted on...the Ship Matilda, lying off the Harbour....you are authorized to
examine and search said Vessel, and if you find (them) bring them on Shore and give
this Board Information thereof....
    Treasurer pay to Henry Miles 159 Ł.16s.6d. to be delivered to sundry persons
for salt manufactured...
    Archives of Maryland Vol. 48, p. 87.

March 5, 1782
    Council ordered that the Issuing Commissary deliver to William Slye, a Soldier
in the Maryland Line who was wounded at Camden one months rations.
    Treasurer pay to Capt. John Mills 434 Ł.17s.5d. due on Certs. issued...
    Archives of Maryland Vol. 48, p. 92.

March 6, 1782
    Council to the Inspectors of Nanjemoy, Chandlers & Chaptico Warehouses
    Deliver to Maurice Simmons, Esqr...to be shipped (by) Flag of Truce for
Charlestown the Tobacco in your warehouse... (for) Maryland Officers while
prisoners in Charlestown....
    Archives of Maryland Vol. 48, p. 94.

March 7, 1782
    Council ordered Treasurer pay to Elisha Burroughs (Burris) & Thomas Wise each
10 Ł.13s.4d. and Cuthbert Jones 10 Ł.3s.4d.
    Archives of Maryland Vol. 48, p. 94.

March 12, 1782
    Council ordered Treasurer pay to John Blair 10 Ł.5s.6d., Stratton (Stourton)
Edwards 10 Ł.10s., William Wilkinson 7 Ł. 1s.6d....John Shanks 1 Ł.15s. due them
per Accounts passed.
    Archives of Maryland Vol. 48, p. 96.

March 13, 1782
    Council ordered Treasurer pay to Henry Briscoe 12 Ł.3s.4d. Ignatius Mattingly
9 Ł.8s.4d. Zachariah Newton 6 Ł.13s.4d. Jeremiah Herbert 10 s. Joshua Bennett
14 Ł. 16s.8d and David Meddiss 12 Ł.6s.8d...due them p. Acct.
    Council to Messrs. Thomas Bond, Wm. Kilgour & John De Butts
    We are favoured with yours of the 12th Utl. and regret that our late Arrangement
of the Orphans Court in St. Mary's has been the Source of so much Uneasiness. In
Justice however to your representatives it is incumbent on us to assure you that they
did not interfere farther than recommend who should fill up the Vacancies. Our only
reason for naming first on the List, the two new Appointments was because they were
senior Magistrates in the County Courts. We have adopted the same Rule in other
Counties....Should it be inconsistent with your Feelings to continue...we shall
lament the Loss to the Court...but we cannot...make any Alteration.
    Archives of Maryland Vol. 48, p. 98, 100.

March 15, 1782

   Council ordered Treasurer pay to ... Ignatius Fenwick 26 £.13s.11d. Jeremiah Hazel 8 £.1s.8d Edward Hazel 8 £.1s.8d. Joseph Brown 10 £.8s.4d. Peter Jarboe and Barney Payne each 10 £.5s. Robert Jarboe 11 £.1s.8d. William Pike 10 L.1s.8d. Charles Gough 11 £.13s. 4d. Baptist Gough 10 £.6s.8d. Dennis Flannigan 2 L.5s.2d...due them per Accounts passed.

   Council to Colo. Richard Barnes

   We are favored with yours of the 12th Inst. and are greatly obliged by the Information it contains. The first moment we had any certain Accounts of the Enemy's Depredations we took measures to put the Barges in Motion and we expected three of them would have been in Readiness by this Time to proceed against the Enemy but are disappointed; however we flatter ourselves that by Tuesday or Wednesday next we shall be able to afford effectual Security against the present Force in the Bay to all above the Mouth of Potowmack.

   Archives of Maryland Vol. 48, p. 101, 102, 103.

March 19, 1782

   Council ordered Treasurer pay to John Norris 10 £.10s., Ignatius Bryan 9 £.8s. 4d., Henry Norris 7 £.15s....Ignatius Howard 10 £... due them per Accounts passed.

   Archives of Maryland Vol. 48, p. 106.

   Council ordered Treasurer pay to Colo. Forrest 17 £.15s.4d. for use of Lieut. William Rapour (Rapier) & his Detachment of Militia, 6 £.13s.4d. for use of Lieut. John Reeder & his men...and also 24 £.15s.5d....due...Also pay Colo. Uriah Forrest 1219 £.11s.6d. specie...

   Council to the Count De Kergariou Loemaria, Commanding his mo. Chrn. Majys. Fleet in the Chesapeake

   Enemy committing depredations in the Bay and on the Shores as high up as Sharp's Island above the mouth of Patuxent and have made a number of captures; hope you can take effectual measures to strip this contemptible enemy of their plunder; the State has several Barges but are not in condition for use.

   Archives of Maryland Vol. 48, p. 106, 107.

March 20, 1782

   Council ordered Treasurer pay to Colo. Uriah Forrest 1219 £.11s.6d...due him..

   Archives of Maryland Vol. 48, p. 107.

March 21, 1782

   Council ordered Treasurer pay to....Moses Adams 9 £.8s.4d., John Sewall (Sule) and Wm. Adams each 9 £.18s.4d., Charles Taney 13 £.14s.2d., Edward Monarch 9 £.13s.4d....John Brewer 25 £.3s. ...

   Archives of Maryland Vol. 48, p. 108.

March 23, 1782

   Council ordered Treasurer pay to Ignatius Payne 10 £.10s. and Ignatius Adams 17 £.10s...

   Archives of Maryland Vol. 48, p. 109.

   Bartholmew Roach (Roche) Pvt. in the 5th. Reg. Md. Line

   Archives of Maryland Vol. 18, p. 422, 471.

March 23, 1782

   Ignatius Adams a Substitute from St. Mary's County to serve 'till the 10th December, having this Day applied for a Discharge is therefore Discharged.

   Archives of Maryland Vol. 48, p. 110.

March 28, 1782
          Council ordered Treasurer pay to...Solomon Dixon 6 Ł.13s.4d., John Coachman
10 Ł.5s. James Williams 104 Ł.19s.7d...
          Also pay...41 Ł. 13s.4d...for the use of Nicholas Thomas Esqr. for one months
Salary on Account.
          Archives of Maryland Vol. 48, p. 114.

April 2, 1782
          Council ordered Treasurer pay to Nathaniel Kahill a Draft from St. Mary's
County 9 Ł.15s...due him.
          Archives of Maryland Vol. 48, p. 119.

April 9, 1782
          Council ordered Treasurer pay to Athanasius Ford 27 Ł.7s....for the use of Capt.
Edward Mattingly and his Company per pay roll....
          Archives of Maryland Vol. 48, p. 127.

          Council ordered Treasurer pay to Thomas Curtis 11 Ł.3s.4d. due...
          Archives of Maryland Vol. 48, p. 127.

April 10, 1782
          Council ordered Treasurer pay to Wm Coombs 7 Ł.15s. due...
          Archives of Maryland Vol. 48, p. 128.

April 11, 1782
          Council ordered Treasurer pay to...Capt. Francis Millard 65 Ł.2s., 7 Ł.15s. to
William Coombs....19.2.6. to Capt. William Barton Smoot....
          Archives of Maryland Vol. 48, p. 128.

April 13, 1782
          Council ordered Treasurer pay to...Joseph Reswick 7 Ł.13s.4d... Arnold
Norris 19 Ł.18s.4d., Samuel Thompson and Robert Thompson 23 Ł. due them per
Accounts passed.
          Archives of Maryland Vol. 48, p. 129, 130.

May 1, 1782
          John Bond, Pvt. enlisted in the 2nd. Reg. Md. Line for the duration of the war.
          Archives of Maryland Vol. 18, p. 422.

May 2, 1782
          Council ordered Treasurer pay to Capt. John Horn Abell 168 Ł.14s.4d...2 Ł.5s.
for use of Solomon Jones, 3 Ł.15s. for Robert Armstrong and the residue for himself and
Company of Militia per Accounts...

          Council to General Smallwood
          Capt. Abell of St. Mary's has four British Prisoness in the Harbour, they be-
longed to the Barges in the Bay. We shall be much obliged to you to order a Guard
to take Charge of them. The Commissary of Issues (shall) deliver to Capt. Abell 16
rations, so many (as) furnished by him to four British Prisoners for four days.
          Archives of Maryland Vol. 48, p. 152, 153, 154.

May 3, 1782
          Council ordered Treasurer pay to Henry Sewall 16 Ł. 16s.9d. for the use of
Nicholas Sewall due him per Account passed.
          Archives of Maryland Vol. 48, p. 153.

May 6, 1782
          Council ordered Treasurer pay to William Somerville 549 Ł.10s.6d. specie

116

agreeable to the Act to adjust the debts due from this State per certificates adjusted.
Archives of Maryland Vol. 48, p. 155.

May 9, 1782
Council ordered Treasurer pay to John Allen Thomas 127 Ł.6s.9d...to be delivered over as follows, 21 Ł.17s.9d. to John Shanks...42 Ł.11s. to John Shank's Company of Militia and 62 Ł.18s. to Capt. Charles Jordan's Company of Militia p. pay rolls....
Archives of Maryland Vol. 48, p. 160.

May 10, 1782
Council ordered Treasurer pay to Colo. Uriah Forrest 23 Ł.2s.10d. for Capt. James Rapier dues his Company of Militia, 3 Ł. for John Somerville, 10 Ł.10s. for John King, 18 Ł.5s. for Joseph Ford and 18 Ł.17s.3d. for Robert Jarboe per Accounts.
Also pay to Colo. Ignatius Fenwick 202 Ł.6s. and 4 d. specie...due him....
Archives of Maryland Vol. 48, p. 162.

Council ordered Treasurer pay to...William Piercy 12 Ł. on June 12, 1782 he was paid 10 Ł. specie due him.
Archives of Maryland Vol. 48, p. 167.

May 17, 1782
Council ordered Treasurer pay to George Aisquith 12 Ł.6s.1d...11 Ł. 13s.1d. thereof to be delivered over to Thomas Keimer and the residue to Thomas Hall per Acct. Passed.
Archives of Maryland Vol. 48, p. 167.

May 23, 1782
Council ordered Treasurer pay to John Greenwell 34 Ł.5s.2d...for the use of Capt. Bennett Combs & Compy of Militia...
Archives of Maryland Vol. 48, p. 172.

May 25, 1782
Jeremiah Jordan, St. Mary's County to Richard Barnes, Annapolis
Advises by the bearer Lt. Roger Nelson that on the last alarm of the enemy being in the river he tried the public powder and found it weak; recommends applying for more powder if the enemy are expected to return.
Calendar of Maryland State Papers No. 4. Part 3, p. 189 (Item 1219).

May 28, 1782
Council ordered Treasurer pay to James Daffin 10 Ł.12s.6d. due him...
Archives of Maryland Vol. 48, p. 177.

June 10, 1782
Council ordered Treasurer pay to Edmund Plowden 20 Ł.5s...14 Ł.5s. thereof to be by him retained and the residue to be delivered over to William Hammersley due them per Accounts passed.
Also pay to Edmund Plowden for the use of William Hammersley 7536 pounds of Tobacco in St. Mary's County Warehouses for the like Quantity lent in 1780 per certificates adjusted and passed.
Archives of Maryland Vol. 48, p. 188.

June 12, 1782
Council ordered Treasurer pay to Joseph Shanks 38 Ł.15s.7d. Specie...due him.
Pay to Edmund Plowden Esq. 5882 pounds of Tobacco in St. Mary's County Warehouses for so much lent in 1780...
Pay to Joseph Ford 98 Ł.15s.7d... per Accounts passed. Also pay to Joseph Ford 759 bushels of Wheat to be delivered in St. Mary's County in lieu of 284 Ł.13s.6d. due him per Account passed.
Archives of Maryland Vol. 48, p. 189.

June 13, 1782
Council ordered Treasurer pay to...John Blair 8 Ł.18s.10d. specie...
Archives of Maryland Vol. 48, p. 190.

June 14, 1782
        Council ordered Treasurer pay to Jeremiah Jordan, Esqr. 97 Ł.2s.7d...due on Certificates settled and adjusted.

        Council to Abraham Skinner, Esqr. Commy. of Prisoners
        Requested to arrange for exchange of Josiah Biscoe and Thomas Griffin, captured off Capes of the Chesapeake.
        Archives of Maryland Vol. 48, p. 191, 192.

June 17, 1782
        Council ordered Treasurer pay to Colo. Forrest 41 Ł.11s....to be delivered over as follows: 12 Ł. to   Kenelm Bolt Watts, 8 Ł.4s. to Matthew Wise, 8 Ł.13s. to Thomas Dillon and 12 Ł. 14s. to John Abell, the Bounty allowed for making Salt per Accounts passed and pay Charles Cole 10 Ł.10s. due him and Philip Evans 118 Ł.6s.5d. due...Also pay Colo. Uriah Forrest $150.00...due him for half Pay from the 1st. January to 31 of May inclusive...
        Archives of Maryland Vol. 48, p. 193, 194.

June 18, 19, 1782
        Council ordered Treasurer pay to John Dunbar 3 Ł. also to Henry Jarboe 6 Ł. due them...
        Pay to John Smith 13 Ł., William Langley 6 Ł.6s., Thomas Biscoe 2 Ł.4s.... Bounty for making Salt...also to Isaac Simmons and Jesse Hebb each 10 Ł...for making Salt...
        Archives of Maryland Vol. 48, p. 194, 195.

June 22, 1782
        Council ordered Treasurer pay to John Fenwick 1 Ł.13s.4d. & Sarah Blake 1 Ł. 13s.6d...due them...
        Archives of Maryland Vol. 48, p. 198.

June 28, 1782
        Richard Fitzjeffrey paid bounty by the State for making salt.
        Archives of Maryland Vol. 48, p. 201.

June 29, 1782
        Council ordered Treasurer pay to Jesse Hebb 39 Ł... to be delivered over as follows: 20 Ł. to Senate Duvaul, 8 Ł. to Jeremiah Gibson, 5 Ł. to Joshua Gibson and 6 Ł. to Herbert Blackiston the Bounty allowed for manufacturing Salt p. Acct. passed.

        Council to Jeremiah Jordan, Esqr.
        We request you will be pleased to inform us what Gentlemen of your County have qualified as Magistrates under the last Commission and who have qualified on the Orphan's Court. We understand many People are suffering for Want of an Orphan's Court and we are therefore desirous of appointing other Gentlemen immediately in the Room of those who may not choose to qualify.
        Archives of Maryland Vol. 48, p. 203, 204.

July 3, 1782
        Council ordered Treasurer pay to Jesse Hebb 83 Ł.10s....to be delivered over as follows: 10 Ł. to George Guy, 12 Ł.8s. to Richard McKay, 4 L.10s. to John McLaland, 5 Ł.4s. to Joshua Redman, 5 Ł. to Thomas Hebb, 15 Ł. to Caleb Hebb, 24 Ł.8s. to Thomas Waughop, and 7 Ł. to George Cole, the Bounty allowed for Manufacturing Salt per Accounts passed.
        Archives of Maryland Vol. 48, p.205, 206.

July 8, 1782
        Council ordered Treasurer pay to Samuel Theobald 33 Ł.11s...11 Ł.6s. thereof to be by him retained and the residue to be delivered over as follows: 3 Ł.4s. to

John Hill, 3 £.3s. to Thomas Briscoe, 2 £. to Thomas Jones, 18s. to Joseph Milburn, 6 £.10s. to Basil Hopkins, 3 £.10s. to Richard Barnhouse and 3 £. to James Richardson the Bounty allowed for manufacturing Salt per Accounts passed.
> Archives of Maryland Vol. 48, p. 208.

July 9, 1782
> Council ordered Treasurer pay to Charles Cole 10 £. 10s. due...
> Archives of Maryland Vol. 48, p. 209.

July 10, 1782
> Council ordered Treasurer pay to Nicholas Sewall 33 £.7s.4d...25 £. 16s. to be by him retained for manufacturing Salt and the residue to be delivered over to Nicholas Levin Sewall due him....
> Also pay to Thomas Allen, 12 £.1s.9d., Bartholomew Roach 1 £. and George Clarke 5 £. due them per Accounts passed.
> Archives of Maryland Vol. 48, p. 209.

July 15, 1782
> Council ordered Treasurer pay to John Brewer 13 £.10s. of the Bills emitted under the Act for the Emission of Bills of Credit &c. to be delivered over as follows: 4 £. to John Goldsmith, 4 £. to John Blackiston, 3 £. to Thomas Howard, 2 £. to John Gardiner and 10s. to Thomas Gardiner the Bounty allowed for manufacturing Salt per Accounts passed.
> Archives of Maryland Vol. 48, p. 214.

July 18, 1782
> Council ordered Treasurer pay to Colo. Uriah Forrest 91 £. specie for the like sum paid to the Treasurer by him for Caution Money as appears by a Certificate.
> Archives of Maryland Vol. 48, p. 217.

July 24, 1782
> Council ordered Treasurer pay to Benjamin Williams 44 L.14s...to be delivered over as follows: 1 £.16s. to Richard Taylor, 1 £.10s. to Richard Thompson, 5 £.15s.6d. to Richard Fenwick, 5 £.16s. to Solomon Jones, 10 £. to Joseph Leigh, 2 £.5s. to Edmund Basey, 4 £.10s. to Vincent Kelly, 10 £. 17s. to John Fenwick and 2 £.4s.6d. to William Langley due them per Accounts passed.
> Archives of Maryland Vol. 48, p. 220, 221.

July 25, 1782
> Council ordered Treasurer pay to William Watts 16 £.10s...to be delivered over as follows, 3 £.10s. to Moses Flower, 6 £. to John McKay and 7 £. to William Barton Smoot due them per Accounts passed.
> Also the Treasurer pay to William Watts Surgeons Mate in the Maryland Line 60 L...in lieu of two suits of Cloaths and eight Shirts for the last & present years on Account.
> Archives of Maryland Vol. 48, p. 222.

July 27, 1782
> Commissions issued to Ignatius Taylor, Hanson Briscoe, John Shanks, John Ireland and Ignatius Fenwick appointed Judges of the Orphan's Court of St. Mary's County.
> Archives of Maryland Vol. 48, p. 223.

August 2, 1782
> Council ordered Treasurer pay to James Atwood 104 £.11s.6d... 6 £.10s. thereof to be by him retained and the residue to be delivered over as follows: 6 £.2s. to George Beane, 5 £.17s.6d. to William Beane, 1 £.12s. to Austin Massey, 4 £.10s. to Thomas Clarke, 10 £.3s. to William Loker, 8 £.7s.6d. to Moses Davis, 4 £.1s to Robert Beane, 7 £.8s.6d. to William Sanner, 6 £.17s. to Stephen Milburn, 1 L.15s. to

Jona. Evans, 4 Ł. to John Beane, Jr. 12s. to John Tallen, 5 Ł.10s. to Richard Milburn, 4 Ł.10s. to Jonathan Thorp, 5 Ł.4s. to Robert Daffin, 13 s. to Charles Atwood, 4 Ł.17s. to Henry Jarboe, Jr., 3 Ł.2s. to Thomas Sanner and 13 Ł.1s.6d. to William Leigh due them for Bounty on Salt per Accounts passed.
Archives of Maryland Vol. 48, p. 228, 229.

August 9, 1782
Council ordered Treasurer pay to Colo. Uriah Forrest 60 Ł. specie out of the money arising from the specie Tax due him on Certificate given him by Mr. Robert Bowie, one of the persons appointed agreeable to the "Act to furnish the Southern Army with twenty Dragoon Horses".
Archives of Maryland Vol. 48, p. 230.

August 20, 1782
Council ordered Treasurer pay to Athanasius Ford 66 Ł.3s.3d. specie...
to adjust the Debts due from this State....
Also pay him 25 Ł.6s.10d...per Accounts passed.
Archives of Maryland Vol. 48, p. 238.

September 2, 1782
Council ordered Treasurer pay to Benedict Spalding 8 Ł.14s., Richard Jarboe 6 Ł.12s. Isaac Clark, 3 Ł.12s. Francis Kirby 1 Ł.12s. Anthony Baxter 6 Ł., John Shadrick 12 Ł.12s., Thomas Gibbins 1 Ł.16s., John Miles Duvall & Robert Nugent 27 Ł.10s....
Archives of Maryland Vol. 48, p. 251.

September 13, 1782
Council ordered Treasurer pay to Charles Lansdale 19 Ł.16s...for the use of George Aisquith per Account passed.
Archives of Maryland Vol. 48, p. 262.

September 16, 1782
Council ordered Treasurer pay to Henry King 25 Ł.9s...2 Ł.14s. to be delivered over to Ignatius Moore and the residue 22 Ł.15s. to William Jenkins Hager.
Archives of Maryland Vol. 45, p. 254.

September 26, 1782
Council to Captn. Zedekiah Walley
There being some Cruzers of the Enemy in the Bay, which have done and may do considerable Injury, it is our Desire that you proceed immediately down the Bay with the Barges under your Command and do every Thing which Prudence will dictate to put a Stop to their Depredations and to protect the Citizens on the Shores and the Bay Trade.....
Archives of Maryland Vol. 48, p. 269.

September 28, 1782
John Swailes, Pvt. enlisted in the Northern Detachment, Capt. Horatio Clagett's Company and served to 11/15/1783.
Archives of Maryland Vol. 18, p. 427, 465, 501, 557.

October 16, 1782
Benjamin Morgan, George Howell Leigh and Patrick Carberry were presented and fined at a County Court held in St. Mary's County in November 1781 for suffering several people to game in their houses; after consideration by the Council were "discharged from the Fines" and dismissed on their paying the Legal Fees.
Archives of Maryland Vol. 48, p. 286.

Council ordered Treasurer pay to Nicholas Sewall 42 Ł.11s.2d. specie agreeable

to the "Act to adjust the Debts"....
> Archives of Maryland Vol. 48, p. 286.

October 17, 1782
> Commission issued to Samuel Abell, Jr., elected Sheriff of St. Mary's County.
> Archives of Maryland Vol. 48, p. 287.

December 4, 1782
> Daniel of St. Thomas Jenifer, Intendant's Office to Gov. Wm. Paca.
> Has contracted with Col. Uriah Forrest for 400 suits of soldiers' clothing, provided there is no objection to it; is to pay in tobacco; for 40 or 50 more suits he is to pay in money.
> Calendar of Maryland State Papers No. 4, Vol. 3, p. 197 (Item 269).

> Wm. Paca in Council to Honble, Intendant
> Presuming that the Barges will be kept in Service and that the Assembly will either supply the men with Cloathing or that the Men will gladly take those you have purchased in Part of their Pay, we have no objection to the Contract you have made with Colo. Forrest.
> On December 20, Wm. Paca wrote, "The barge Men and Soldiers are so distressed for Cloathing that...(we) direct the Bales purchased of Messrs. Forrest and Key be opened...
> Archives of Maryland Vol. 48, p. 313, 326, 340.

December 7, 1782
> Council ordered Treasuere pay to George Plater 91 Ł.2s.7d. specie agreeable to the Act to adjust the Debts due from this State per Certificate and Account passed.
> Archives of Maryland Vol. 48, p. 316.

December 18, 1782
> Council ordered Treasurer pay to Philip Ford 4 Ł.10s...
> Archives of Maryland Vol. 48, p. 324.

December 19, 1782
> Commissions issued by the Council of Maryland to:

Jeremiah Jordan	Vernon Hebb	Ignatius Taylor
Hanson Briscoe	John Shanks	John Ireland
Ignatius Fenwick	Robert Watts	Thomas Bond
William Killgore	John Mackall	John De Butts

> Justices of the Peace for St. Mary's County

Vernon Hebb	Hanson Briscoe	Ignatius Fenwick
Thomas Bond	John De Butts	

> Justices of the Orphan's Court of the said County.
> Archives of Maryland Vol. 48, p. 325.

December 26, 1782
> W. Paca, Governonr, in Council to Majr. John Davidson
> The Enemy's Barges being still in the Bay and Committing Depredations upon the Inhabitants on the Shores, we find it necessary to send down our Barges....as Barges are not completely manned, we must request the assistance of the Continental Soldiers...25 will be sufficient....we will engage to pay them...at the Rate of Ł. 3 pr. month (in addition to regular pay).
> Archives of Maryland Vol. 48, p. 328.

January 1, 1783
> John Alvey, Pvt. enlisted in the 7th Co. Md. Line and served until 11/15/1783.
> Traverse Alvey, Pvt. enlisted in the 4th Co. Md. Line, deserted (A.W.O.L.) 4/29/1783 but was pardoned and was discharged 11/15/1783.
> Archives of Maryland Vol. 18, p. 490, 494.

Major John Davidson retired from the 5th. Md. Reg.
Archives of Maryland Vol. 18, p. 481, 519.

Ignatius Adams, Pvt. enlisted in the 8th. Co. Md. Line 8/1/1780 and served until 11/15/1783.
Archives of Maryland Vol. 18, p. 522.

January 20, 1783
William Paca in Council to Honble. Intendant
Your letter of this day we have received and have no Objections to the Offer made you by Messrs. Forrest & Co. for 400 Hogsheads of Tobacco....
Archives of Maryland Vol. 48, p. 346.

January 21, 1783
Major John Davidson appointed Maryland State Intendant (Comptroller) by Gov. William Paca.
Calendar of Maryland State Papers Vol. 4., No. 1, p. 211 (Item 1224).

February 8, 1783
Nicholas Lewis Sewall, Mattapany to Richard Barnes, Leonardtown
Three Privateers, 2 Sloops and a Schooner from the British Fleet have captured a "Bay Craft" at Cedar Point; they came up the Patuxent; haste in moving property delayed this report.

Richard Barnes, Leonardtown to Gov. William Paca
Three British barges have been sighted near Young's Ferry; on way down the Potomac they landed on St. Georges Island; rumors of peace are afloat; enemy fleet is manned by an "abandoned Set of Men"; Negroes have been taken as well as other plunder; letter of Nicholas Lewis Sewall is enclosed.
Calendar of Maryland State Papers No. 4, Part 1, p. 211 (Items 1226, 1227).

February 19, 1783
Wm. Paca in Council to the Merchants of Baltimore Town.
You cannot be strangers to the Depredations daily committed by the Enemy in our Bay, Not content with interrupting our Trade, they are guilty of the most wanton Destruction of Property on the Shores...there is no Force belonging to Government able to oppose them....we solicit (you) to lend three Armed Sloops or Schooners of 8 or 10 Guns and upwards, completely manned and 150 Men over and above the Crews of these Vessels....to man three Barges belonging to the State....there are 13 Barges, one Sloop and two Schooners belonging to the Enemy now in the Bay....there are Vessels now in Patuxent doing great Damage....
(Total Maryland Fleet will be the Pole Cat, Ship?, a French Brig of 14 Guns, 3 Sloops or Schooners of 8 or 10 Guns each and 3 Barges).
Archives of Maryland Vol. 48, p. 360, 361, 364, 365.

February 21, 1783
Wm. Paca in Council to His Excellency General Washington
....On Thursday last, a Party under the Command of (Joseph) Whaland went up the Patuxent, plundered the Town of Benedict and burnt and destroyed the dwelling House and out Houses of Mr. Benjamin Mackall with his furniture, Tobacco and other moveable Property, Col. Plater was also plundered of some of his Negroes....
Archives of Maryland Vol. 48, p. 365, 366.

March 7, 1783
Wm. Paca in Council to Colo. Richard Barnes
Yours be the Post of the first Instant was just now handed us. It gives us great Concern to hear that the Enemy's Barges continue their Depredations. There can be no Doubt but what all Expences on Account of the Militia will be paid by the State: nothing can be more reasonable and our Endeavours to have them paid shall be

faithfully exerted. We have now some money in the Treasury and we have begun to enlist Men for the Barges but cannot say when we shall be able to equip them fit for Service. Altho' the French Commodore was so obliging as to promise us an armed Vessel, yet she is not come, possibly, as he informed us Repairs were wanting, that Circumstance may still detain her. The Post is not yet come in and therefore can say nothing of Intellignece from the Northward: we are still left in Suspence as to Peace or War.

> Archives of Maryland Vol. 48, p. 376.

February 26, 1783

John Goddard, Pvt. who re-enlisted in the 3rd. Reg. M.d. Line on 2/2/1780 was discharged.

> Archives of Maryland Vol. 18, p. 115, 430, 512, 536.

February 28, 1783

Commissions issued to Ignatius Taylor, Hanson Briscoe, John Shanks, John Ireland and Ignatius Fenwick, Justices of the Orphan's Court of St. Mary's County.

> Archives of Maryland Vol. 48, p. 371.

March 21, 1783

Council ordered Treasurer pay to Edmund Plowden 9 Ł.9s.3d. for one year's Interest on a Certificate for 150 Ł.13s.7d. issued agreeable to the "Act to adjust the Debts due from this State".

> Archives of Maryland Vol. 48, p. 387.

Council ordered Treasurer issue to Francis Plowden a Certificate agreeable to the "Act proposing to the Citizens of this State, Creditors of Congress on Loan Office Certs. &c" for 8 Ł.2s.2d. due him on a Continental Loan Office Certificate adjusted by the Aud. Genl.

> Archives of Maryland Vol. 48, p. 386, 387.

March 26, 1783

Council ordered Treasurer pay to John Blair 10 Ł.5s.6d. specie...per acct.

> Archives of Maryland Vol. 48, p. 390.

April 12, 1783

Council ordered Treasurer issue Certificates to Ignatius Craycroft for 266 Ł.13s. 2d. due him on Continental Loan Office Certificates....

> Archives of Maryland Vol. 48, p. 397.

April 22, 1783

Governor William Paca issues Proclamation - peace treaty signed with Great Britain on February 3, 1783, and proclaimed by the Congress April 11, 1783.

> Archives of Maryland Vol. 48, p. 398, 399, 400.

April 25, 1783

Wm. Paca in Council to the Sheriffs of the Several Counties

We beg Leave to congratulate the good People of St. Mary's County upon the Glorius Event of a General Cessation of Hostilities among the Powers at War, which their Virtuous exertions have so greatly contirbuted to bring about; and we desire you will announce it to them, on an appointed Day, by reading to them in the most public place, the enclosed Proclamation.

> Archives of Maryland Vol. 48, p. 401.

April 30, 1783

Council ordered Treasurer pay to Capt. Ignatius Fenwick 17,350 pounds of nett Tobacco at George Town and Bladensburg Warehouses due him for the like Quantity lent the State in November 1780 per Certificates adjusted by the Depy. Aud.

> Archives of Maryland Vol. 48, p. 405.

May 6, 1783
   Brice T. B. Worthington and Philip Key Esquires from the House of Delegates acquaint his Excellency, the Governor that there is a sufficient number of Members convened to compose a house....
   Archives of Maryland Vol. 48, p. 406.

May 10, 1783
   Council ordered Treasurer pay to Edward Abell 2 Ł.10s. specie agreeable to "Act to Adjust Debts"...
   Archives of Maryland Vol. 48, p. 418.

May 13, 1783
   Council ordered the Treasurer issue a Certificate to Richard Barnes, Esqr.... for 170 Ł.6s.11d. due him on Continental Loan Office Certificates....
   Archives of Maryland Vol. 48, p. 412.

   Council ordered Treasurer issue a Certificate to Robert Briscoe....for 119 Ł.... 8d. due on 14 Continental Loan Office Certificates...
   Archives of Maryland Vol. 48, p. 412.

May 16, 1783
   Ordered Treasurer to issue a Certificate to Zachariah Forrest for 120 Ł.7s... Also deliver to Francis Plowden 5865 pounds of nett Tobacco at Coles Creek Warehouse in St. Mary's County for the like Quantity lent the State by Henrietta Plowden July 1780. ...
   Archives of Maryland Vol. 48 , p. 414.

May 20, 1783
   Council ordered Treasurer pay to John Allen Thomas, Esqr. for the use of Nicholas Thomas, Esqr. 200 L. Current Money for 6 months Salary due him as one of the Judges of the Gen'l. Court to the 1st. Inst.
   Archives of Maryland Vol. 48, p. 417.

July 2, 1783
   Council ordered Treasurer issue Certificate...to Miss Willey Slye for 13 Ł.19s. 4d. due on Continental Loan Office Certificates....
   Archives of Maryland Vol. 48, p. 436.

July 4, 1783
   Council ordered Treasurer issue a Certificate to John Brewer Senr...for 27 Ł.4s. due him on Continental Loan Certificates....
   Archives of Maryland Vol. 48, p. 436.

September 7, 1783
   George Biscoe, Esqr. is mentioned as Naval Officer for the Patuxent.
   Archives of Maryland Vol. 48, p. 452.

September 19, 1783
   Council ordered Treasurer pay to Wm. Chiverall, Adm. of John Chiverall 52 Ł. 6s. current money due him per acct. passed.
   Archives of Maryland Vol. 48, p. 455.

October 9, 1783
   Council ordered Treasurer issue a Certificate to John Shanks....for 23 Ł.5s.8d. due on Continental Loan office Certificates...
   Archives of Maryland Vol. 48, p. 461.

October 16, 1783
Council ordered Treasurer issue a Certificate to Bladen Craycroft....for 36 Ł. 4s.3d....due on Continental Loan Office Certificates....
Archives of Maryland Vol. 48, p. 469.

October 30, 1783
Archibald Campbell, Balto. to Daniel St. Thomas Jenifer
Col. Uriah Forrest has not yet received sum due him from Philip Key and others; Campbell wishes a copy of this account.
Calendar of Maryland State Papers No. 4, Part 3, p. 206 (Item 1337).

November 8, 1783
Council ordered Treasurer pay to Edmund Plowden, Esqr., 11 Ł.11s.9d. current money for one year's interest on a Certificate issued under the "Act to adjust Debts due from this State"....
Archives of Maryland Vol. 48, p. 479.

Council ordered Treasurer issue Certificate...to Thomas Bolt (Boult) for 40 Ł. 17s.1d., Robert Armstrong for 37 Ł.18s.11d. and to John Armstrong for 35 Ł.10s. due on Continental Loan Office Certificates adjusted by the Auditor General....
Archives of Maryland Vol. 48, p. 479.

December 3, 1783
Council ordered Treasurer issue Certificate to William Somerville for 269 Ł.8s. 5d.3f.... due .
Archives of Maryland Vol. 48, p. 485.

December 19, 1783
Council ordered Treasurer pay to Philip Key 11 Ł.6s.1d. specie... also for 7 Ł. 11s.8d. due him on Continental Loan Office Certificates... and 282 Ł.5s.5d. specie. ...due on two Certs from Audrs. Office...
Archives of Maryland Vol. 48, p. 493, 494.

Council ordered Treasurer issue a Certificate to John Manley...for 35 Ł.8s.10d. due on Continental Loan Office Certificates adjusted by the Aud. Genl. the 11th November last.
Archives of Maryland Vol. 48, p. 494.

----- 1785
Beginning about 1785 there was a considerable migration of County people, particularly from the St. Inigoes area, to Kentucky. British depredations along the waterfront had ruined many of the Planters, their sons had been killed in battle, their unworked fields had grown up, many of their slaves and much of their stock gone and homes and farm buildings burned, many decided to try a new frontier. While several hundred families migrated to Kentucky from the Southern Counties over the years to 1810, a few families moved to Georgia and North Carolina, The population in St. Mary's County dropped from 8502 in 1790 to 8005 in 1810.
"The Centenary of Catholicity in Kentucky " by Ben J. Webb, "The Jesuit Missions of St. Mary's County" by Edwin W. Beitzell; McSherry's History of Maryland.

March 12, 1792
Thomas Tabbs, St. Mary's County to John Davidson, Annapolis.
Writes concerning the "poor man", John Morris of St. Mary's County, of the 3rd. Maryland Regminent, who was wounded "through the groin" while serving under General Daniel Morgan at Cowpens, S.C.; he has a wife and five children to support and his present condition is "truly deplorable"; he would be satisfied with half pay from the time of his discharge.
Calendar of Maryland State Papers No. 5, p. 148 (Items 1088-1091).

CHARLOTTE HALL SCHOOL

The central section was a replica of the
first school, which burned in 1896. The entire
building burned in 1927.

Courtesy of Robert E. T. Pogue.

This school was authorized and founded
by the General Assembly of Maryland for St.
Mary's, Charles and Prince George's Counties
on April 16, 1774. The first Trustees of St.
Mary's County were: George Plater, Esq., the
Reverend Mr. George Goundrill, John Reeder,
Thomas Bond, Richard Barnes, Philip Key and
Henry Greenfield Sothoron.

(Archives of Maryland Vol. 64, p. 377-379)

ALL FAITH CHURCH
1767   Near Charlotte Hall

BATCHELOR'S HOPE
c. 1668

MISCELLANEOUS DATA

Peter Ford, Pvt. served in the 2nd. Artillery of the Continental Troops 1781-1783.
From a study of the Ford Family by Mrs. Paul A. Jaccard,
U.S. National Archives, Pension Case #597.

George Clarke Somerville, Surgeon, of Mulberry Fields, served in the Revolution under Dr. Benjamin Rush, probably about 1781.
Chronicles of St. Mary's Vol. 5, No. 10.

John Greenwell, Pvt. served as a Minuteman in a Company of St. Mary's County Militia in April 1781 and from Aug. 2, 1781 in the 3rd. Reg. Md. Line until Dec. 3, 1781. He was at Yorktown at the surrender of Gen'l. Cornwallis. After the war, he moved to Kentucky, and there applied for a pension in 1831.
U.S. National Archives, Kentucky Pension No. 27640 and U.S. Pension No. S.31076.

Ignatius Greenwell, Pvt. served in the St. Mary's County Militia, Capt. John Greenwell's Company in 1776 and later in the same year was a member of Capt. John Allen Thomas' Company, the 5th. Independent Co. and was called out several times during the war and served altogether at least two years. After the war he moved to Missouri and there applied for a pension in 1831.
U.S. National Archives, Missouri Pension No. 19752 and U.S. Pension No. S.16836. The data on both John and Ignatius Greenwell is from a study of the Greenwell Family by Mr. Lewis H. Greenwell, Jr.

List of Men Blown Up in the Barges (undated).
While this list contains the names of only two St. Mary's County men, Joseph and William Sewall, both Charles E. Fenwick and the writer have seen another list that contained the additional names of Richard Fenwick, Enoch Medley, Richard Yates and Lt. Vachel Yates. The explosion occurred prior to April 6, 1778 for on that date the Will of Richard Fenwick was probated.
Archives of Maryland Vol. 18, p. 615, Wills, Liber JJ#1 f.54.

Since the Revolutionary War records of St. Mary's County were lost in the Court House fire of 1831 the following important records are excerpted from the "Chronicles of Colonial Maryland" by James Walter Thomas:
St. Mary's (County) was quick to respond to the suggestion to elect a "Committee of Safety and Correspondence" for the County and the following is the record of the meeting for that purpose, held December 23rd., 1774.
St. Mary's County
On public notice being given for the gentlemen, freeholders and others of the said County to meet at the Court House at Leonard-Town, on Friday, the twenty-third day of December last, met agreeable to said notification a considerable number of the most respectable inhabitants, when it being proposed that, for the more orderly and effectually carrying on the present business, it would be necessary to make a choice of a chairman, as also to appoint a clerk to officiate for the day. Mr. Jeremiah Jordan was thereupon unanimously elected to the chair and Timothy Bowes appointed clerk to the said meeting,
Mr. Jeremiah Jordan in the Chair
Mr. Timothy Bowes, Clerk
Several of the proceedings of the Continental Congress being read, as well as the late resolves of the provincial convention, which were unanimously approved of. The Chairman, addressing himself to those assembled, informed them that the intent and design of the present convention, among many other things, was principally to make choice of a general committee for the country - a committee of correspondence - as also a committee, to meet, if necessary, the provincial committee, to be held at

126

Annapolis on Monday, the 24th day of April next, in order to carry into execution the association agreed on by the Continental Congress, as well as the resolves of the late provincial convention upon which the following gentlemen were chosen as a _general committee_ for the County, to wit:

Major William Thomas
Mr. Wm. Hammersly
Mr. Gerard Bond
Mr. Wilfred Neale
Mr. Richard Bond
Mr. Athanasius Ford
Mr. John Barnes
Mr. William Williams
Mr. Vernon Hebb
Mr. George Guyther
Mr. John Mackall
Mr. William Taylor
Mr. James Adderton
Mr. Richard Clark ?
Mr. William Jenkins, Jr.
Mr. William Cavenaugh
Mr. Robert Watts
Mr. John Abell, younger
Mr. Edward Abell, Jr.
Mr. Thomas Forrest, Sr.
Mr. Enoch Fenwick
Mr. Thomas A. Reeder
Mr. William Bruce
Mr. Robert Hammett
Mr. Jeremiah Jordon
Mr. Samuel Abell, Sr.

Mr. Cornelius Barber
Mr. John Llewellin
Mr. John Shanks, Jr.
Mr. William Bond
Dr. John Ireland
Col. Abraham Barnes
Mr. Richard Barnes
Mr. John Fenwick
Mr. William Watts
Mr. Ignatius Combs
Mr. John Black
Mr. Maffey Leigh
Mr. Robert Armstrong
Mr. Edward Fenwick
Mr. Nicholas Sewall
Mr. Jenifer Taylor
Mr. Henry Carroll
Mr. Samuel Jenifer
Mr. Peter Urquhart
Mr. Ignatius Fenwick (Coles)
Mr. John Reeder, Jr.
Mr. Wm. Killgour
Mr. Henry Tubman
Mr. Herbert Blackiston
Mr. William Bayard
Mr. Samuel Abell, Jr.

Major Zachariah Bond
Mr. James Eden
Mr. John Eden
Mr. Meveril Lock
Mr. Cyrus Vowles
Dr. Henry Reeder
Mr. Timothy Bowes
Mr. John Greenwell
    of Ignatius
Mr. John McLean
Mr. John De Butts
Mr. George Cook
Mr. Bennet Biscoe
Mr. Thomas Griffin
Mr. Nicholas L. Sewall
Mr. Ignatius Taylor
Mr. Hugh Hopewell
Mr. John Abell, Sr.
Mr. John H. Read
    Mr. John Smith
    (Patuxent)
Mr. John H. Broome
Mr. Henry G. Sothoron
Mr. John A. Thomas
Mr. Joseph Williams
Mr. Hugh Hopewell, Jr.

A general committee for the county elected, the next step taken was making a choice of a committee of correspondence when the following gentlemen were chosen with power for any three or more of them to act as occasion should require to wit:

Col. Abraham Barnes
Mr. Athanasius Ford
Mr. Jeremiah Jordan

Mr. Richard Barnes
Dr. Henry Reeder
Mr. John A. Thomas

Timothy Bowes
Mr. John De Butts
Mr. John Black

This business completed, a committee was choosen (sic) to meet the provincial committee, to be held at Annapolis on Monday, the 24th of April next, if necessary, when the following gentlemen were elected for that purpose, to wit:

Mr. Jeremiah Jordan
Mr. John Barnes
Mr. Henry G. Sothoron

Mr. Richard Barnes
Mr. John A. Thomas

Mr. John Reeder, Jr.
Mr. John De Butts

Signed per
Timothy Bowes, Clerk
(from the Maryland Gazette, January 5, 1775).

....on the reorganization of the "Maryland Line" in 1794, in compliance with an Act of Congress, the following officers from St. Mary's County were elected. Brig. Genl. John Hanson Briscoe; Lieut. Cols. George Plater and Henry Neale; Majors William Thomas, John Armstrong, William Somerville and Francis Hamersly....

The members of the committee from St. Mary's County appointed by the General Assembly to draft the famous Resolutions declarative of the Constitutional rights and privileges of the people, and also, the instructions for the government from Maryland of the Stamp Act Congress of 1765, and which passed the "Remonstrance to Parliament", were the Hon. Edmund Key and the Hon. Daniel Wolstenholme.

In 1774, St. Mary's County raised by private subscription for the Maryland "Revolutionary Fund", the sum of £. 600 sterling, the fifth largest contribution made by any county in the State....

The representatives from St. Mary's, in the first General Assembly held after the Declaration of Independence and which formally established in 1777, the first State Government in Maryland were the Hons. William Thomas, James Jordan, Athanasius Ford, and John Hatton Read. The Senator was the Hon. George Plater. The election, the first in Maryland as a State, was held in Leonardtown on November 25th for Senate electors and on December 18th (1776) for members of the House of Delegates, the judges of election being Major Henry Tubman, Abraham Barnes and Hugh Hopewell. The representatives from St. Mary's in the convention which framed the first constitution of the State were, Hon. George Plater, Ignatius Fenwick, Richard Barnes and Jeremiah Jordan. The representatives in the Convention for the ratification of the Constitution of the United States and of which George Plater was president were the Hons. George Plater, Richard Barnes, Nicholas L. Sewall and Charles Chilton.

The first local officers for St. Mary's County under the State Government in 1777 were, County Lieut. Richard Barnes, Justices of the County Court, Jeremiah Jordan, John Reeder, Jr., Henry Greenfield Sothoron, Richard Barnes, Henry Reeder, Vernon Hebb, Igantius Taylor, Henry Tubman, Bennet Biscoe, John Shanks, John Hanson Briscoe, John Ireland, Ignatius Fenwick, Robert Watts, Nicholas L. Sewall and Robert Armstrong. The Judges of the Orphans Court were Henry Greenfield Sothoron, Richard Barnes, Henry Reeder, Vernon Hebb and John Reeder, Jr.; Sheriff, Jenifer Taylor; Clerk, Daniel Wolstenholme; Register of Wills, Jeremiah Jordon; Surveyor, Jesse Lock; Coroners, James Mills, Thomas Greenfield, Stephen Tarlton, John Attaway Clark and Mackelery Hammett...

Thomas also records that "the brig Mary and Tom from London, with tea, consigned to Robert Findlay and other" was turned away from the landing in St. Mary's River in August 1774.
Chronicles of Colonial Maryland, p. 278-285.

PENSIONERS 1818

     Josias Alvey, Md. Line
     George Dent, Md. Line
     Charles Goldsborough, Md. Line
     John Jordan, Md. Line
     Nicholas Milburn, Md. Line
     John McKay, Md. Line
     Henry Spalding, Md. Line
     Jonathan Woodburn, Md. Line

A Report of the Names, Rank and Line of Every Person Placed on Pension List.

PENSIONERS 1840

     George Dent, age 83
     Thomas Haywood, age 84

Census of Pensioners for Revolutionary and Military Services.

Burials of Revolutionary Patriots

John H. Abell
     St. George Episcopal Church, Poplar Hill. No stone but name appears in Church register, d. 2/8/1801.

Abraham Barnes)
Richard Barnes)
     In the yard at Tudor Hall, Leonardtown. "Tudor Hall...was...originally the home of the Barnes Family and on it may still be seen the ancient tombstones covering the graves of Major Abraham and Colonel Richard Barnes two of early Maryland's most distinguished sons. Near it is a grove of stately oaks, sentinels of the primeval forest, one of which, a majestic white oak, is said to measure 29 feet in circumference".
     Thomas, Chronicles of Colonial Maryland (1900) p. 318.
     Note: Both trees and tombstones have disappeared and the roadway that
           encircles Tudor Hall covers the small private cemetery in front of the
           house.

Timothy Bowes
     Old St. Aloysius Cemetery, North end of Leonardtown. No stone but the grave was pointed out to Charles E. Fenwick by Mr. Thad Yates.

*Dr. John Hanson Briscoe
     Christ Church Cemetery, Chaptico. A stone here reads "Sacred to the memory of John Briscoe, who died May 29, 1822, aged 81 years, emphatically it may be said that his life was a life of scrupulous integrity, rigid Justice and temperance with great moderation and self denial."

Sergt. John Hanson Briscoe
     Christ Church Cemetery Chaptico. No stone but it is likely that he is buried here. 2nd. Reg. Md. Line. The British raided here in the War of 1812 and damaged both Church and cemetery.

*John Carpenter
     Christ Church Cemetery, Chaptico. A stone here reads "In memory of John Carpenter who departed this life 25th. Feby. 1803, age 68.

George Dent
     St. Andrews Episcopal Church, near Leonardtown. A tombstone marks his grave. He also   served in the War of 1812.

Col. Ignatius Fenwick
     Buried in Newtown Cemetery. Stone with name but no dates.

*James Fenwick
     St. Inigoes Cemetery at St. Inigoes, Md. The stone reads "Here lies the body of James Fenwick, who died on the third day of Feb. 1806 in the 56th. year of his age. He was a worthy, candid, honest and generous and truly attached to the liberties of his country. His fore-fathers were among the first settlers of this ancient County and he left a numerous connection; for all of whom he felt like a Father. May his virtues be long revered and perpetuated among them."

*Richard Fenwick
     St. Inigoes Cemetery. The stone reads "Sacred to the memory of Richard Fenwick who departed this life April 10, 1799, aged 52 years."

*Vernon Hebb

Private cemetery at Porto Bello, Drayden. The stone reads, "Vernon Hebb, Son of William and Ann Hebb, Departed this Life Oct. 26 in the 60th (?) year of his age.

*Robert Jarboe

St. Nicholas Cemetery, Patuxent Naval Air Station. The stone, now buried, reads, "Sacred to the memory of Robert Jarboe, who died Mar. 21, 1803, Age 51 years, 2 months & 18 days."

*Philip Key

In the vault at Christ Church Cemetery, Chaptico. This vault was desecratated by the British during the War of 1812. No stone.

*Samuel Maddox

Probably buried at Christ Church Cemetery. His name appears on a stained glass window of the Church.

*John Mackall

Helen W. Ridgely recorded in 1908 that John Mackall, who died Aug. 18, 1813, aged 75 years lies buried in an unmarked grave "on the left hand side of the road leading from Trinity Church to St. Inigoes in what is known as the Grave yard Lot."

Thomas McWilliams

Private cemetery at his plantation, Broad Neck, in St. Clements Bay. Two very old stones but the inscriptions are worn off.

*Gov. George Plater

Thomas records in his Chronicles of Colonial Maryland in 1900, that "Gov. George Plater died at Annapolis Feb. 10, 1792. His remains, attended by the Council and State officials were taken next day by way of South River to Sotterley where he is buried in what is now an open field and without a simple slab to mark the last resting place of a son of Maryland whose statesmanship and zeal are so closely interwoven with her government and whose life from the dawn of early manhood to the grave was conspicous for disinterested devotion and distinguished service to the State and Nation. Oh! Spirit of Liberty, where sleeps your thunder!" (p. 300). Ridgely in her "Historic Graves" states the Governor was buried in the rose garden at Sotterley(p.30).

Edmond Plowden

There can be little doubt that Edmond Plowden lies buried in the old portion of Sacred Heart Church Cemetery, near his estate, Bushwood Manor. The stone, if there was one, has disappeared.

*Dr. Henry Reeder

Private cemetery at "Ellenborough" near Leonardtown. He is buried in an unmarked grave beside his wife, Judith Townley Reeder.

John Shanks

Private cemetery near River Springs, the home of the Blackistone Family. He died Nov. 22, 1825 (Blackistone Family records).

William Barton Smoot

There seems little doubt that he is buried in the family plot at St. George Episcopal Church, Poplar Hill, but there is no stone.

Dr. George Clarke Somerville, Died Dec. 13, 1800)
William Somerville, Died Dec. 30, 1806   )

Both are buried at St. George's Episcopal Church, Poplar Hill. There are no stones, but both appear in the Church register.

*<u>Henry Greenfield Sothoron</u>
   Private cemetery at The Plains on the Patuxent River in the Charlotte Hall area. He is buried in an unmarked grave beside his wife, Mary Bond Sothoron.

*<u>James Thomas</u>   )
*<u>William Thomas, Sr</u>)
 *<u>William Thomas, Jr.</u>)
   Buried in Private cemetery at Deep Falls, near Chaptico.

*<u>Benjamin Williams</u>
   Probably buried beside his wife, Mary Williams, in St. Inigoes Cemetery. No stone.

* See Helen W. Ridgely, Historic Graves of Maryland p. 27-49.

APPENDIX A

Chronology of St. Mary's County, Maryland in the American Revolution

Subscribers to the Oath of Allegiance - 1778
St. Mary's County, Maryland

The following list is a revised arrangement of an earlier compilation by Mr. Frank F. White, Jr., of Riverdale, Maryland, that was published in the National Genealogical Society Quarterly. Mr. White has granted permission to Mr. Crolian Wm. Edelen to arrange this alphabetical listing for publication in the "Chronicles of St. Mary's". The individual oaths may be found in the returns of officials of St. Mary's County in 1778 now on deposit in Box #94 of the Scharf Papers at the Maryland Historical Society.

In addition to serving as a substitute for the 1776 Census of St. Mary's County by reason that all male residents, eighteen years of age and over who were not then in service, are included; the list serves as evidence to qualify descendants of the various individuals for membership in several patriotic societies. The taking of this oath was considered treason against the Crown of England and was an overt act of resistance on the part of the subject.

The form of the oath of allegiance was as follows:

I do swear that I do not hold myself bound to yield any Allegiance or obedience to the King of great Brittain his heir or Successors; And that I will be true and faithful to the State of Maryland, and will to the utmost of my power support, maintain and defend the freedom and independance thereof and the Government now Established Against all open Enemies and secret and traitorous conspiraces and will use my utmost Endeavours to disclose and make known to the Governor, or some one of the Judges, or Justices thereof, all Treason and Traitorous conspiraces, attempts or Combinations against this State or the Government thereof, which may come to my knowledge
SO HELP ME GOD --

The officials who administered the oath in the various districts of St. Mary's County were as follows:

1.	Robert Armstrong	8.	Henry Reeder
2.	Richard Barnes	9.	John Reeder
3.	Bennett Biscoe	10.	John Shanks
4.	Ignatius Fenwick, Jr.	11.	Henry G. Sothoron
5.	Vernon Hebb	12.	Jenifer Taylor
6.	John Ireland	13.	Henry Tubman
7.	Jeremiah Jordan	14.	Robert Watts

The number following the name of each citizen who took the oath identifies the official who administered the oath. This arrangement was resorted to in order to eliminate the duplication of official's names.

Arthur Abell 2	Henry Abell 2	Samuel Abell 2
Barton Abell 8	John Abell, of Samuel 7	Samuel Abell, Youngest 2
Clarke Abell 14	John Abell, Youngest 14	Thomas Abell 7
Cuthbert Abell 14	John Booth Abell 14	Zacharias Abell 4
Cuthbert Abell 14	John Horne Abell 3	John Adams 7
Cuthbert Abell 14	Joshua Abell 6	George Aisquith 14
Edmund Abell 8	Philip Abell 14	John Aisquith 14
Enoch Abell, Jr. 2	Robert Abell 7	John Allison, Jr. 3
George Abell 8		Thomas Allstan 7

Thomas Allstan, Jr. 10
James Alvey 6
Jesse Alvey 6
Joseph Anderson 5
John Armstrong 5
Joseph Arthurs 3
Nathaniel Askum 11
James Atkinson 14
James Attwood 3
John Aud 2
Joseph Aud 2
William Aud 2
John Avery 10
James Baccus 11
John Bailey 10
Thomas Bailey 3
Archibald D. Barber 9
Cornelius Barber 13
Richard Barnhouse 1
Rudolph Barnhouse 3
Zacharia Barnes 9
Edmund Bassey 3
Joseph Baxter 3
William Bayard 10
Benjamin Bean 5
Robert Bean 5
Henry Belwood 14
William Belwood 14
John Bending 3
Joseph Bennet 1
Joseph Bennett 1
Richard Bennet 1
Robert Bennet 1
John Bial 3
Allen Billingsley 9
James Billingsley 13
Zachariah Billingsley 13
Bennet Biscoe 3
George Biscoe 14
Ignatius Biscoe 1
Ignatius Biscoe, Jr. 14
James Biscoe 3
James Biscoe, Jr. 3
Jonathan Biscoe 1
Joseph Biscoe 1
Mackay Biscoe 1
Stephen Biscoe 1
Thomas Biscoe 1
Thomas Biscoe 1
Thomas Biscoe of John 3
Herbert Blackistone 10
John Blundell 3
John Boarman 10
Richard Boarman 9
Sylvester Boarman 10
John Bolds 2
Jeremiah Bond 10
John Bond 10

John Bond, Jr. 10
Thomas Bond 7
William Bond 11
Samuel Bonfield 4
Joseph Booker 11
Basil Booth 2
George Booth 6
James Booth 2
John Booth 5
John Booth, Sr. 2
Joseph Booth 2
Leonard Booth 2
Richard Booth 2
John Bothick 6
William Boulds 6
Thomas Boult 5
Mark Bourn 10
Ignatius Bowles 8
William Bowling 10
James Boyd 7
James Bradburn 2
John Bradburn 6
John Bradburn, Jr. 6
William Bradburn 8
Thomas Branson 4
Enoch Breeden 14
George Brewer 5
James Brewer 9
John Brewer 6
John Brewer 8
John Baptist Brewer 11
Mark Brewer 9
Thomas Brewer 8
William Brewer 8
Zacharias Brewer 8
Thomas Bridget 7
Thomas Bridgett 11
James Bright 7
John Bright 2
John B. Bright 2
John Hooper Brome 9
Francis Brooke 4
Michael Brooke 6
Hooper Broome 11
Cornelius Brothers 2
Anthony Brown 2
Basil Brown 2
George Thomas Brown 7
Ignatius Brown 2
James Brown 2
James Brown 10
John Brown 9
Nicholas Brown 8
Peter Brown 8
Peter Brown, Jr. 8
William Brown, Jr. 7
Ignatius Bryan 14

Philip Bryan 9
William Bryan 11
Robert Buckler 7
Charles Buckman 7
Ignatius Buckman 7
Joseph Budd 6
George Bullock 10
Benjamin Burroughs 13
Benjamin Burroughs, Jr. 13
George Burroughs 13
Hezekiah Burroughs 13
James Burroughs 13
John Burroughs, Jr. 13
John Burroughs, Sr. 13
Joseph Burroughs 13
Matthew Burroughs 13
Richard Burroughs 13
Samuel Burroughs, Jr. 13
William Burroughs 13
Williamson Burroughs 13
Nicholas Byrn 1
Michael Byrne 3
Thomas Cain 3
Archibald Campbell 8
Edward Campbell 6
Enoch Campbell 9
Joseph Carberry 8
Patrick Carberry 6
Peter Carberry 6
Justinian Card 7
Thomas Card 7
William Card 13
George Carpenter 7
George Carpenter 2
John Carpenter 7
John Carpenter, Sr. 6
William Carpenter 2
William Carpenter 3
Ambrose Carr 9
James Carter 7
John Cartwright 9
Ignatius Chamberlain 8
Gerard Cheseldine 10
Kenelm Cheseldine 10
William Cheseldine 10
John Chesley 13
Seneca Chezeldine 14
George Chilton 5
Henry Chilton 5
James Chittim 10
Jesse Chiverill 3
Barton Cissell 6
Bernard Cissell 2
Bennett Cissell 6
Francis Cissell 2
Ignatius Cissell 2
James Cissell, Jr. 2

John Cissell 2
John Cissell 8
John B. Cissell 8
John Baptist Cissell 6
Raphael Cissell 6
William Cissell 2
Abraham Clarke 8
Cuthbert Clarke 2
John Clarke 6
John A. Clarke 5
Kenelm Clarke 14
✓ Matthew Clarke 9 Reeder
✓ Philip Clarke 14
✓ Richard Clarke 2
✓ Richard Clarke 2
✓ Robert Clarke 1
✓ Robert Clarke 9
✓ Robert Clarke 8
✓ Roger Clarke 14
✓ Thomas Clarke 3
✓ Thomas Clarke 10
✓ William Clarke 4
Thomas Clayton 7
Bennett Closher (Clocker?) 3
James Coad 3
John Coad 3
Joseph Coad 3
Edward Cole 8
George Cole 5
Isaac Cole 3
John Cole 5
Robert Cole 8
Valentine Cole 5
William Collins 7
Bennet Combs 8
George Combs 3
Philip Combs 8
Alexander Cooke 11
John Cooke, Sr. 6
Ignatius Coombs 3
Samuel Cottreal 1
Bennett Cox 10
Peter Craig 6
Rubin Craige 6
James Armstrong Crain 5
William Crain 3
Fielder Crampfoot 4
Thomas Crane 5
James Crawley 3
Edward Craycroft 4
Ignatius Craycroft 8
John Crocker 3
James Curtis 7
Joseph Curtis 7
James Daffin 14
Robert Daffin 14
William Daffin 14
Ignatius Daft 6

Matthew Dafft 6
William Daft 2
John Baptist Dant 6
John Dart 3
James Davis 9
John Davis 6
Joseph Davis 11
Moses Davis 2
Stephen Davis 6
Walter Davis 6
James Dean 4
John Dean 4
Thomas Dean 4
William Dean 4
Thomas Dennison 1
Charles Dent 14
George Dent 13
John Dent 13
Francis Diddle 11
John Dillahay 11
Roda Dillahay 11
Thomas Dillehay 6
*(Thomas Dillen 14
*(Took Oath at Baltimore
(per certificate from
(Isaac Van Bibber
Henry Dixon 3
Peter Dixon 11
William Rooke Dixon 3
James Dorsy 3
John Dorsey 3
John Dossey 2
Joseph Downs 3
Austin S. Doxey 1
William Doxey 3
Robert Drewry 9
Thomas Drewry 9
John Drudge 6
Enoch Drury 6
Enoch Drury, Sr. 6
Ignatius Drury 6
James Drury 4
John B. Drury 4
John Drury, Sr. 7
Michael Drury 4
Philip Drury 4
John Dunbar 3
Joseph Dunbar 6
John Duncaster 2
John Dunnard 4
Benet Duvall 7
John Miles Duvaul 3
William Eadie 7
John Edley 8
Benjamin Edwards 13
Hezekiah Edwards 13
Ignatius Edwards 13
Jeremiah Edwards 2
Jesse Edwards 13

John Edwards, of John 13
John Edwards, of Robert 13
Stourton Edwards 11
John Egerton 3
Thomas Egerton 3
Matthew Ellet 3
Richard Elliot 4
James Ellis 7
John Ellis 7
Thomas Ellis 7
William Ellis 7
Joshua Estep 13
Philamon Estep 13
Philip Evans 4
Philip Evans 3
Richard Evans 14
William Evans 3
William Evens 6
Benjamin Fenwick 4
Bennett Fenwick 14
Cuthbert Fenwick 4
Edward Fenwick 3
Enoch Fenwick 8
Enoch Fenwick, Jr. 4
Francis Fenwick, of Ben. 4
Francis Fenwick, of I. 4
George Fenwick 4
Ignatius Fenwick 5
Ignatius Fenwick, of E. 4
James Fenwick 6
James Fenwick 5
John Fenwick 6
John Fenwick 4
John Fenwick 1
John Fenwick, Jr. 1
Joseph Fenwick 8
P. Fenwick, of Enoch 2
Philip Fenwick, of P. 4
Richard Fenwick 3
Robert Fenwick, of John 2
Thomas Fenwick 8
William Fenwick 4
William Fenwick 2
Thomas Ferrill 7
William Ferrill, Jr. 7
William Ferrill, Sr. 7
Nicholas Fielder 14
Leonard Fields 9
William Fields 6
Christopher Fisher 14
William Fitzgo 14
Charles Fitzjeffers 3
Joseph Fitzjeffery 1
Richard Fitzjeffery 1
Henry Fletcher 3
Joseph Flood 10
Jeremiah Flower 7
Thomas Flower 7
Jesse Floyd 4

134

Raphael Foard 6
Henry Ford 2
John Ford 2
John Ford 14
John Ford 8
John Ford, Jr. 2
John Ford of Peter 8
Peter Ford 8
Philip Ford 8
Richard Ford 8
Robert Ford, Sr. 6
Robert Ford, C.H. 2
William Ford 7
Thomas Forrest 4
Thomas Forrest, Jr. 6
Zachariah Forrest 8
Zeph. Forrest 2
Thomas Foyer 11
Benedict French 6
Ignatius French 6
Raphael French 6
Daniel Friend 6
Edward Gadden 9
Jeremiah Gadden 9
Richard Ellis Gadden 9
Clement Gardiner 10
John Gardiner 10
Simon Gardiner 3
Thomas Gay 6
Francis Gibbons 5
John Gibbons 11
Jeremiah Gibson 10
John Gibson 7
John Gibson, of William 6
Joshua Gibson 7
Roswell Gibson 7
William Gibson 7
Henry Gill 3
Barton Goddart 9
Ignatius Goddart 9
Ignatius Goddart, Jr. 4
John Goddart 4
John Baptist Goddart 9
Jonathan Goldsbury 4
John Goldsmith 7
John Goldsmith of Ben. 7
Michael Goldsmith 10
Notley Goldsmith 7
Thomas Goldsmith 7
Thomas Goldsmith 11
John Goodman 14
Matthew Goodwin 7
William Goodwin 7
Bennett Gough 10
George Gough 3
Ignatius Gough 8
Ignatius Gough 10
James Gough 2
Stephen Gough 2

John Gowing 14
Jeremiah Graves 6
John Graves 6
Joshua Graves 6
John Gray 9
John B. Greaves 6
James T. Greenfield 13
Nathaniel T. Greenfield 13
Archibald Greenwell 6
Barnaby Greenwell 11
Bennett Greenwell 8
Clement Greenwell 8
Cuthbert Greenwell 2
Edmund B. Greenwell 8
Edward Greenwell 2
Enoch Greenwell 8
George Greenwell 8
Henry Greenwell 8
Ignatius Greenwell 8
Ignatius Greenwell, of Henry 8
Ignatius Greenwell, Jr. 4
James Greenwell 2
John E. Greenwell 8
John Greenwell of George 2
John Greenwell, of James 2
John Greenwell, Jr. 2
John Greenwell, Sr. 2
Joseph Greenwell 2
Joseph Greenwell 8
Joshua Greenwell 2
Joshua Greenwell 8
Justinian Greenwell 7
Leonard Greenwell 8
Nicholas Greenwell 8
Raphael Greenwell 2
Robert Greenwell 4
Stephen Greenwell 2
Stephen Greenwell 8
Thomas Greenwell 6
Thomas Greenwell 2
William Greenwell 8
William Greenwell 8
William Greenwell 8
William Greenwell 8
Robert Greeves 3
Sabbaston Griggs 3
Abraham Griffin 3
Thomas Griffin 3
Richard Gristy 11
George Guyther 5
Rodolph Hacket 2
Thomas Haft 3
Robert Hagan 4
William Jenkins Hager 14
Aquila Hall 14
Arthur Hall 14
Basil Hall 11
Ignatius Hall 14

John Hall 14
Joseph Hall 2
Richard Hall 7
Thomas Hall 6
James Hamilton 9
William Hamilton 13
Caleb Hammett 14
Cartwright Hammett 14
Richard Hammett 14
Robert Hammett 11
William Hammett 5
Zachariah Hammett 11
William Hancock 9
James Haney 8
Ignatius Harbert (Herbert?) 3
William Harbert (Herbert?) 3
John Baptist Harden 10
Joseph Hargiss 6
James Harper 11
John Harper 8
Josias Harris 8
Samuel Harris 2
Benjamin Haskins 6
John Haskins 6
John Haskins 10
Lawrence Hatter 7
Clement Hayden
Francis Hayden 8
George Hayden 8
James Hayden 7
William Hayden 9
William Hayden, of George 6
Thomas Haywood 3
Bennet Hazel 9
Edward Hazel 9
Jeremiah Hazel 4
John Hazell, Jr. 4
Cuthbert Head 11
Ignatius Heard 7
Ignatius Heard 8
James Heard 7
James Heard, of W. 4
John Heard 6
John Heard, of Mark 14
John Basil Heard 8
Luke Heard 8
Matthew Heard 6
William Heard 4
William Heard 6
William Heard, Jr. 6
James Heath 3
Caleb Hebb 5
Jesse Hebb 10
John Hebb 5

Joseph Hebb 5
Thomas Hebb 5
William Hebb 5
Caleb Hennen 3
George Hennick (?) 11
Elias Henry 3
Nathaniel Hickman 3
John Higdon 7
John Baptist Hill 14
Zachariah Hill 11
Francis Hilton 14
Francis Hilton 10
John Hilton 10
William Hilton 14
Judiah Hinnen 3
Nathan Hinnen 3
Thomas A. Hinnen 3
Henry Hone 9
John Hooton 7
Bennett Hopewell 6
George Hopewell 14
Hugh Hopewell 12
James Hopewell 14
Edward Hopewood 1
Basil Hopkins 1
Jacob Hopkins 13
Henry Horrell 2
John Horrell 9
Thomas Horrell 9
Austin Howard 2
George Howard 2
James Howard, Sr. 6
Jonathan Howard 6
Joseph Howard 6
Leonard Howard 2
Peter Howard 10
Peter Howard of Thomas 6
Peter Howard, of
  Thomas (Bay Side) 6
Thomas Howard 10
William Howard 4
John Hughes 3
Bennet Hutchins 8
John Hutchins 2
Bennett Hutchinson 11
Bennet Jarboe 2
Charles Jarboe, Jr. 4
Henry Jarboe 3
Henry Jarboe, Jr. 3
John Jarboe 11
John Baptist Jarboe 3
Joshua Jarboe 2
Mark Jarboe 11
Matthew Jarboe 8 q
Peter Jarboe 8
Philip Jarboe 8
Richard Jarboe 2
Robert Jarboe 14

Robert Jarboe, Jr. 2
Rodolph Jarboe 3
Stephen Jarboe 3
Thomas Jarboe 8
John Jeans 10
Thomas Jeans 3
Whitten Jeffery 1
Parke Jenifer 1
Samuel Jenifer 14
Augustin Jenkins, of
  Richard 6
Edmund Jenkins 8
George Jenkins 3
Henry Jenkins 14
John Jenkins 3
Thomas Jenkins 3
William Jenkins 14
David Johnson 9
William Johnson 6
John Jones 11
Matthias Jones 1
Morriss Jones 3
Solomon Jones 1
Charles Jordan 7
James Jordan 7
John Jordan 6
Samuel Jordan 10
William Jordan 7
Justinian Joseph 9
William Joseph 9
Athenatius Joy 9
Charles Joy 4
Enoch J. Joy 4
Ignatius Joy, Jr. 4
Ignatius Joy, Sr. 4
Peter Joy 4
Peter Joy 6
Timothy Keach 3
James Keech 13
John Keech 9
Thomas Keimer 5
Joseph Keirk (?) 1
Zacharias Kendruk 5
William Keough 14
William Kilburn 3
Barton King 11
Charles King, Jr. 14
Francis King 4
George King 6
Henry King 14
Henry King, Jr. 3
*(James King 4
*(Resident of Harford County
James King, of John 6
John King, Jr. 14
John King, of Thomas 8
Richard King 14
Robert King 10

Thomas King 4
William King 9
John Kinnaman 11
James Knott 14
John Knott 11
John Lake 12
John Lancaster 6
Raphael Lancaster 10
Henry Langley 7
Josiah Langley 5
William Langley 1
Matthew Latham 2
Thomas Leach   4
William Leach 6
James Leake 10
Charles Lee 3
Hance Lee 7
John Lee 9
Philip Lee 10
Samuel Lee 7
Thomas Lee 10
Christopher Leigh 3
George Leigh 3
George H. Leigh 3
Joseph Leigh 1
Joseph Leigh, Jr. 1
William Leigh 3
Charles Lewellin 7
John Lewellin 7
Joseph Lewis 3
James Lithgow 7
George Lock 7
Meveral Lock 7
Thomas Lock 11
Thomas Loker 3
James Long 7
Jeremiah Long 7
John Long 7
Perry Long 7
Robert Long 7
Samuel Long 7
John Longson 7
John Baptist Low 10
Bennett Lowe 3
Ignatius Lowe 3
John Lucas 9
John Lynch 3
Richard Jones Lynch 3
John McClean 11
Benjamin McKay 3
Richard McKay 5
John McLean 2
Henry McMullin 7
Kenelm McWilliams 7
Thomas McWilliams 7
John Mackall 3
Daniel Mackintush 3
John Maddox 7

Samuel Maddox 7
Raphael Magee 4
Basil Mahoney 9
John Smith Mahoney 9
James Maitiland 3
William Mallepone, of
  Thomas 6
John Manley 3
Matthew Manley 3
John Manning 2
William Martin 5
Richard Mason 6
Henry Mattin 6
Bennet Mattingley
Benjamin Mattingley 3
Clement Mattingley 7
Edward Mattingley 6
Francis Mattingley 6
Ignatius Mattingley, Jr. 6
James Barton Mattingley 10
Luke Mattingley, Sr. 6
Robert Mattingley 6
Enoch Medley 3
George Medley 2
Henry Medley 8
John Medley 8
Joseph Medley 2
Philip Medley 2
William Medley 8
Austin Milburn 3
Edward Milburn 14
Jeremiah Milburn 2
Joseph Milburn 3
Richard Milburn 14
Stephen Milburn 14
Henry Miles 9
Philip Miles 9
Joseph Millard 8
Joshua Millard 8
Ignatius Mills 2
James Mills 7
James Mills, of John 6
John Mills, of Jesse 2
John Mills, 3rd. 7
Joseph Ignatius Francis Mills 9
Joshua Mills 9
Justinian Mills 7
Nicholas Mills 2
William Mills
William Mitchell 2
Benedict Moore 3
George Moore 13
James Moore 4
Jesse Moore 4
John Moore 3
John Moore 4
Leonard Moore 4
*Joseph Moreman 6

*Joshua Moreman 6
*William Moreman 6
*Zachariah Moreman 6
*Probably Mareman
Benjamin Morgan 8
James Morgan 6
John Morgan, Sr. 6
William Morgan 6
William Moulds 7
Joseph Mudd 13
Thomas Mudd 2
William Muir 7
Valentine Murrain 7
Bennett Neale 10
Charles Neale 11
Henry Neale 7
James Neale, Youngest 7
Jeremiah Neale 7
Raphael Neale 7
Raphael Neale, Jr. 6
Wilfred Neale 10
Senna (?) Nelson 6
Charles Nevitt 11
John Nevitt 7
John Baptist Nevitt 7
Joseph Nevitt 7
Joseph Nevitt 10
Bernard Newton 2
Delbert Newton 8
Gabriel Newton 6
Ignatius Newton 4
Ignatius Newton 6
Zachariah Newton 6
James Nivison 7
Thomas Noakes 10
Joseph Nobel 3
George Noe 13
Riahard Nokes 14
Bennet Norris 8
Clement Norriss 2
Edmund B. Norris 8
Henry Norris 2
Ignatius Norris 6
Ignatius Norris 2

James Norris 2
John Norris 2
John Norris 8
Mackelva (McKelvie?)
  Norris 5
Mark Norris 2
Mark Norris, Sr. 2
Matthew Norris 14
Philip Norris 6
Rodolph Norris 8
Thomas Norris 8
Thomas Norris 6
William Norris 3

Benjamin Nottingham 8
John Basil Nottingham 4
Philip Nottingham 8
James Nowles (Vowles?) 2
Bernard O'Neill 7
Joseph Owens 7
Clement Parsons 9
James Parsons 4
Francis Payne 2
James Payne 6
James Payne, of Richard 2
John Payne 10
John Baptist Payne 8
Raphael Payne 6
Richard Payne 2
Vincent Payne 2
William Payne 10
Ignatius Peacock 4
Paul Peacock 8
Augustin Peake 2
Baptist Peake 14
Ignatius Peake 8
John Peake 2
Peter Peake 6
Philip Peake 14
Robert Peake 2
Richard Pearcy 7
Bennett Perran 6
Samuel Phearson 7
Henry Phillips 9
Jonathan Phillips 9
Henry Pike 8
Richard Pinkerton 4
Edmund Plowden 7
Francis G. Plowden 4
James Plummer 9
Bennet Price 3
John Pusy 3
Basil Raley 4
Bennett Raley 14
Henry Silvester Raley 4
John Baptist Raley 2
John Raley,, of H. 4
John Raley, Jr. 4
John Raley, Sr. 4
John W. Raley 4
Richard Jems Rapier 6
William Rapier 8
John Baptist Read 6
Philip Read 2
Joshuary Redman 3
John Reece 3
John Reeder, Jr. 5
Thomas Attaway Reeder 9
William Reeder 3
John Reynolds 8
John Reynolds 4
Abraham Rhodes 14

Barnaby Rhodes 14
John Rhodes 14
Robert Ribbon 13
Thomas Richardson 1
Thomas Richardson 3
Thomas Richardson, Sr. 3
William Richardson 3
Henry Rilely 8
Bennet Rily 2
Joseph Riswick 2
Thomas Riswick 8
Wilfred Riswick 2
James Ritchie 3
James Roach 6
George Roberson 3
Anthony Roberts 6
John Roberts 6
Philip Rocke 6
William Rocke 7
George Rogers 14
William Rooke 3
Peregrine Rose 10
Lazerous Ross 3
James Russell 4
William Russell 2
William Russell, Sr. 2
John Sanner, Jr. 3
William Scott 13
James Seager 13
John Seaton 6
Clement Sewall 2
Henry Sewall 12
Henry Sewell, L.T. 2
N. Lewis Sewall 14
Nicholas Sewall 12
John Shadrick 5
Joseph Shanks 7
John Shanks, Sr. 6
Thomas Shanks 6
William Shaw 6
John Shercliff 6
Joseph Shercliff 14
Thomas Shercliff 6
George Sherley 14
Joseph Shurbentine 3
Anthony Simmes 4
Josias Simpson 7
Bartholomew Smith 3
Basil C. Smith 4
Edward B. Smith 4
Elias Smith 2
James Smith 1
James Smith, S. Master 3
John Smith 3
John Smith 14
John Smith 1
John Smith, Jr. 2
John Smith, of John 3

Peter Pears Smith 1
Samuel Smith 3
Vernon Smith 14
Wat Smith 14
Austin Sanford Smoot 3
Cuthbert Smoot 3
John Smoot, Sr. 3
Thomas Smoot 3
William B. Smoot 5
John Somerville 11
John I. Sotheron 13
Levin Sotheron 11
Richard Sotheron 13
Richard Sotheron, of
   Richard 13
Richard Sotheron, of
   Samuel 13
Samuel Sotheron 13
Alexs. Spalding 9
Benedict Spalding 8
Bennet Spalding 2
Edward Spalding 4
Henry Spalding 9
Henry Spalding, Jr. 9
John Baptist Spalding, Sr. 9
Joseph Spalding 6
Michael Spalding 4
Moses C. Spalding 4
Peter Spalding 4
Philip Spalding 3
Philip Spalding 9
Raphael Spalding 8
Richard Spalding, Jr. 9
Thomas Spalding, Jr. 9
William Spalding 9
William Spalding 3
Edward Spink 8
William Spink 2
Enoch Stone 4
Ignatius F. Stone 4
John Stone 4
Joseph Stone 2
Joseph Stone 2
Joseph Stone, Jr. 4
William Stone 4
William H. Stone 2
William Storr 3
Benjamin Suite 13
Dent Suit, Sr. 11
John Dent Suit 11
Daniel Sulivan 3
Francis Swales 4
John Swales 4
Robert Swales 4
Edward Swan 8
Ignatius Sword 3
Moses Tabbs, A. M. 5
John F. Taney 4
Raphael Taney 4

Bennet Tarlton 3
James Tarlton 5
Joshua Tarlton 5
Thomas Tarlton 3
William Tarlton 3
Henry Taylor 2
Ignatius Taylor 2
James Taylor 2
John Taylor 2
John Taylor, St. Mary's 3
Richard Taylor 1
Thomas Taylor 7
William Taylor 3
Jesse Tennison 6
Jessey Tennison 3
John Tennison 6
Matthew Tennison 10
Samuel Tennison 10
William Tennison 10
Joseph Tewkes 3
James Theobald 3
Samuel Theobald 1
Harbert Thomas 3
John A. Thomas 8
Levy Thomas 3
Philip Thomas 3
Robert Thomas 8
Tylor Thomas 1
John Thomkins 8
Aaron Thompson 10
Arthur Thompson 6
Athanatius Thompson 6
Henry Thompson 10
James Thompson 10
James Thompson 2
John Thompson 2
John B. Thompson 2
John Baptist Thompson 4
John Basil Thompson 6
John Gerard Thompson 2
Joseph Thompson, of Thomas 6
Peter Thompson 3
Raphael Thompson 6
Raphael Thompson 2
Richard Thompson 3
Robert Thompson 2
Thomas Thompson 2
Thomas Thompson 8
Thomas Thompson, Sr. 6
Thomas Thompson, of Thomas
                        6
Willifred Thompson 6
Alexander Thomson 13
Bazil Thomson 9
Joseph Thomson 9
Richard Thomson, of Edward 9
William Thomson 9
Vincent Thornton 8

APPENDIX A

Robert Timms 3
John Tippett 11
John Tippet, Jr. 7
Zachariah Tippett 11
Leonard Trale 11
John True 13
Charles Turner 7
John Turner 10
Joshua Turner 10
Peter Urquhart 14
Thomas Uzzel 14
Thomas Vaughan 1
Jas. Vowles 2
John Vyzmier 9
John Wakelin 11
Henry Walker 6
James Walker 9
Joseph Walker 9
Joseph Walker, of Thomas 6
Thomas Walls 2
Joseph Walters 9
James Walton 10
John Watkin 6
Alexander S. T. Watts 14
Kenelm B. Watts 14
Thomas Watts 14
Thomas Watts 3
William Watts 5
James Waughop 5
Thomas Pal. Waughop 5
William C. Waughop 5
Thomas West 10
Justinian Wharton 7
Francis Wheatley 6
Francis Wheatley 13
James Wheatley 8
John Wheatley 2
John Wheatley 13
Richard Wheatley 13
Thomas Wheatley 13
Francis Wheeler 2
Ignatius Wheeler 7
Junsinian Wheeler 6
Abner Wherritt 3
John Wherritt 3
Nicholas Wherritt 5
Thomas Wherritt 5
Thomas Wherritt 5
James White 3
Cornelius Wildman 9
John Wildman 9
James Wilkinson 4
William Wilkinson 4
Benjamin Williams 1
Gabriel Williams 4
George Williams 7
Henry Williams 7
Hugh Williams 4

James Williams 2
Joseph Williams 7
Simpson Williams 3
Ignatius Wimsatt 2
James Wimsatt 2
James Wimsatt 2
John Wimsatt 8
John Wimsatt 2
John Baptist Wimsatt 6
Richard Wimsatt 2
Robert Wimsatt 2
Stephen Wimsatt 2
William Wimsatt 2
Adam Wise, of Adam 14
Matthew Wise, Sr. 14
Matthew Wise, of Matthew 14
Thomas Wise 14
William Wise 14

Richard Wiseman 14
John Wood 13
Leonard Wood 13
John Woodard 8
Daniel Woodburn 11
John Woodburn 13
Jonathan Woodburn 11
William Woodward 10
Edward Yates 6
James Yates 2
John Yates 4
Martin Yates 2
Robert Young 14

APPENDIX B

Records of the Major William Thomas Chapter
Daughters of the American Revolution
Compiled by Mrs. Margaret K. Fresco and Mrs. Winifred Russell

List of Patriots from St. Mary's Co., Maryland during the American Revolution

Abell, Cuthbert – Sergt. 1759-1794 St. M. Co., s of Capt. Robert Abell, m Mary
Simmonds 1785

Service: Enlisted in Flying camp Aug. 4, 1776 (Arch. of Md. V 18
                      p 34)
                      Enlisted 7th Regt., Md. Line 1 Feb. 1780; discharged
                      1 Nov. (Archives of Md. V 18 p 154)
                      1st Md. Regt. (Arch. Md. V 18 p 389); Sgt. 5th Co., 1st
                      Battn. Md. Line (Arch. Md. V 18 p 437) Sgt., served
                      betw. Aug. 1780 & Jan. 1783 (Arch. Md. V 18 f 523)

Abell, Enoch – 1st. Lt. 1745-1784 St. M. Co., s of John & Elizabeth Abell; m Judith–

Service: 1st Lt. in Capt. Ignatius Abell's Company, St. M. Co.
                      (Ref: "Military Officers in Md. 1778-79" unpubl. records
                      of Md. p 3 at MHS: "Chronicles of Colonial Md." by
                      Thomas p 342.

Abell, John – 1st. Lt. 1746-1794 St. M. Co., m Elizabeth

Service: Mem. Comm. of Safety & Corres. St. M. Co. 12/23/1774
                      1st. Lt. in Capt. Samuel Jenifer's Company 8/26/1777
                      Refs: "Chron. of Colonial Md." p 342 & "Militia Offcrs.
                      in State of Md." p 3, MHS

Adams, James – Private 1737-1795 St. M. Co.; m Jane Brinam 1756

Service: Joined troops at Annapolis July 28, 1781 (Arch. Md. V 18
                      p 384)

Barber, Barnet White – Private b 1748 St. M. Co., drowned 1802; m Elizabeth Story
                      Briscoe

Service: Private mms of militia list, MHS (Balto)

Biscoe, James Sr. – Private 1730-1796 St. M. Co., s of George Biscoe; residence Rev.
                      St. M. Co.

Service: Private in St. M. Co. Militia in 1780 (Unpubl. mms. Rcds.
                      of Md. V 6 p 1)

Blackistone, Nehemiah Herbert – Patriot 1740-1816 St. M. Co.; s of John Blackistone &
                      Eleanor Dent; m Mary Cheseldine 1772

Service: Member Comm. of Safety & Corres. St. M. Co. 12/23/1774
                      Made prisoner tho exempt from military duty, on account
                      of physical infirmity. His dwelling was burned & his
                      stock appropriated by the British because of his rebellious
                      sympathies, emphasized by his refusal to sell anything
                      or accept any pay for what they took by force.
                      Ref: Scharf's History of Md.; Archives of Maryland V 43
                      p 295, 296

APPENDIX B

Briscoe, Dr. John Hanson - <u>Major</u> 1752-1796 St. M. Co. near Chaptico; m Mary Eliza-
<u>Brig. Gen</u>.   beth Attaway Bond

       Services: Elected Jan. 6, 1776 by Convention of Md;
Major of Upper Battalion of St. M. Co. w/Col. Jeremiah
Jordon commanding. Was commissioned Surgeon in Con-
tinental Army on 1/1/1777 & served as such in 2nd. Md.
Regt., Maj. Gen. Smallwoods Div. from which he & others
withdrew 1/11/1778 in consequence of some unwise re-
solves of Field Ofcrs. of Div. Then assigned to hospital
duty. Charge of gov't. hospital in Phila.
Commissioned Brig. Gen. in 1794.
(Refs: Arch. Md. V 12 pp 142 & 242; "Records of Md.
Troops in Continental Service" p 30; "History of Western
Md."; "Side Lights of Md. History"; "Colonial Families
of Amer".

Briscoe, Philip - <u>Private</u> 1729 (born after) St. M. Co. Chaptico; s of John (1678-1734)
Residence during Rev: St. M. Co.; m Chloe Hanson
abt. 1750

       Service: In Lt. James Peale's Co.
1st Md. Regiment on Foot; Enlisted 6/3/1778 & on Muster
Roll 9/2/1778 at <u>White Plains</u>
Discharged 4/5/1779
Archives of Maryland Vol. 18, p. 82

Burroughs, Hezekiah - <u>Pvt</u>. 1747-1806 St. M. Co; s of Richard Burroughs, m Ann
Sothoron 1768

       Service: St. Mary's County Militia Soldier 1780
(Ref: Md. Rev. War Militia List: at Md. Hist. Soc.
Balt. p 236)

Carpenter, John - <u>Capt</u>. 1735-1803 St. M. Co.; son of Jos. & Susanna Carpenter, m
Susanna Turner

       Service: Enlisted as private 5/23/1778 & served till 4/1/1779
Enlisted 4/4/1779 (Arch. Md. V 18 pp 96 & 329)
(In DAR Scrapbook noted "Promoted to Captain in militia
in 1780)

Cheseldine, Seneca Nelson - <u>Pvt</u>. abt. 1750-1816 St. M. Co., m (1) Elizabeth Biscoe
1779 (2) Elizabeth Turner 1798

       Service: Militiaman of St. M. Co. in 1780
(Ref: Orig. papers, Scharf Papers at Md. Hist. Soc.,
Box 94 V 2 p 10 & V 4 p 7; & "Index of Md. Rev. War
Militia List" MHS p 249

Clarke, Ignatius - <u>Private</u> 1750-1789 St. M. Co.; s of Thos. Clarke d 1777 & Julia-
m Frances Leigh (1752-70) in 1772

       Service: Private enlisted in 2nd. Reg. Md. Line May 30, 1778 from
St. Mary's, discharged 4/3/1779
(Arch. of Md. V 18 p 330)

Clarke, Joshua - Pvt. 1750-1823 m Mary Thompson (b 1753) dau. of Thomas Thompson who d 1777.

       Service: Militia from St. M. Co. 1780 (soldier)
Ref. "Original manuscript entitled "Return of Militia for Each County, 1780" p 8

Combs, Ignatius - 2nd Lt. 1740-1790 from St. M. Co.; son of Enoch Combs & Mary Manning, m Mary Fenwick 1761

       Service: Commissioned 2nd Lt. in St. M. Co. Militia on Aug. 26, 1777 (Arch. of Md. V 16 p 346)
Member of General Committee of St. M. Co. 1774 (Comm. of Safety & Corres.)
Member of the Council of Safety & Assn. of Freemen (American Archives, Series 1, vol 1, p 1060)

Dent, George - Captain 1756/7-1845 St. M. Co. s of Thos. Dent & Elizabeth Edwards m Elizabeth Mills 1790
Residence during Rev. - St. M. Co.

       Service: He served as a private in the 1st. Reg. Md. Line from May 25, 1778 until Apr. 3, 1779; Served in the U.S. Congress from Mar. 4, 1793 to Mar. 3, 1801; elected Speaker pro tempore Apr. 20, 1798 and served during the illness of Speaker Dayton; appt'd. U.S. Marshall for the Potomac District in 1801; in the War of 1812 he was Capt. of the Home Guard of St. Mary's Co. on the pension lists in 1818 and 1840
Ref: Archives of Md. Vol. 18, Letter of Geo. B. Dent 2/10/1902; Speakers of the House of Rep. of U.S. by Wm. Henry Smith.

Dent, John - Brig. Genl. 1735-1830 Charles County; m Violette Winnert in 1753

       Service: Member of the 1st Provincial Congress 1775. Declined command of the Md. Troops.
Ref. Scharf's "History of Md." V 2 pp 152, 153 & 165.
In command of the Maryland Militia in St. Mary's County during the attempted invasion by Lord Dunmore in July 1776.

Dunbar, Joseph - Cooper aboard ship. 1719-1801 son of Wm. & Eliz. Dunbar. St. M. Co., m abt. 1760 Henrietta---. Residence during Rev.- Upper St. Clements, St. M. Co.

       Service: Served as cooper on the ship "Defence" 19 Sep. 1776 to Dec. 31, 1777
Ref: Archives of Md. V 18, p 607 & 656
    Archives of Md'. V 16, p 463
    Misc. Naval Records

Fenwick, Ignatius - Colonel 1736-1792 St. M. Co. m (1) Sarah Taney 1761/2

       Service: Lower Battalion Aug. 26, 1777
Ref: "Officers State Militia 1778-1779", at MHS Balto.
    Unpubl. Rev. Records of Md., compiled by Margaret
    Roberts Hodges; v 1 p 2; DAR Libr., Wash.,DC

142

APPENDIX B

<u>Ford, Philip</u>   1750-1806 St. M. Co., lived in Leonardtown, s of John Ford & Harriet
Neale. m Mary Eleanor Thompson 1770

       Service: Signed Oath of Allegience 1778
Manuscript List of Rev. Militia of St. M. Co.; MHS
Arch. of Md. V 16 p 536

<u>Forrest, Zachariah</u> – <u>Captain</u> 1742-1817 s of James & Henrietta Forrest. Residence
during Rev. – St. M. Co., m Ann (Nancy) Edwards

       Service: Commissioned Captain 22 June 1780 (Arch. of Md. V 43
p 201)
Commissioned 1st Lt. 26 Aug. 1777 (Arch. of Md. V 16
p 345)
Member of Committee of Safety (Amer. Archives, series 1,
V 1 p 1060)
Appointed by Governor & Council as Associate Justice to
the Bench, 21 Dec. 1790 (Scharf's "History of Md." V 2
p 573)

<u>Jordan, Justinian Townshend</u> – <u>Private</u> 1743-1789 St. M. Co., s of Justinian Jordan &
Elizabeth Eden. m Elizabeth Bond 1753

       Service: Pvt. Justinian Townshend Jordan enlisted in Continental
Army on Apr. 8, 1777 for 3 yrs. (Ref. Muster Roll of Capt.
Armstrong)
Promoted to Sgt. Apr. 2, 1778 (Arch. of Md. V 18 p 127 &
298) & "Records of Md. Troops in Continental Army."
"Muster of Md. Troops" Vol. 1; 3rd. Regt., beginning
1779 shows "Pvt. Justinian Jordan May 25, 1779"

<u>Llewellyn, John</u> – <u>Patriot</u> 1716-1785 St. M. Co. m Elizabeth Jordan who d 1811
Residence during Rev. – "Brambly" St. M. Co.

       Service: Member of Committee of Safety and Correspondence of St.
M. Co. 1774
Inspector of Tobacco Warehouse 1781
Refs: Journal of Council of Safety V 77 p 344;
Archives of Md. V 47 p 231 & "Chronicles of Colonial
Md." p 279

<u>Locke, Jesse</u> – <u>Pvt.</u> 1755-1815 St. M. Co; s of Meverel & Eliz. Locke. Res. during
Rev. – St. M. Co.; m Sarah Bruce

       Service: Soldier in St. M. Co. Militia
Ref. Rev. War Militia List for St. M. Co. 1780 – p 237;
MHS, Balto.

<u>Loker, Thomas</u> – <u>Patriot</u> 1751-1803 m Rebecca Mackall (1757-1824) Res. during Rev.
St. M. Co.

       Service: Surveyor of St. Mary's Co. 1777
Signed Oath of Allegience in St. M. Co. in 1778
Property destroyed by the British in 1781

Maddox, Samuel - <u>Lt.</u> 1728-1798 St. M. Co. m Lydia Turner abt. 1750

Service: Signed Oath of Allegience
2nd. Lt. Upper Battn. St. M. Co. Militia, Capt. Charles Jordan's Co. 8/26/1777, promoted to 1st. Lt. 11/2/1779
Archives of Maryland Vol. 16 p 345; Vol. 43 p 18.

Milburn, Joseph - <u>Patriot</u> 1755-1818 St. M. Co.
Property destroyed by the British 1781
Paid bounty by the State for manufacturing salt 1782.

Plowden, Edmund - <u>Captain</u> 1751-1804 St. M. Co.; m Janette Hammersley 1779

Service: Captain in Upper Battalion of Militia of St. M. Co.
(Ref. Archives of Md., V 16 p 345, 6 & V 12 p 215)
June 1781. As member of Md. House of Delegates, sub-scribed to 500 pounds "to defray expenses of present campaign" (Arch. of Md. V 47 p 326). Presidential Elect-or, 4th Pres. Election, 1801 (History of Md., Scharf, V 2 p 602)

Reeder, Thomas Attaway - <u>Captain</u>. d 1806 Residence during Rev. St. M. Co.
m Catherine Vemere, dau. of a French Factor of Port Tob.

Services: Mem. of Comm. of Safety & Corres. St. M. Co. 12/28/1774
Captain Upper Battn. St. Mary's Co. Militia 8/26/1777
Captain in Gen. Smallwood's 1st Battalion 11/18/1779
Ref: Chronicles of Colonial Md. by Jas. W. Thomas, p 340 & 342.

Sanner, John V - <u>Pvt.</u> Militia of St. M. Co. 1760-1842 s of John IV & Mary Sanner
m Elizabeth Abell 1785

Service: Militia of St. M. Co.
Ref: "Unpubl. Rev. Rcds." by Margaret Roberts Hodges, V 2 p 59, 61, 69.

Shemwell, William - <u>Private</u> 1755-1824 served in St. M. Co., m Ann Billingsley
abt. 1787.

Service: St. Mary's Co. Militia 1780
Ref: mss copy of Md. Militia in Md. Hist. Soc.

Smith, William - <u>Private</u> 1757-1829 St. M. Co.; m Margaret Williams 1796; son of
John Smith and Amy Leigh

Service: Private William Smith enlisted Jan. 29, 1776, in 9th Co.
Light Inf. Charles County
Ref: Arch. of Md. V 18 p 19

APPENDIX B

<u>Thomas, William</u> – <u>Major</u> of Deep Falls 1714-1795; m Elizabeth Reeves 1751

Service: 1761, 1766-1773 – Representative fm St M Co to House of Delegates.
1774 – Member of Committee of Safety and Correspondence for St M Co
1777 thru 81 – Repre. fm St. M Co in House of Delegates

Major William Thomas, Sr., as indicated above, served as a Delegate in the Maryland Assembly from St. Mary's County in 1761 and again 1766-1773. He was appointed a Justice of St. Mary's County 1773-1774. His name appears first in the list of members of the St. Mary's Committee of Safety and Correspondence formed December 23, 1774. He also represented the County in the first General Assembly held after the Declaration of Independence from 1777-1781. He had three sons in the Revolution whose records are detailed below; a fourth son, George, was born in 1764 and was too young for service.

References: Thomas Family Genealogy; Chronicles of Colonial Maryland by James Walter Thomas; Archives of Maryland Vol. 56, p. xxxiii, 334, 353, 363, 364, 381, 437, 458, 460, 464; Vol. 61, p. 68, 341, 400, 418; Vol. 62, p. 37, 49, 64, 205, 216, 262, 280, 290, 462; Vol. 63, p. xiii, 75, 88, 100, 101, 120, 159; Vol. 64, p. 368.

Thomas, John – Capt. Upper Battn, St. Mary's County Militia 8/26/1777
Apptd to Purchase Provisions for Army 3/25/1778
Lt. Col. Upper Battn. St. Mary's County Militia 11/18/1779
Apptd. Inspector of Tobacco, St. Mary's River 8/30/1780.

Thomas, William Jr. – Adj. 25th Battn of Militia 10/5/1776
2nd Lt. Upper Battn, St. Mary's Co. Militia 8/26/1777
  Capt. John Thomas' Company
1st. Lt. Upper Battn St. M. Co. Militia
  Capt. Francis Millard's Co.   11/18/1779
Supplier to the Army   10/20/1780
Major, reorganization of Md. Line 1794

Thomas, James, Ensign Upper Battn, St. Mary's Co. Militia
Capt. Francis Millard's Co. 11/18/1779
Recruiting Officer
Wounded and captured by the British on the Patuxent 7/1/1781
Exchanged and died, Deep Falls Sept. 1781

Ensign James Thomas was wounded and his Schooner captured by the British at the mouth of the Patuxent while running supplies to the Head of Elk in July 1781. His father, William, Sr. and brother John were successful in having him exchanged for a British prisoner of equal rank from a British prison at Portsmouth, Va., in August 1781 but he died from his wound soon after reaching home and was buried at Deep Falls.
  Archives of Maryland Vol. 47, p. 402; Vol. 45, p. 562.

<u>Turner, Charles</u> – <u>Private</u> 1745-1796 St M. Co., s of Edward Turner & Susanna
  m Mary

Service: Private – Early & Independent Companies
5th Company of the 1st Battalion, with Capt.
Nathaniel Ramsey
(Ref Arch of Md. V 18 p 13 & 640)

APPENDIX B

His Excellancy
Thomas Sim Lee Esqr
  Governor of Maryland

Oct 20 1780 Returns of St. Mary's County's Militia by Col. J. Jordan
                    St. Mary's County Oct 20. 1780

Sir - You have below the returns of the militia of this county - I should have made this long before this - but could not get the officers of the Lower Battalion to apportion the companies equal, or nearly so - and it is not in my power to do it - unless I had been acquainted personnally with every man therein.

                    I am Sir, your very humb. servant,
                         Jeremiah Jordan.

Upper Battalion viz.			Lower Battalion		
Capt. Shanke's Company		71	Capt. Greenwell's Co.		99
Capt. Jordan's	"	79	Capt. Ignatius Abells' Co.		84
Capt. Mills's	"	91	Capt. Aisquith's	"	66
Capt. Millard's	"	83	Capt. Watts	"	89
Capt. Mattingly's	"	68	Capt. Smith's	"	63
Capt. Broome's	"	81	Capt. Smoote's	"	79
Capt. Plowden's	"	87	Capt. Mackalls'	"	85
Capt. Rapier's	"	82	Capt. Jenifer's	"	82
Capt. Edwards'	"	84	Capt. John H. Abells'	"	94
		726			743

                    TOTAL---- 1469

Above list includes both ofcrs & privates.

INDEX

of

Military and Civilian Personnel

of St. Mary's County, Maryland in the American Revolution

(For Alphabetical List of St. Mary's Countians who took the Oath of Allegiance in 1778, see Appendix A, p. 131)

Abell, Aaron, Pvt. Enlisted in Calvert Co. Militia, Capt. John Brooke's Co. 8/23/1776   23

Abell, Cuthbert Enlisted in Calvert Co. Militia, Capt. John Brooke's Co. 8/23/1776
*Sgt. 7th Md. Reg. 2/1/1780-11/1/1780
*Recruit in 7th. Md. Reg. 4/18/1780
*Sgt. 1st. Md. Reg. Southern Army, Capt. Beatty's Co. 2/1/1780-8/1781
Sgt. 1st. Battn. 5th Co. Md. Line, Capt. Lloyd Beall's Co. 1/1/1782-2/1/1783   23, 68, 70, 111, 139
*Probably two individuals of same name

Abell, Cuthbert Collector of the Tax, St. M. Co. 9/8/1780   74

Abell, Edw., Capt. Mem. Comm. of Safety & Corres. St. M. Co. 12/23/1774 Mem. Comm. of Observation, St. M. Co. 7/23/1776
Capt. St. M. Co. Militia 9/5/1776
                8, 16, 24, 48, 123, 126

Abell, Enoch, 1st. Lt. Lo. Battn. St. M Co. Militia 8/26/1777
Capt. Ignatius Abell's Co.   38, 139

Abell, George, Supplier for Army 10/20/1780   77

Abell, Henry, Ensign, Lo. Battn. St. M. Co. Militia. Capt. Barton Abell's Co. 5/7/1781   95

Abell, Ignatius, Capt. Lo. Battn, St. M. Co. Militia 8/26/1777
Resigned 4/22/1780
Appt. Inspector of Tobacco, Leonardtown 8/30/1780   38, 71, 73, 139, 145

Abell, John, Jr. Mem. Comm. of Safety & Corres. St. M. Co. 12/23/1774
1st. Lt. Lo. Battn. St. M. Co. Militia 8/26/1777, Capt. Sam'l. Jenifer's Co.
                38, 126, 139

Abell, John, Sr., Mem. Comm. of Safety & Corres. St. M. Co. 12/23/1774
Paid bounty by the State for making Salt 6/17/1782   117, 126

Abell, John Barton, 2nd. Lt. Lo. Battn, St. M. Co. Militia 8/26/1777, Capt.
Ignatius Abell's Co.
Capt. Lo. Battn. St. M. Co. Militia 4/22/1780   38, 71, 95, 101, 115

Abell, John Horn, Capt. Lo. Battn. St. M. Co. Militia 8/26/1777
Apptd. Inspector of Tobacco,St. Inigoes 8/30/1780 38, 73, 94, 95, 115, 128, 145

Abell, Robert Supplier for Army 10/20/ 1780   77, 139

Abell, Samuel, Jr. Maj. Mem. Comm. of Safety & Corres. St. M. Co. 7/23/ 1774   Mem. Comm. of Observation St. M. Co. 7/23/1776
Sheriff of St. Mary's Co. 12/23/1776
                8, 16, 30, 56, 120, 126

Abell, Samuel, Sr. Mem. Comm. of Safety & Corres. St. M. Co. 12/23/ 1774   126

Adams, Enoch, Pvt. Co. of Flying Camp St. M. Co. 7/28/1776   9

Adams, Ignatius, Pvt. 1st. Md. Reg. 5/9/1779-11/1/1780
8th Co. Md. Line 8/1/1780-11/1/1781
Army Substitute 7/23/1781
Discharged Dec. 1781
1st. Battn. 2nd Co.Md. Line Jan. 1, 1782, discharged 3/23/1782
8th Co. Md. Line 1/1/1783-11/15/1783
In Md. Line 1780-1783
        62, 71, 72, 102, 111, 114, 121

Adams, James, Enlisted in Capt. Patk. Sims' Co. Apr. 6, 1776
Pvt. Army Substitute 7/28/1781
                6, 101, 139

Adams, Jr. Pvt. Co. of Flying Camp St. M Co. 7/28/1776   8

Adams, John, Pvt. Continental Army, discharged 1781   111

Adams, Moses Pvt. Co. of Flying Camp St. M. Co. 7/28/1776
Army Substitute 7/31/1781
Cont. Army, discharged Dec. 1781
                9, 102, 111, 114

Adams, Nathan Pvt., Cont. Army 5/22/ 1778   55

Adams, Wm. Pvt., Co. of Flying Camp St. M. Co. 7/28/1776
Army Draught 7/27/1781
Cont. Army, discharged Dec. 1781
                8, 102, 111, 114

INDEX

150

INDEX

INDEX

154

INDEX

156

INDEX

162

INDEX

INDEX

(Continued)

INDEX

172

INDEX
of
Other Persons and Places, Events, Battles, Ships, etc. appearing in this Book

(For Alphabetical List of St. Mary's Countians who took the Oath of Allegiance in 1778, see Appendix A, p. 131)

178

INDEX

ST. MARY'S COUNTY BICENTENNIAL COMMISSION

Mary Combs Barber, Secretary

Edwin W. Beitzell

F. Elliott Burch, Sr., Treasurer

Henry J. Fowler, ex officio

J. S. Guy, Jr.

Michael E. Humphries

J. Patrick Jarboe, M.D.

Bernard I. Johnson

Marvin C. Joy, Chairman

Frederick L. McCoy, Vice-Chairman

Jonathan Nelson

John G. Norris

Bruce A. Perrygo

Robert E. T. Pogue

John P. Rue

R. Oakley Winters

Theresa Young

The

MARYLAND BICENTENNIAL COMMISSION

for the

Commemoration of the American Revolution

Endorses
the activities of

THE ST. MARY'S COUNTY BICENTENNIAL COMMISSION

for its book

**St. Mary's County, Maryland, in the American Revolution
Calendar of Events
by Edwin W. Beitzell**

Louise Gore
Commission Chairman

Marvin Mandel
Governor

SAINT MARY'S COUNTY

19

76

BICENTENNIAL

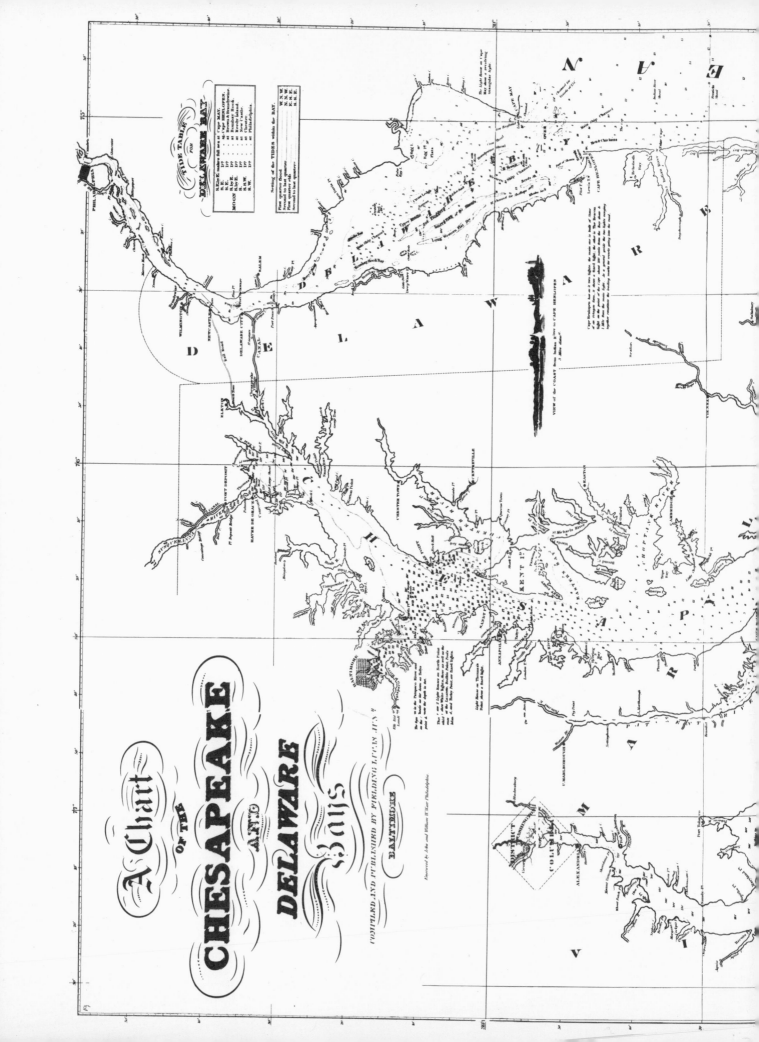